EXPLORE THE
AMERICAS

DISCOVER 60 FANTASTIC TRAVEL EXPERIENCES

Costa Rica's imposing Arenal volcano, capped with cloud.

CONTENTS

Bison grazing in a valley in Yellowstone
National Park, USA.

6

EXPLORE. DREAM. DISCOVER.

**The sky is a perfect blue with puffy clouds like a
children's drawing** and I'm blasting through Amarillo,
Texas on Route 66, past the giant cowboy sign advertising
the Big Texan Steakhouse. I'm hoping to make Albuquerque
by lunchtime and the state line of California by nightfall.
The radio's on, and I feel so free I'd float away if my
seatbelt wasn't holding me down.

Is this not the great American adventure?

Yes, but it's not the only one. Not by far. America – The
Americas – is a land of almost unimaginable variety.
Variety of landscape, of people, of climate, of experience.
We're talking, after all, about 35 countries spread
over more than 16 million sq miles (41 million sq km),
stretching from far northern Canada to the subantarctic
islands of South America.

The European explorers of the 16th century called these
two vast continents – which, along with their islands,
encompass nearly 30% of Earth's landmass – the New
World. But they weren't new, of course, not to the people
who lived here already. People have inhabited these lands
for at least 15,000 years, when they crossed a long-gone
land bridge from Siberia to Alaska. From there they spread
everywhere. From the frigid tundra of arctic Canada to the
wind-blasted tip of Argentina, from the arid canyons of
northern Mexico to the dripping Amazon rainforest, from
the great grass seas of the US Midwest to the aqua waters
of the Bahamas. And then, in ever-growing waves, people
came from elsewhere. Polynesians reached Hawaii on
canoes. The Spanish landed in the Caribbean and pushed
on to South America. Africans were brought in the holds

of slave ships. And on and on and on. Conquerors and refugees, pilgrims and prisoners, rich and poor, willing and unwilling. They all made the Americas what they are today.

This book offers you the very best of this sublimely diverse land. It showcases adventures in the classic sense: trekking through the ancient red rock canyons of Utah, diving the gin-clear, dizzyingly deep cenotes of Mexico's Yucatán, kayaking past glaciers in Antarctica. It also offers adventures that have more to do with the mind – or the belly: admiring the soaring architecture of Chicago, sipping your way through the cabernets of Chile's Colchagua Valley, binging on poutine in Québec City. It invites you to discover the continents' history, from the mountaintop Inca citadel of Machu Picchu to the cobblestone streets of Revolutionary War-era Boston. And it allows you to follow

in the trailblazing footsteps of great explorers of yesteryear, whether that's down the Mississippi with Mark Twain, or through South America with Che Guevara.

So use this book as a jumping off point to explore the places that inspire you most, in the ways that fit you best. That could mean a chill weekend trip of chowing on cioppino and sourdough in San Francisco. That could mean 10 days of cycling around the elysian meadows and shorelines of Canada's Prince Edward Island. Or that could mean tossing your notice on your boss's desk and taking off for a year of cruising the Pan-American Highway, exploring the Americas from top to bottom. Just think: nearly 30,000 miles (48,000km) of open road, with arctic peaks, lush cloud forests and Patagonian grasslands rolling by your window. Don't say you aren't tempted. **EMILY MATCHAR**

PAN-AMERICAN

1 TOUR THE PAN-AMERICAN HIGHWAY

EXPLORE THE AMERICAS

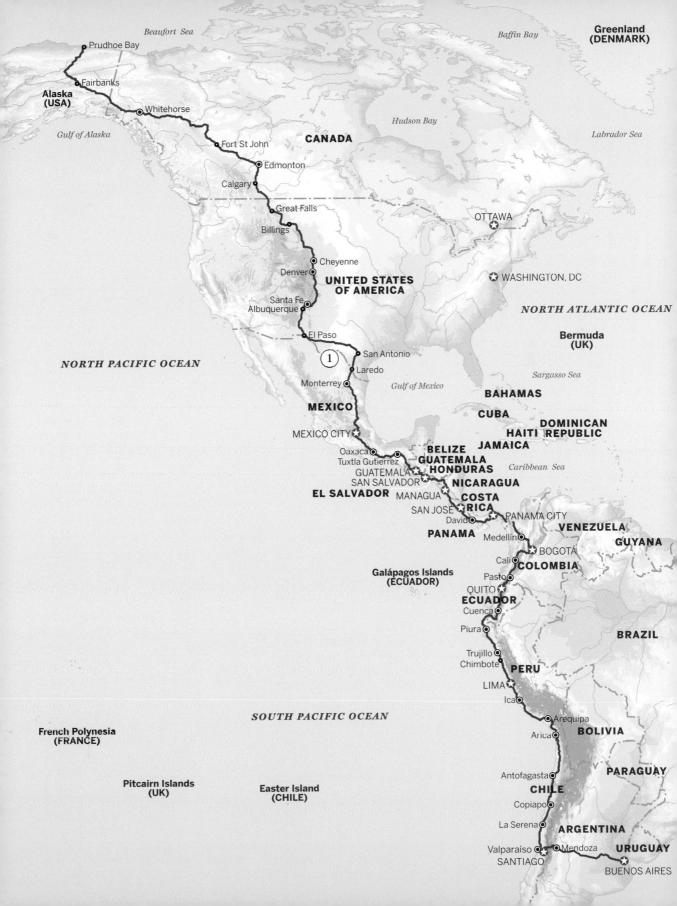

TOUR THE PAN-AMERICAN HIGHWAY

THIS DELICIOUSLY CROOKED LINE, WITH MORE WRONG TURNS THAN RIGHT ONES, CUTS THROUGH THE GREAT TEMPERATE FORESTS OF THE NORTH, SKIRTS MOUNTAIN RANGES ON TWO CONTINENTS, AND JOINS ICY SEA WITH ICY SEA, FROM PRUDHOE BAY TO TIERRA DEL FUEGO.

Make no mistake, there is an official Pan-American Highway, its name emblazoned on (relatively) easy-to-follow signage. It stretches from Monterrey, Mexico's second-largest city and its northern economic hub, to Buenos Aires. First imagined as a railroad as early as 1889, the idea grew legs at the Fifth International Conference of American States in 1923. Mexico was the first country to hold up its end of the bargain, but still didn't complete its branch until 1950. Gradually, all the other countries fell in line and when the original and official route was completed it ran from Monterrey through Mexico City, and down the Pacific coast of Central America until petering out at the Darién Gap – that no-man's land of swampy jungle separates as much as it links Panama with Colombia. Several attempts have been made to bridge the gap, but environmental concerns shelved it once in the early 1970s and again in the early 1990s, when armed drug smugglers were also rumored to have roamed these jungles. The road did (and does) pick up again in Colombia before rolling through the Andes and into Quito, Ecuador where it hugs the Pacific once more before connecting Lima, Peru with Valparaíso, Chile and crossing over to Buenos Aires. Still, the route always felt incomplete, with so much beautiful country extending from either end of the highway. Gradually, several unofficial routes sprung up. One extends south from Buenos Aires to Tierra del Fuego, and two more extend north from Monterrey, one heading through the Rocky Mountains via Denver and Calgary, the other veering east through Dallas and Minneapolis. Eventually the North American routes converge in Edmonton and join the Alaska Highway north to Fairbanks and the Dalton Highway to Prudhoe Bay. All told, the route is 29,800 miles (47,958km). The fastest known trip from point to point? Just under 24 days.

ESSENTIAL EXPERIENCES

❋ **Rumbling through the remote Arctic north and glimpsing the Brooks Range from Atigun Pass on the Dalton Highway.**

❋ Glimpsing epic Mayan ruins and experiencing lush cloud forests, echoing with the call of the howler monkeys, in Chiapas and Guatemala.

❋ **Canyoning in Nicaragua's oft overlooked Cañón de Somoto in the Northern Highlands, then staying overnight here or in the nearby college town, Estelí.**

❋ Rolling through grasslands and over steep Andean passes as you journey from sexy Cali, Colombia to laid-back Quito, Ecuador.

❋ **Moving from the tasteful cosmopolitan glamour of Buenos Aires to the exquisite desolation of Tierra del Fuego.**

10

DISTANCE 29,800 MILES (47,958KM) | **COUNTRIES COVERED** CANADA, USA, MEXICO, GUATEMALA, EL SALVADOR, HONDURAS, NICARAGUA, COSTA RICA, PANAMA, COLOMBIA, ECUADOR, PERU, CHILE, ARGENTINA | **IDEAL TIME COMMITMENT** 12 WEEKS | **BEST TIME OF YEAR** AUGUST TO JANUARY | **ESSENTIAL TIP** DARIÉN GAP REMAINS IMPENETRABLE; TAKE A FERRY FROM PANAMA CITY TO COLOMBIA.

THIS WAY OR THAT?

There's an alternative route through South America to consider if you're an ambitious driver who wants to see Brazil and Venezuela. Starting from Tierra del Fuego, you'll hop on a ferry from Buenos Aires to Colonia del Sacramento, Uruguay, and continue north to Pelotas, Brazil where Highway 116 leads to Rio de Janeiro. Continue north and you'll reach Bogotá, Colombia, and then Venezuela, where Highway 9 ends at Güiria on the Caribbean coast. This run includes the Simon Bolivar Highway, connecting the two capitals of Caracas, Venezuela and Bogotá.

MIRAFLOR NATURAL RESERVE

Its namesake is a small mountain lake, around which
the Area Protegido Miraflor unfurls with waterfalls,
blooming orchids, coffee plantations, swatches of
remnant cloud forest home to hold-out monkey
troops, hiking trails, and dozens of collective
farming communities that welcome tourists. Nature
is glorious here, and the chance to participate
in rural Nicaraguan life – making fresh tortillas,
milking cows, harvesting coffee, riding horses
through the hills with living, breathing *caballeros*
(cowboys) – is unforgettable. But Miraflor, best
accessed from Estelí, also has a past. When the
US-trained Contras snuck over the Honduran border
with a plan to march into Managua and seize political
power, a large contingent came through these
mountains, hoping to sack Estelí. But the farmers
rose up in resistance, and helped win the war.

THE JOURNEY TODAY

Begin your drive on the shores of Prudhoe Bay in the Arctic Ocean, and bump along a rough, gravel road for 489 miles (788km) south to Fairbanks. Things get more, ahem, civilized, as you carve through Canada's Midwest to the prairie town of Calgary. Cross the US border where the I-25, nicknamed the Pan-American Freeway, skirts the Rockies past Billings, Montana, through Denver, gorgeously groovy Taos, artsy Santa Fe, and into Albuquerque. You'll want to move quickly through the border regions of Mexico and down to Mexico City, replete with art galleries, museums and *zócalos* (plazas). Head east on Highway 190 through the indigenous-influenced state of Oaxaca, the jungles of Chiapas, and into Guatemala where the 190 becomes Central American Highway 1, which zags across the Continental Divide and onward into the Sierra de los Cuchumatanes.

Continue through El Salvador and Honduras and into Nicaragua's Northern Highlands. You'll want to soak up colonial Granada and snap photos of Lake Nicaragua on your left before buzzing through Rivas and into Costa Rica, where the highway separates two national parks and passes through the shadows of Arenal, which is one of the world's most active volcanoes. You'll then take a ferry from Panama City to Buenaventura, Colombia, 71 miles (115km) north of Cali. With its reputation as a hot, gritty city with great restaurants and an infectious passion for life, charming Cali is worth a stop. You can make it from here to Quito, Ecuador's Andean capital, in one long day. The laid-back city of Cuenca, a Unesco World Heritage Site, is even more charming and your last Ecuadorean stop before you hug the Peruvian coast on Peru Highway 1 through Lima to the Chilean border, where you'll continue along the coast on Chile's Highway 5. In Valparaíso, pick up Ruta 60, which links with Argentina's National Route 7 to Buenos Aires. Regal and cosmopolitan, Buenos Aires is where you can explore 48 districts influenced by Spanish, Italian, Jewish, German, Syrian, and Lebanese Argentinians. From here cut along Argentina's Atlantic Coast on Highway 3 to rugged Tierra del Fuego National Park.

SHORTCUT

On a highway this expansive it's easy to find a bit that suits your schedule. The most romantic choices would be the Dalton Highway into the Alaskan Arctic from Fairbanks to Prudhoe Bay, where car rental is easy to find. The run from Buenos Aires to Tierra del Fuego is equally remote and alluring. If you want a blast of the official highway, however, pick it up in northern Colombia, rolling through Cali and into Quito.

DETOUR

From Fairbanks, it's an easy drive to the Chena River State Recreational Area, where there are a number of trails, including the impressive Granite Tors Trail, a 15-mile (24km) loop. End the day at Chena Hot Springs Resort, where you can soak those sore feet or enjoy a cold one in the Aurora Ice Museum, which is the world's only year-round ice palace.

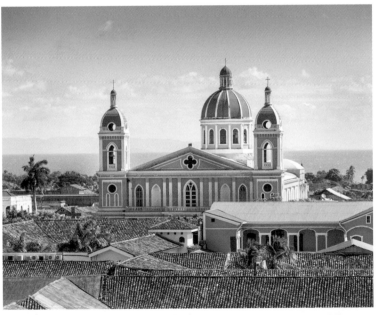

MLENNY PHOTOGRAPHY | GETTY IMAGES ©

OPENING SPREAD On the open Highway through the Atacama Desert, Chile.
ABOVE Granada Cathedral in Nicaragua. **LEFT** Costa Rica's active Arenal volcano.

13

ARMCHAIR

✳ **Road Fever** (Tim Cahill) This high-speed travelogue documents travel-writer Cahill and professional long-distance driver Garry Sowerby's record-breaking run from the southernmost tip of Tierra del Fuego to the northernmost terminus of the Dalton Highway in a camper-shelled GMC Sierra.

✳ **Long Road South** (Joseph R Yogerst) A touch more serious, and illustrated by *National Geographic* photographers, this book follows Yogerst's journey along the original and official Pan-American Highway from Mexico to Argentina.

✳ **Obsessions Die Hard** (Ed Culberson) Because someone had to ride a motorcycle through the Darién Gap and write a book about it.

✳ **The Motorcycle Diaries** (Ernesto Che Guevara) Not all of Che's iconic postgraduate road trip followed the Pan-American Highway, but some of it certainly did.

CANADA

✻

EXPLORE THE AMERICAS

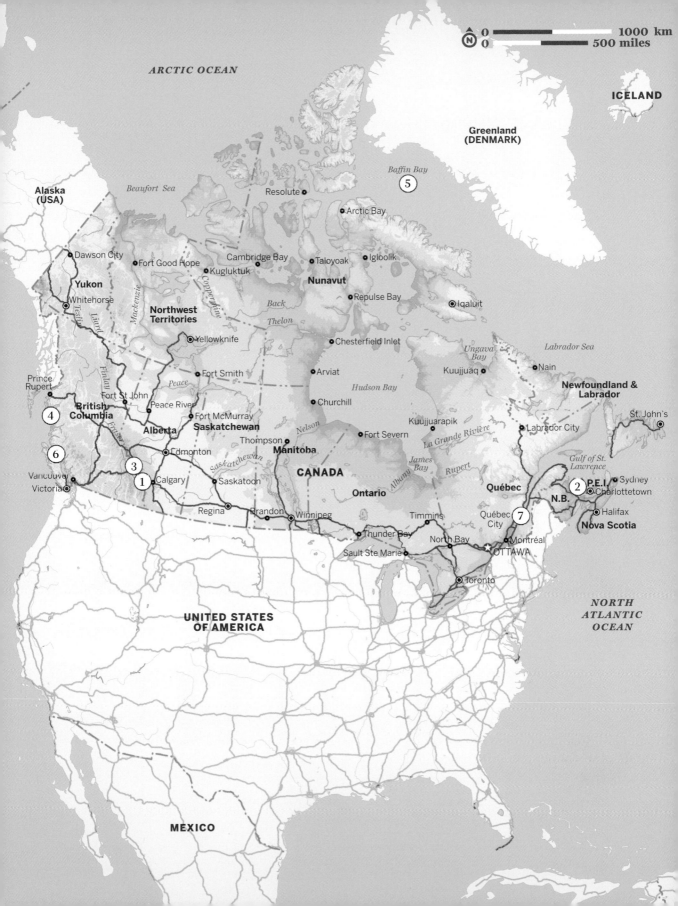

ARCTIC OCEAN

ICELAND

Greenland
(DENMARK)

Baffin Bay

⑤

Beaufort Sea

Resolute

Alaska
(USA)

Arctic Bay

Dawson City

Fort Good Hope

Cambridge Bay

Taloyoak

Igloolik

Kugluktuk

Yukon

Coppermine

Nunavut

Whitehorse

Northwest
Territories

Repulse Bay

Iqaluit

Back

Thelon

Yellowknife

Fort Smith

Chesterfield Inlet

Ungava
Bay

Labrador Sea

Prince
Rupert

Peace

Arviat

Hudson Bay

Kuujjuaq

Nain

Fort St John

Churchill

④

British
Columbia

Peace River

Fort McMurray

Saskatchewan

Nelson

Fort Severn

La Grande Rivière

Newfoundland &
Labrador

Alberta

Kuujjuarapik

Labrador City

St. John's

⑥

Thompson

Edmonton

Manitoba

CANADA

James
Bay

Gulf of St.
Lawrence

③

Saskatchewan

Rupert

②

P.E.I.

Vancouver

①

Calgary

Saskatoon

Ontario

Québec

Sydney

Victoria

Albany

Québec
City

⑦

N.B.

Charlottetown

Regina

Brandon

Winnipeg

Timmins

Halifax

Thunder Bay

North Bay

Montréal

Nova Scotia

UNITED STATES
OF AMERICA

Sault Ste Marie

OTTAWA

NORTH
ATLANTIC
OCEAN

Toronto

MEXICO

0   1000 km
0   500 miles

ICE CLIMB AT BANFF

SCALE FROZEN WATERFALLS STUCK TO THE ROCK FACES AND CANYONS AROUND THE CANADIAN TOWN OF BANFF, A METROPOLIS OF OUTDOOR ADVENTURE. IN WINTER, THE ONLY THINGS THAT FLOW HERE ARE THE ARMS AND LEGS OF ASCENDING CLIMBERS.

When winter grips North America in its icy claws, most climbers pack away their hardware for another season. But a hardy, rugged few see winter conditions as just another climbing challenge. It's no longer about rock, however. Instead, their goal is ice, climbing step by pointed step up the frozen streams of waterfalls – not just walking on water, but climbing it.

Laced with winter ice routes, the area around the evergreen Canadian mountain resort of Banff is held by many to be the finest waterfall-climbing destination on the planet. So prominent is ice climbing here that one Banff youth hostel even sets up a 39ft (12m) ice-climbing wall each winter.

The climbing opportunities in the region are seemingly endless, with ice routes around Canmore, Lake Louise, Yoho National Park, the Icefields Parkway and Kananaskis Country. You can even climb the waterfalls inside ever-popular Johnston Canyon, one of Banff National Park's tourist beauty spots. There's ice around Banff to suit all abilities, from the climbing nursery at the Junkyards near Canmore, up to the famed Polar Circus, a nine-pitch, 2297ft (700m) climb with an exposed, 328ft (100m) vertical sheet of ice at its top – it's one of the most prized ice routes in the world.

Ice climbing may sound more confronting than rock climbing but, at its core, it's a simpler task. While rock climbers are often forced to meander across walls in search of hand- and footholds, ice climbers can usually ascend in more straightforward lines. Their tools are a pair of ice axes and a set of crampons, hammering the axes into the ice for support and then stepping up by kicking the front points of their crampons into the ice – process by process, step after step, until they've hauled themselves over the head of the waterfall, climbing mission complete.

ESSENTIAL EXPERIENCES

* Hanging from your new metal fingers and toes – ice axes and crampons – on a frozen waterfall along King Creek.

* **Seeing the Johnston Canyon waterfalls from a very new perspective... clipped onto them.**

* Heading out on the Icefields Parkway to at least witness others scaling the Polar Circus, near the Weeping Wall.

* **Practicing your front-pointing on the ice-climbing wall at the HI-Banff Alpine Centre.**

* Enjoying the après-climbing scene in buzzing Banff.

ELEVATION 4593FT (1400M) ABOVE SEA LEVEL | **LOCATION** BANFF, ALBERTA, CANADA | **IDEAL TIME COMMITMENT** TWO TO SEVEN DAYS | **BEST TIME OF YEAR** MID-DECEMBER TO MID-MARCH | **ESSENTIAL TIP** WEAR A HELMET; IT'S VERY EASY TO PULL ICE DOWN ON YOURSELF WITH YOUR AXE.

MEC ICE CLIMBING FESTIVAL

Every January or February, Banff resounds even more loudly to the noise of axes and crampons as the ice world descends for the MEC Ice Climbing Festival, part of the town's annual SnowDays celebrations. Previously known as the Knucklebasher Ice Fest, the event features climbing competitions, gear demonstrations, tradeshows and a host of clinics that cover skills such as lead climbing and mixed climbing. The centerpiece is a 40ft (12m) freestanding ice wall in the middle of town. It's just the place to get you practiced, prepped and pretty damn excited about heading off to the waterfalls.

ICE GRADING

To help you know what you're letting yourself in for, the Canadian Rockies has a grading system for ice climbs, beginning at WI2 – easy, low-angled climbs – and going up to WI7 – highly technical vertical or overhanging ice. Gradings aren't as definitive as they are on rock, however. Conditions can change year by year, depending on how generous or stingy nature has been with ice; a climb that was grade seven last year might only be grade four this year. Likewise, routes tend to get easier as others climb them, leaving ice-axe and crampon marks in the ice that will help others to pick the line. As an example, Junkyards is rated WI2-3, while Polar Circus is WI5.

THE ADVENTURE UNFOLDS

The sky is clear and it's 21°F (-6°C) as you walk in from the trailhead on Kananaskis Hwy. Between narrowing gorge walls you follow King Creek, winding upstream. Finally you reach a large bulb of blue ice – a small waterfall frozen against the gorge wall. It's brittle ice. Technique will be important today.

You test out the ice with a couple of low traverses, repeatedly swinging with your axe to punch holes into the waterfall that will hold your axe and your weight. Ice is shattering into hundreds of pieces, shards flying past you. You feel more like an ice sculptor than a climber.

Finally you begin to get a read on the ice – the small pockets in the ice from previous climbers that best hold the axe, the tiny ice ledges to support your crampons – and you begin to ascend, chopping at the ice with your axe, the front points of your crampons clawed into the waterfall. Slowly you creep higher, re-stapling yourself to the ice at every step. Clip, unclip, clip. You hang back on the axes as the ice briefly bulges into an overhang, and then you are over the lip.

You abseil back into the gorge and head upstream, soon rounding a corner to where a high frozen waterfall seems to drip down the gorge wall like melted wax on a candle. This waterfall is around 148ft (45m) high, about double the height of the previous climb, and looking about twice as difficult.

Clip, unclip, clip – you begin again, dragging yourself slowly toward its ever-steepening top. Your arms have gone almost floppy from the effort, but finally you drag yourself over the head of the waterfall, where the view is extraordinary. If you didn't climb for climbing's sake, this panorama of snow-smothered mountains enclosing the Kananaskis Valley would be reason enough to justify the effort.

MAKING IT HAPPEN

Several companies offer guided ice climbing in Banff and nearby Canmore. Yamnuska is one of the most experienced, and leads two-day basic courses for novices, and also five-day multipitch programs on grade-five ice. There are also courses on mixed climbing (ice and rock). Experienced climbers can hire equipment from Mountain Magic Equipment in Banff.

DETOUR

For more ice climbing, head north to the Alaskan town of Valdez. Near to town, Keystone Canyon is a famous ice-climbing spot. The canyon offers a variety of multipitch routes, most famously Keystone Greensteps (four pitches) and Bridal Veil Falls (five pitches), right by the road. These routes are for experienced climbers, but there's ice for all abilities. Valdez hosts an ice-climbing festival in late winter or early spring, conditions permitting.

OPENING SPREAD An ice-climbing guide leads by example while his student looks on at Johnston Canyon, Banff National Park. **ABOVE** Winter sunrise in the Rocky Mountains presents a colorful spectacle. **LEFT** A lone climber gets to grips with the steep ice walls at Johnston Canyon.

ARMCHAIR

❉ *Banff, Jasper & Glacier National Parks* (Lonely Planet) Lonely Planet's guidebook has extensive coverage of activities around Banff, including ice climbing.

❉ *Ice & Mixed Climbing* (Will Gadd) A great introduction to life on ice, written by a noted Alberta climber.

❉ *Banff National Park* (Whitecap Books) Pictorial tribute to Canada's first national park, from a variety of photographers.

❉ *Waterfall Ice: Climbs in the Canadian Rockies* (Joe Josephson) More than 800 ice routes in Alberta and British Columbia.

❉ *Brokeback Mountain* (2005) The mountain scenes featured in this Oscar-winning film were shot around Canmore and Kananaskis Country.

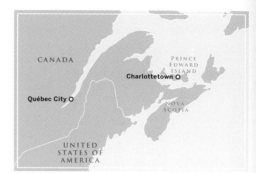

CYCLE PRINCE EDWARD ISLAND

PEDAL ACROSS CANADA'S SMALLEST PROVINCE, FOLLOWING ONE OF THE WORLD'S ORIGINAL RAIL TRAILS OR BRANCHING OFF TO EXPLORE THE GLEAMING COASTLINES AND THE SURPRISINGLY COSMOPOLITAN SMALL CAPITAL OF CHARLOTTETOWN.

Tiny Prince Edward Island, known almost universally as simply PEI, has the honor of being the only North American region to ban motor vehicles, which happened for a short time in the early 1900s. It's therefore unsurprising that it's grown into one of the finest cycling destinations on the continent.

The backbone of PEI's cycling network is the Confederation Trail, a 173-mile (279km) route that bisects the island. The trail was conceived as an idea after the closure of PEI's railway in 1989, and was developed as a cycling rail trail throughout the 1990s. The hard-rolled dirt path was finally completed in 2000 and now stretches from Elmira to Tignish, the island's most eastern and western tips.

The trail cuts through PEI's rural heartland, only flirting with the coast between Morell and St Peters in the east. A web of side trails and quiet backroads branch out to the coast, however, making PEI's trail network a great spot on which to idly meander – to hurry is not a PEI thing. Recommended side trips include Souris and the beaches at Basin Head Provincial Park; the seaside play town of Cavendish; and the capital city of Charlottetown, home to just 40,000 people but with wine bars, architecture, and restaurants to rival many major cities.

A second bike trail heads along the north coast through Prince Edward Island National Park, following the line of the dunes behind Brackley Beach and showcasing some of PEI's finest coastal scenery.

Adding to PEI's cycling appeal is the island topography. Its highest hill reaches just 466ft (142m) above sea level, making for predominantly flat cycling (although if you ride against the grain of the land – south to north or vice versa – there are some steep short climbs).

ESSENTIAL EXPERIENCES

* ✳ **Cycling atop the sandstone cliffs and endless beaches of Prince Edward Island National Park near Cavendish.**

* ✳ Wandering the boardwalk to the coastal sand dunes at Greenwich.

* ✳ **Donning a bib for a traditional lobster supper at St Ann, New Glasgow or North Rustico.**

* ✳ Detouring into Charlottetown for a big-city fix in a small-town setting.

* ✳ **Celebrating PEI's lack of hills as you cut through the center of the island on the Confederation Trail.**

DISTANCE 173 MILES (279KM) | **LOCATION** PRINCE EDWARD ISLAND, CANADA | **IDEAL TIME COMMITMENT** ONE TO TWO WEEKS
BEST TIME OF YEAR JUNE TO SEPTEMBER | **ESSENTIAL TIP** THE PREVAILING WINDS ON PEI BLOW FROM THE WEST AND SOUTHWEST.

SEAFOOD SUPPERS

Food is like a religion on Prince Edward Island, which becomes especially apparent when you see a 'fully licensed' sign hanging outside a village church. Across the island, in churches, dining halls and community centers, you'll encounter PEI's classic dining experience: no-frills lobster suppers. The lobster is served unadorned – no sauces or fanfare – with a slew of accompaniments, from chowder to mussels to PEI's famed potatoes. Lobster suppers are held daily from roughly mid-June to mid-October, and the most renowned are in New Glasgow, St Ann and North Rustico in central PEI.

THE ADVENTURE UNFOLDS

At the entrance to the national park, cars are stopping to pay fees, but you just pedal on through to the bike lane that begins as soon as you enter the park.

Along the foot of the Brackley Beach dunes there's barely a tree in sight, just the coastal grasses and the sound of the ocean beyond the dunes. Soon enough you're turning back off the coast, wondering at the piety of this island where road signs warn of 'Church Traffic Ahead' as you rejoin the Confederation Trail at Tracadie.

At the town of Mt Stewart, built in the fork of the old railway, you pedal through the salt marshes above the Hillsborough River. Over the river, a bald eagle is perched to attention atop a spruce tree. The trail takes you back to the coast just beyond Morell, sometimes just meters in from the shores of St Peters Bay, a host of birdlife stirring its protected waters. Past St Peters, there are miles of ruler-straight track. Out here, alone in the woods, passing beaver ponds, it's hard to believe PEI is Canada's most densely populated province.

The names of the rural settlements are as entertaining as the chipmunks that bounce about the track: Bear River on this island with no animals larger than a beaver; New Zealand; and Harmony Junction, where you depart the main trail, following a branch line to the south coast in Souris.

You keep pedaling east, to Basin Head and the beach so many rate as the finest on the island. Red cliffs drop to white sands and blue seas, and a crowd of bodies bake in the sun, looking like sausages on a barbecue. Elmira – ride's end – is just a few miles away, but for this it can wait.

MAKING IT HAPPEN

Cycling independently is a simple task on Prince Edward Island. Bike rentals are available from Outside Expeditions in North Rustico and MacQueen's Bike Shop in Charlottetown – MacQueen's also offers transfers. Full planning details, including maps and trail descriptions, can be found via Tourism PEI.

AN ALTERNATIVE CHALLENGE

Strapped in and ready for something really big? In creating the Confederation Trail, PEI was the first province to complete its section of the mammoth Trans Canada Trail, or Great Trail, a near 15,000-mile (24,000km) coast-to-coast path across the entire country. Beginning at North America's most easterly point, Cape Spear, the trail (also known as the Great Trail) extends right across to Victoria on Vancouver Island, crossing through every one of the Canadian provinces on its way. Officially connected cross-country in August 2017, it is the world's longest network of trails, half as long as the Earth is round.

VADIM PETROV | SHUTTERSTOCK ©

ALL CANADA PHOTOS | ALAMY ©

OPENING SPREAD The road clings to the coast at Orby Head, Prince Edward Island. **ABOVE (L)** The West Point Lighthouse Museum (and inn) at Cedar Dunes. **ABOVE (R) & LEFT** The PEI's flat terrain, beautiful scenery and excellent cycling trails make it perfect for two-wheelers.

ARMCHAIR

✳ **Anne of Green Gables** (Lucy Maud Montgomery) To know Prince Edward Island is to know the red-haired orphan who's more famous than the island.

✳ **Flavours of Prince Edward Island: A Culinary Journey** (Jeff McCourt, Allan Williams & Austin Clement) PEI is foodie heaven, and here are recipes and tales from its chefs, farmers and fishers.

✳ **Prince Edward Island Book of Everything** (Martha Walls) If you

wanted to know anything about PEI, it's probably in here, from the strange place-names to the origins of all that red dirt.

✳ **Prince Edward Island: An (Un)Authorized History** (Boyde Beck) A PEI historian recounts some of the island's best historical yarns.

✳ **Nova Scotia, New Brunswick & Prince Edward Island** (Lonely Planet) Your indispensable travel companion.

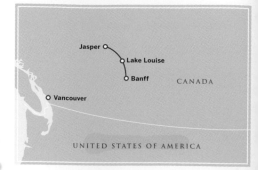

DRIVE THE ICEFIELDS PARKWAY

MARKETERS HAVE DUBBED CANADA'S ICEFIELDS PARKWAY THE 'MOST BEAUTIFUL ROAD IN THE WORLD'. IT SEEMS LIKE AN OVERSTATEMENT ONLY UNTIL YOU'VE DRIVEN PAST THE PIN-SHARP PEAKS AND DUCK-EGG-BLUE LAKES THAT DEFINE THIS SLICE OF THE ROCKY MOUNTAINS.

Linking Lake Louise to Jasper – and, in effect, a connection between the evergreen resort towns of Banff and Jasper – the Icefields Parkway began as a Great Depression infrastructure project in 1931. Construction crews worked from both ends of the road, finally meeting at Big Bend, below Sunwapta Pass, eight years later. The 143-mile (230km) road opened in 1940 as the unsealed Banff–Jasper Hwy, before being sealed and given its sexier new name in the early 1960s. Early road workers called it 'the road through the clouds,' while, soon after its opening, a local newspaper christened it '20 Switzerlands in one,' in reference to its wealth of mountain sights and cerulean lakes.

Threading through creases in the Rocky Mountains, it is arguably the most spectacular mountain road-trip in North America, and among the finest in the world. It offers the full glossary of mountain features – shapely peaks, glacial lakes, glaciers, copious wildlife, wildflower meadows, open passes, the massive Columbia Icefield – as it crosses between Banff National Park and Jasper National Park.

Today, it's said that around 400,000 vehicles travel the parkway each year. The road transitions between alpine and subalpine zones, with the dazzlingly colored lakes ever-present, and the icefields sat like frosting across the tops of the mountains. Numerous roadside stops allow you to take in the parkway's natural features and viewpoints. And, though this road takes you about as close as you're ever going to get to the Rockies' craggy summits and gushing waterfalls in a vehicle, you needn't just admire the views from the road. The parkway is stitched with 19 trailheads heading away into various wildernesses and national parks; stop your car, get out into the fresh air, and follow one of the walking trails, and you'll feel as though you're on top of the world within a matter of hours.

24

ESSENTIAL EXPERIENCES

* **Sneaking a dawn view of Lake Louise before the daily crowds arrive.**

* Wandering to the Peyto Lake viewpoint for an elevated look across one of the world's most beautiful mountain lakes.

* **Stepping quietly around the Waterfowl Lakes for the rare chance to spot moose.**

* Taking a special bus or a guided hike onto the ice of Athabasca Glacier.

* **Listening to the roar of thundering Athabasca Falls, pouring over a 75ft (23m) drop.**

* Riding the Jasper SkyTram to the summit of Whistlers Mountain for a view that extends up to 47 miles (75km) south along the parkway.

DISTANCE 144 MILES (232KM) | **COUNTRIES COVERED** CANADA | **IDEAL TIME COMMITMENT** THREE TO FOUR DAYS
ESSENTIAL TIP DRIVE IN THE EARLY MORNING OR LATE AFTERNOON FOR THE BEST CHANCE OF SPOTTING WILDLIFE.

THE COLUMBIA ICEFIELD

Tourism operators here will tell you that the Columbia Icefield (the main block of ice that gives the parkway its name) is the largest mass of ice south of the Arctic Circle. This tends to overlook a little place called Antarctica, but it is nonetheless an impressive chunk of frozen water. Icing the mountains to the west of the road, it is North America's largest icefield, covering an area of 125 sq miles (325 sq km). Its meltwater drains away to three oceans, the Pacific, Atlantic and Arctic, while 11 of the Canadian Rockies' 22 highest peaks rise around the icefield.

CYCLING THE PARKWAY

Cycling the Icefields Parkway has become so popular that, at times, you might even see more bikes than cars on the road. Due to the terrain, it's easier to cycle north. Most cyclists begin in Banff, adding the Bow Valley Parkway to the trip, making for a journey of around 190 miles (300km). Five days is an ideal commitment – a workable itinerary is Lake Louise, Waterfowl Lakes, Athabasca Glacier, Honeymoon Lake, and Jasper. The road has two major climbs, Bow Summit and Sunwapta Pass, both ascending around 1640ft (500m). The first is spread across 25 miles (40km), while the latter is shorter and sharper, reaching the pass in 9 miles (15km).

■ THE JOURNEY TODAY

The brilliance of the Rocky Mountains has been imprinted onto your windscreen for the past couple of hours. You fueled up at Saskatchewan River Crossing, the only petrol stop along the parkway's length, and are ready for yet more of this mountain march-past. As you drive upstream, the rock walls close around the road, and you're reminded of the vast rock faces of Yosemite. Waterfalls drop from the heights but the wind, funneling through the valley, carries them away before they reach the ground.

The road climbs towards Sunwapta Pass, and you edge around a pair of cyclists who seem to move as slowly as the glaciers. Atop the pass, 1640ft (500m) above the Saskatchewan Valley, a wind comes from the north, chilled by the Columbia Icefield. Away below, the icefield makes a guest appearance, spilling into the valley in the crumbled shape of the Athabasca Glacier, one of just six glaciers that drip off the edge of the Columbia Icefield.

The descent is intoxicating, but soon you are back into low gears as the road makes the short, steep climb to Tangle Hill. Tangle Falls lurch down the slopes but the sight that stops the traffic, literally, is the bighorn sheep. Atop the hill, they wander along the road itself and, while the sight is no longer unusual – bighorn sheep are one of 53 mammal species along the road, and you've already been stopped by elk and, most gloriously, a bear sow and cub – you pull off and listen to the tap-dance of hooves on asphalt. It's a classic Rockies' scene, enhanced by the vision across the valley of the multi-layered Stutfield Glacier (another of the Columbia Icefield's arms) gouging its way down 2950ft (900m) of cliff faces. They could easily have called this road by any number of names – Wildlife Parkway, Glacier Parkway, Wow Highway – but right now you accept that they might just have it right. This may be the most beautiful road in the world.

■ SHORTCUT

You can barrel along the whole parkway in a day, but if you just want to see or touch the main icefield that gives the road its name, you need only drive 60 miles (100km) south from Jasper to the Athabasca Glacier. Here, the Columbia Icefield breaks through a gap in the mountains, spilling down the rocky slopes toward the valley floor, almost to the road itself.

■ DETOUR

Continue south from Lake Louise and you can follow the other parkway – Bow Valley – into evergreen Banff. This 40-mile (65km) road parallels Hwy 1, but has fewer cars and more critters. It follows the banks of the Bow River beneath the watchful gaze of bald eagles and in the possible company of elk, bighorn sheep and bears. Be sure to wander up into Johnston Canyon to view its waterfalls, which roar in summer and freeze in winter.

OPENING SPREAD Driving the Icefields Parkway through the towering Rocky Mountains. **ABOVE (L)** Visitors on a guided tour of the Athabasca Glacier. **ABOVE (R)** A bull elk stands his ground in this wildlife-rich region. **LEFT** The glacier-fed Peyto Lake in Banff National Park.

ARMCHAIR

❊ **On the Roof of the Rockies** (Lewis Freeman) Classic account of a 70-day trip in the 1920s exploring the region around the yet-to-be-built parkway.

❊ **50 Roadside Panoramas in the Canadian Rockies** (Dave Birrell) A panoramic vision of some classic views, with detailed notes and histories. Icefields Parkway scenes include Sunwapta Pass, Bow Lake, and the Alexandra River Flats.

❊ **Bow Lake: Wellspring of Art** (Jane Lytton Gooch) A celebration of Bow Lake's artistic traditions, from the explorer Jimmy Simpson through to the modern artists in residence.

❊ **Jimmy Simpson** (EJ Hart) Biography of the Rockies' legend, whose lodge became the modern-day Num-Ti-Jah Lodge on Bow Lake.

FIND AN ISLAND IDYLL IN THE GREAT BEAR RAINFOREST

DESERTED ISLAND DREAMS NEEDN'T NECESSARILY BE ABOUT DEPRIVATION. NOT WHEN THAT ISLAND IS CANADA'S PRINCESS ROYAL ISLAND, ENCASED IN WILDERNESS AND WILDLIFE AND HOME TO A FLOATING LUXURY LODGE.

Who doesn't love a good uninhabited island, an untouched, water-lapped piece of paradise that encapsulates those hard-to-shake fantasies about leaving the world and its worries behind? Princess Royal Island may well be that fantasy in reality.

Hard against the coast of British Columbia, south of the town of Prince Rupert, Princess Royal Island is part of the Great Bear Rainforest, one of the largest tracts of temperate rainforest in the world (covering an area about the size of Ireland). For eight months of the year the island is an untouched wilderness with not a person or human structure on it; then each June, the luxurious King Pacific Lodge is towed from Prince Rupert and anchored by the island's shores in Barnard Harbour.

The location is extraordinary, facing away from the mainland and looking out over the protected waters of the harbor to Gil Island. Bald eagles peer down from the treetops and it's not unusual to see humpback whales rising from the water just meters from the barge on which the lodge sits.

It's these sorts of wildlife encounters that are central to the lodge experience. Humpbacks and orcas cruise the straits, along with Dall's porpoises and Steller sea lions. Boat across to Campania Island and you might see black wolves right on the beach. Otters prowl beside the barge. Grizzlies, black bears and – most enticingly – spirit bears roam the islands. You can fish for salmon or trout, kayak among the whales or helicopter out to hike on a distant snow-wrapped ridge.

When you return to the lodge, no luxuries are overlooked. The large rooms feature king-size beds, slate bathrooms and deep baths with views. Dinners meld Pacific Northwest cuisine with native and traditional recipes, paired with quality wines. Later you can zone out in the lodge spa, the fireside library, or once more view the parade of wildlife through the telescope.

ESSENTIAL EXPERIENCES

* **Watching a humpback whale lift its huge body out of the water.**

* Standing by the banks of a stream as spirit bears and black bears paw at a feed of salmon.

* **Sipping a wine or liqueur on the lodge deck as whales surface in the still harbor, bald eagles perching on dead branches above.**

* Searching for wolf-paw prints in the beach sands of Campania Island, across the water from Princess Royal Island.

* **Dropping a line into a crystalline stream in pursuit of trout.**

* Trading the day's wildlife sightings with other guests as you dine in view of the harbor and the dark forest.

28

LOCATION PRINCESS ROYAL ISLAND, BRITISH COLUMBIA, CANADA | **BEST TIME OF YEAR** THE LODGE IS OPEN JUNE THROUGH SEPTEMBER | **IDEAL TIME COMMITMENT** FOUR TO SEVEN DAYS | **ESSENTIAL TIP** STUDYING UP ON THE WILDLIFE WILL ENHANCE THE EXPERIENCE | **PACK** LODGE PACKAGES ARE ALL-INCLUSIVE; PACK LIGHT.

THE GREAT BEAR RAINFOREST

Dubbed 'Canada's Amazon,' the Great Bear Rainforest encompasses a wild region of mountains, islands, and fjords along British Columbia's coast. One of the largest areas of intact temperate rainforest in the world, it covers an area of around 24,700 sq miles (64,000 sq km) from the Alaska border down to near Campbell River on Vancouver Island. Home to grizzly bears, wolves and spawning salmon, its most famous inhabitant is the emblematic spirit bear, which gives the forest its name. Remote valleys are lined with forests of old Sitka spruce, Pacific silver fir and various cedars that are up to 330ft (100m) tall and 1500 years old.

HUMPBACK HIGHWAY

The star of the sea around Princess Royal Island is undoubtedly the humpback whale. Each fall, humpbacks migrate from Alaskan waters to Hawaii, a journey of around 3400 miles (5500km), which they then make in reverse around June. It's during this return to cooler, nutrient-rich waters (the whales give birth around Hawaii but go months without eating while there) that they are observed along the British Columbia coast. Humpbacks can grow to around 52ft (16m) in length, and watching them breach – propelling themselves out of the water and then slamming back down – is one of the finest wildlife sights on earth.

■ THE PERFECT GETAWAY

The sense of seclusion begins at once. The only way to reach King Pacific Lodge is by float plane, skimming over islands, looking down onto the seas that harbor the marine life you've come to see. The lodge is spectacular – native timbers, a stone fireplace and cathedral-high ceilings in the Great Hall; suites that might overlook the surrounding temperate rainforest, the ocean or maybe a waterfall – but it's what's beyond the barge that will fill your days.

Intimate whale-watching is one of the prime experiences. Throughout June and July, resident orcas cruise past the island in pursuit of spawning salmon. As the orcas are departing, the nutrient-rich seas begin to fill with humpback whales, returning from winter seasons in warmer waters around Hawaii. Humpbacks are frequently seen in Barnard Harbour itself; in Whale Channel, the strait that separates Princess Royal and Gil islands, expect awesome breaching displays.

Wildlife viewing hits a peak in September, when bear sightings become frequent. Bears roam Princess Royal Island but the population is less concentrated than on smaller islands such as Gribbell. Here guests can wander to the edge of a stream, watching from just meters away as black bears feast on spawning salmon from the shallow water. The prize sightings are spirit, or Kermode, bears, a rare subspecies of the black bear with cream-colored fur. They are endemic to the Great Bear Rainforest, with the population estimated at fewer than 1000, making these animals rarer than giant pandas. All of this with your palatial room, the spa, a liqueur by the fire, the plunge pool – or simply a quiet hour or two in the perfect silence of the barge deck that's awaiting you back in Barnard Harbour.

■ PLAN IT

King Pacific Lodge offers three-, four-, and seven-night packages. Guests take a private charter flight from Vancouver to Bella Bella, connecting with a float plane to the island. The lodge has 17 rooms and suites, allowing for a maximum of 34 guests, and stays are all-inclusive. The resort is open only four months of the year (June to September), so plan your visit well ahead; bookings can be made through the lodge website.

■ DETOUR

Spirit bears might be cute and unusual, but if you want to see the grand master of the ursine world – the grizzly bear – Knight Inlet Lodge is about the pick of Canada's stays. Set on British Columbia's longest fjord, this floating lodge, around 185 miles (300km) southeast of Princess Royal Island, is in prime grizzly territory – it boasts that in salmon season there can be up to 50 grizzlies within a few miles of the lodge.

OPENING SPREAD The extremely rare spirit bear is endemic to the Great Bear Rainforest. **ABOVE (L)** A bald eagle rules its roost in Bella Coola Valley. **ABOVE (R)** King Pacific Lodge on Princess Royal Island. **LEFT** The tail end of a humpback whale's shallow dive off the Rainforest shore.

DECKCHAIR

❋ **Spirit Bear: Encounters with the White Bear of the Western Rainforest** (Charles Russell) A photographic ode to spirit bears, featuring images from Princess Royal Island. The book is part of a push to have the island declared a reserve for this bear species.

❋ **The Great Bear Rainforest: Canada's Forgotten Coast** (Ian McAllister, Karen McAllister and Cameron Young) Beautifully photographed book about the Great Bear Rainforest and its bears.

❋ **I Heard the Owl Call My Name** (Margaret Craven) Best-selling novel about a dying vicar sent to a First Nations community inside the Great Bear Rainforest.

❋ **Exploring the North Coast of British Columbia** (Don Douglass) Get an idea of the waters and islands from this boatie's guide to the waterways around Princess Royal Island.

SAIL THROUGH THE NORTHWEST PASSAGE

SAIL THROUGH THE MOST LEGENDARY SHIPPING ROUTE ON EARTH, FOLLOWING IN THE WAKE OF A HOST OF VICTORIAN-ERA EXPLORERS SEEKING THE OCEAN'S HOLY GRAIL: SAFE BOAT PASSAGE ACROSS THE FROZEN TOP OF NORTH AMERICA TO THE RICHES OF ASIA.

For centuries it was the great marine dream: to find an open passage through the Arctic, creating a sea lane for traders between Europe and Asia to reduce the sailing time between the two continents. A course was sought through the tangle of ice-bound islands and straits across the top of Canada, the so-called Northwest Passage. The search began as far back as the late 15th century, but it was ramped up in the 18th and 19th centuries. James Cook sought it in vain in 1776, sailing with the likes of George Vancouver and William Bligh.

Through the first half of the 19th century, various expeditions chipped away at the route, slowly getting further and further, including the fabulous failure of the Franklin expedition (see the boxed text opposite). The tales of ineptitude and possible cannibalism from this voyage have made it one of the most famous adventure stories in history, up there with Robert Scott's Antarctic expedition.

In 1903, Norwegian explorer Roald Amundsen, who later became the first person to reach the South Pole, set out through the Northwest Passage. Taking a smaller ship and crew, Amundsen spent two winters on King William Island before finally becoming the first person to navigate through the passage in 1906. Such were its difficulties, though, it had already been abandoned as a feasible trading route, and superseded by the Panama Canal, which began construction while Amundsen was in the ice.

In recent years the Northwest Passage has returned to the forefront of shipping minds. Melting polar ice has opened up the Arctic waters, and the European Space Agency noted that in 2007 the passage had been fully clear of ice, and, for the first time since records began in 1978, fully navigable. Numerous vessels, including cargo ships and even cruise liners, now travel the famous route.

ESSENTIAL EXPERIENCES

* **Wandering through the Northwest Passage Historical Park at Gjoa Haven, where you'll find traces of Amundsen's expedition as well as the graves of several of Franklin's crew members.**

* Stopping in at Beechey Island, a national historic site east of Cornwallis Island, where the Franklin expedition wintered in 1845–46 before vanishing forever – traces of the men and their unsuccessful rescuers remain.

* **Viewing the remains of Roald Amundsen's schooner Maud in the harbor of Cambridge Bay, where Northwest Passage explorers often took shelter.**

* Contemplating the northern hardships as you visit Marble Island and its graveyard for James Knight and his crew, who sought the Northwest Passage in the 18th century.

DISTANCE APPROXIMATELY 3000 NAUTICAL MILES | **COUNTRIES COVERED** CANADA, GREENLAND, UNITED STATES | **IDEAL TIME COMMITMENT** TWO TO THREE WEEKS | **BEST TIME OF YEAR** JULY AND AUGUST | **ESSENTIAL TIP** PACK WARM; EVEN IN AUGUST THE AVERAGE TEMPERATURE IN CAMBRIDGE BAY IS AROUND 48°F (9°C).

THE FRANKLIN EXPEDITION

The most celebrated of all Northwest Passage journeys – even if only for the mystery surrounding it – was the British expedition led by Sir John Franklin. The two-ship expedition sailed into the Passage in 1845, seeking to find a way through the last few hundred miles of unnavigated waters. The expedition, and its entire crew of 129 men, never returned and disappeared without trace. The ships, HMS *Erebus* and HMS *Terror*, were eventually found to have been trapped in ice off King William Island, but the reasons for the deaths of the crew – lead poisoning, cannibalism – remain debated.

■ THE JOURNEY TODAY

Although several cruise liners now navigate the entire Northwest Passage, taking nearly a month to do it, it's more likely that any trip here will sample only a snippet of the famed shipping route.

Your 21st-century journey through a 19th-century obsession begins in Greenland, weaving through the fjords that fray its west coast. Through Baffin Bay you enter Parry Channel, the closest thing this region has to a direct line of passage, and quickly you have cause to be grateful that it's an ice-strengthened vessel. Within hours there's a thump; you have smacked into your first iceberg. Welcome to the Arctic.

The world here is reduced to a jumble of islands: snapped, fractured, raw, rugged chunks of land brutalised by the harsh conditions. And yet so very beautiful.

Through the Franklin Strait – its name alone replete with tragic Northwest Passage history – and a jigsaw of fragmented ice, the ship docks at Gjoa Haven, which is the only settlement on King William Island, all but resting against the mainland coast of Canada. As evidenced by the name – Amundsen's ship was named the Gjoa – it was here that Roald Amundsen wintered in 1904 and 1905, learning vital Arctic travel and survival skills from the local Inuit people, before finally punching a way through the Passage in 1906.

You are now nearing the cruise's end at Cambridge Bay, across on Victoria Island, Canada's second-largest, but there's still much excitement to be had ahead. The following dawn you head out from the ship in inflatable Zodiacs, skimming close to the island shores, when you sight movement on a ridge. You slow, watching as the two figures descend to the ice

ARMCHAIR

❋ **Arctic Labyrinth: The Quest for the Northwest Passage** (Glyn Williams) Charts the history of the quest to find a route through the Northwest Passage.

❋ **The Man Who Ate His Boots: The Tragic History of the Search for the Northwest Passage** (Anthony Brandt) Another tale of the quest to punch through the Passage, focusing on the personalities and hardships of those who attempted it.

❋ **Frozen in Time: The Fate of the Franklin Expedition** (Owen Beattie & John Geiger) The definitive account of the most famous – and ill-fated – British expedition through the Passage.

❋ **My Life as an Explorer** (Roald Amundsen) Autobiography of the Norwegian explorer who first navigated the Passage, and was also the first person to reach the South Pole.

ledge ahead of you. These waters and islands may still shelter the undisturbed ghosts of past explorers and sailors, but this polar bear and her cub are far more real.

SHORTCUT

You can skip the ship travel, and the seasickness, by flying direct into the Northwest Passage, though you'll be limited to single stops. First Air flies into several small island communities, including Gjoa Haven, Cambridge Bay and Resolute Bay (on Cornwallis Island), giving you the briefest of glimpses both from the air and on the ground.

DETOUR

If you've made it to Resolute Bay, and have a fortune to squander, keep heading north to Ellesmere Island and remoter-than-remote Quttinirpaaq National Park, Canada's second-largest national park. Highlights include 24-hour daylight; Cape Columbia, North America's northernmost point; and Mt Barbeau, which at 8583ft (2616m) is the highest peak in eastern North America. Hikers can strike out on trips from Lake Hazen Basin, a thermal oasis where animals, unfamiliar with humans, are strangely tame. Wilderness expertise is crucial.

ACWO | SHUTTERSTOCK ©

OPENING SPREAD Arctic wilderness of Auyuittuq National Park in the Canadian island province of Nunavut. **ABOVE** Navigating icebergs by kayak in Greenland. **BELOW** A polar bear surveys its surroundings from an ice floe in Baffin Bay.

POLAR BEARS

In the Canadian province of Nunavut, which incorporates the bulk of the islands through the Northwest Passage, polar bears aren't just found on the license plates. The region is home to almost half the world's population of *nanuq* (the Inuit name for polar bears). Worldwide, there are estimated to be around 20,000 polar bears, but it's a population now threatened by global warming and melting sea ice – it's on sea ice that the bears hunt and breed. Unlike grizzly and black bears, polar bears actively prey on people, so inquire about bear sightings before you go trudging about, or go with a shotgun-toting guide.

WATCH ORCAS FROM A KAYAK IN BRITISH COLUMBIA

WITNESS ONE OF NATURE'S GREAT SPECTACLES AS YOU SIT ON THE ROLLING OCEAN IN A KAYAK, OBSERVING ORCAS SWIMMING THROUGH JOHNSTONE STRAIT IN PURSUIT OF SALMON RETURNING TO THEIR BIRTHPLACE TO SPAWN. THESE AWESOME PREDATORS ARE BIGGER THAN YOUR BOAT, AND THEY'RE SO QUIET...

Welcome to the food chain as a spectator sport. Each summer, masses of salmon funnel through narrow Johnstone Strait, between Vancouver Island and the British Columbia mainland, on their way to spawning grounds in the Fraser River near Vancouver. This is said to be the world's most prolific salmon-spawning river, with up to 50 million fish returning here each year. And in their wake comes a host of predators, none more spectacular than orcas. More killer whales are said to pass through here than through any other waters on Earth.

Inside Passage cruise liners travel through the strait, but the most intimate way to witness the orcas is from a kayak. Whether you're kayaking across the strait, which narrows to less than 1.9 miles (3km) at points, or simply following the kelp lines along the shores of Vancouver Island, orca sightings are almost certain. There are thought to be around 250 whales in the strait during summer, and you'll probably also get to see the likes of bald eagles, Steller sea lions, Dall's porpoises and perhaps even a minke whale.

Trips here usually involve camping behind the rocky beaches that line the strait, where the orcas' sounds by night are almost as impressive as the sight of them by day. Days are spent poking along the coast of Vancouver Island, which is smothered in tall forest, or heading across the strait, where the topography is like that of an underwater canyon, plunging to 1640ft (500m) on islands such as West Cracroft and Sophia.

It's also just as likely that you'll observe orcas from the shore; salmon commonly swim near to the nutrient-rich kelp lines with pods of orcas inevitably in tow, sometimes bringing them to within just several feet of the Vancouver Island coastline.

36

ESSENTIAL EXPERIENCES

* **Dodging salmon as they leap from the waters around your kayak.**

* Watching as a pod of orcas rises silently from the waters in front of you.

* **Taking a break from the water to hike among giant cedars on West Cracroft Island.**

* Falling asleep in your tent to the sound of passing orcas.

* **Paddling the shores of Vancouver Island in sight of bald eagles, Steller sea lions and Dall's porpoises.**

LOCATION JOHNSTONE STRAIT, BRITISH COLUMBIA, CANADA | **IDEAL TIME COMMITMENT** THREE TO SIX DAYS | **BEST TIME OF YEAR** JUNE TO SEPTEMBER | **ESSENTIAL TIP** REMEMBER THAT KAYAKERS ARE NOT PERMITTED TO PADDLE INSIDE THE ROBSON BIGHT (MICHAEL BIGG) ECOLOGICAL RESERVE; THE AREA IS HEAVILY PATROLLED.

ORCAS

Orcas have long been given a bum rap. In the oldest known description, written during the days of the Roman Empire, the so-called killer whales were portrayed as 'an enormous mass of flesh armed with menacing teeth.' In the 1970s, US Navy diving manuals warned that orcas will 'attack human beings at every opportunity.' And yet there has never been a recorded attack on humans in the wild. Orcas, which can grow to 30ft (9m) in length and are the largest member of the dolphin family, are generally classified into two major types: transient, which hunt marine mammals; and resident, which feed almost exclusively on fish. The orcas in Johnstone Strait are resident whales, which means you need only be nervous if you're a salmon.

ROBSON BIGHT

Most kayaking companies concentrate their trips around the fringes of Robson Bight, a small bay about 9 miles (15km) southeast of Telegraph Cove. They do so with good reason. Robson Bight is noted for its 'rubbing beaches', where orcas swim up to the shores to rub against the smooth pebbles – it's the only place in the world where they're known to do this. In 1982 the Robson Bight (Michael Bigg) Ecological Reserve was established as the world's only dedicated orca sanctuary. Boats and kayaks aren't allowed to enter the reserve, which is patrolled by wardens.

■ THE ADVENTURE UNFOLDS

The orcas have sounded again, like an alarm clock. The sun has just risen and, from your tent, you can hear the rush of air as a pod surfaces just offshore. It's like having visitors from the deep knock at your front door. You breakfast on the beach, watching salmon pop from the strait like corn. The orcas have moved on – you saw their enormous fins heading into Robson Bight – and a Steller sea lion darts about the ocean surface in their place. It's enjoying its breakfast even more than you, tossing unlucky salmon about like a shot putter.

It's mid-morning by the time you ready the kayaks. You slide out from the smooth, rounded rocks of the beach, turning north, away from the bight, hugging the shores and hoping not to be brained by a leaping salmon – already one has clattered into your kayak. From the tops of the trees, a bald eagle watches you pass, while cruise liners parade past in the distance.

You've paddled only several hundred feet when you hear the sound again – the blow of a whale. Ahead, fins appear, slicing through the water. You stop paddling and glide over to the kelp line, grabbing a strand to anchor you in position atop the water. Regulations prevent you from going within 328ft (100m) of the whales, but watching them from a distance is still a thrilling experience; the kayak giving you a pond-skater's eye-view. The fins disappear for a minute and then resurface, at the same level as where you sit inside your cocoon of fiberglass. A male orca leads the pod, its 7ft (2m) fin rising higher than you, leaning over with the weight of gravity. You feel no bigger than krill. The pod moves so gracefully it's tough to imagine that it's hunting right now.

■ MAKING IT HAPPEN

The remoteness of the area surrounding Johnstone Strait and Robson Bight means that the vast majority of kayakers come here on guided paddles. Port McNeill and Telegraph Cove are the usual starting points, with water taxi transfers to beach camp grounds. Port McNeill and Telegraph Cove are near to Port Hardy, which has Pacific Coastal flights to and from Vancouver.

■ AN ALTERNATIVE CHALLENGE

If you want to mix and match your whale adventures in Canada, head for the northern town of Churchill (famous for its polar bears), where thousands of white beluga whales gather in Hudson Bay each summer. These ghostly white whales are one of the smallest members of the whale family, typically measuring no more than 13ft (4m). They are chatty fellows who squeak, groan and peep while traveling in close-knit family pods. The season for whale-watching runs from mid-June to August. Go kayaking or view them from a boat. You'll probably see polar bears on the trip, too.

CULLENPHOTOS | GETTY IMAGES ©

NICKJKELLY | GETTY IMAGES ©

OPENING SPREAD & ABOVE (L) Southern resident orcas – a variety that mainly feed on fish – in the waters around Vancouver Island.
ABOVE (R) & LEFT Kayaking this part of Canada's Pacific coast is the best way to view the animals, as well as the stunning scenery.

ARMCHAIR

❋ *Listening to Whales: What the Orcas Have Taught Us* (Alexandra Morton) Stories from the author's 20 years as an orca researcher, predominantly in the waters of British Columbia.

❋ *Field Guide to the Orca* (American Cetacean Society) Dedicated guide about viewing orcas, from techniques to facts about the animals.

❋ *Orca: Visions of the Killer Whale* (Peter Knudtson) Portrait-rich book of orcas, with discussion on such issues as the creature's communications, history and environmental threats.

❋ *Passage to Juneau: A Sea and its Meanings* (Jonathan Raban) Campfire reading about the British travel writer's journey through the Inside Passage in a yacht.

❋ *Free Willy* (1993) Yes, that movie – get warm and fuzzy about orcas in this feel-good tug on the heart strings.

EMBRACE QUÉBEC CITY IN WINTER

YEAH, IT'S COLD. BUT WINTER IN HISTORIC FRENCH CANADA IS ALSO COMPLETELY COOL: WHERE ELSE CAN YOU HUG A GIANT SNOWMAN, REFUEL ON CRÊPES AND HAUTE CUISINE, SKI RIGHT IN THE CITY AND SLEEP ON A BED OF ICE?

Ahead: glittering grooves sliced into virgin snow; naked trees, shivering in an icy breeze; a sky so blue it should be X-rated. As for you, you're wrapped in as many layers as a pass-the-parcel, with skinny skis on your feet and poles clasped in your mittens. You could be gliding through a winter wilderness, were it not for the thrum of Québec City just a hockey-puck's throw away.

Québec City is a North American anomaly. The continent, north of Mexico at least, doesn't really do old towns. But the capital of Canada's Francophone province is the exception, founded in 1608 and bequeathed a comely, European-style mish-mash of stone walls and cobbled alleys. To be here is almost to be in Carcassonne, sipping café au lait on terraces amid French voices, lorded over by a château. Yes, just like France – except for the in-city cross-country skiing...

For that is peculiarly Canadian. When most would cower in the nearest heated bar, the Québécois embrace winter. And the best place to do so is the Plains of Abraham. In 1759, this is where General Wolfe's army defeated that of French General Montcalm to claim the place for Britain; now it's the city's premier park, an urban lung of meadows, woodland and – in season – cross-country ski trails.

Fortunately, it's an easy (if energetic) sport to pick up: only the toes of your boots are snapped into skis, so you can step-glide with the help of your poles. The main issue is concentrating on technique when there's so much to look at: the ice-littered St Lawrence River to one side, the city skyline (including iconic Château Frontenac) to the other. As you schwoop along, you'll near-yelp at the novelty of practicing a back-country pastime in a city of 500,000 people.

Better, when you've finished on the Plains, the city's pleasures await you right there: the boutique hotels, the French-accented eateries and the stands selling stodgy poutine (chips, cheese and gravy) – calorific, yes, but you've earned it.

ESSENTIAL EXPERIENCES

* **Tucking into a comforting plate of poutine – the refined, Frenchified version of chips, cheese and gravy.**

* Hugging Bonhomme, the big, jolly mascot of the Québec Winter Carnival.

* **Gliding around the Plains of Abraham on skis, looking out over canyons, treetops and the St Lawrence River.**

* Wrapping up warm for a night in an ice room at the sparkling Hôtel de Glace (Ice Hotel).

* **Riding the ferry over to Lévis, for fine, inexpensive views back to the old city.**

* Taking to the slopes just minutes from the city center.

LOCATION QUÉBEC, CANADA | **BEST TIME OF YEAR** DECEMBER TO MARCH | **IDEAL TIME COMMITMENT** FOUR DAYS
ESSENTIAL TIP SKI IN THE RIGHT DIRECTION: THE PLAINS OF ABRAHAM'S SKI TRAILS ARE ONE-WAY | **PACK** THERMALS, GOOD GLOVES, LOTS OF LAYERS.

CARNAVAL DE QUÉBEC

To truly embrace Québec's Winter Carnival, know some basics. First, don a *ceinture fléchée* — this traditional arrow-weave sash should be tied around the waist. Next, carry a stick — special plastic canes (topped with a bust of carnival mascot Bonhomme) have hollowed-out middles in which to store your favorite tipple. And talking of booze, make it Caribou: when the first settlers here found First Nations people drinking caribou blood, they added wine to make it less icky; now the drink has morphed into a potent mix of wine, liquor, port, maple syrup, and spices — guaranteed to warm your cockles on a cold night.

■ THE PERFECT GETAWAY

No matter the season, your first stop in Québec City must be the hill-tumbling Old Town, still encircled by stone ramparts. This cluster of 17th- and 18th-century houses is where you'll find twisty streets, massive murals and cafes aplenty. Follow the marked, 3.1-mile (5km) VivaCité walking route for an overview and board the ferry across the St Lawrence to Lévis, just for the joy of looking back.

For the most romantic sleep, book into Auberge St-Antoine, a hotel part-housed in the port's original wharf buildings. For something more chilled, the Hôtel de Glace (Ice Hotel) is 10 minutes from the city: its artful snowy suites, sculpted afresh each winter, have Arctic sleeping bags to keep you toasty.

Once oriented, hit the Plains. This green space (white come winter) is the Québécois equivalent of Central Park, an urban playground with abandoned canons, a Joan of Arc garden and a 28-species arboretum. From December to April, 7.8 miles (12.6km) of cross-country trails – suitable for beginners – are cut. Hire some kit, read the rules, and off you go. There are no huge hills, but ascending any slope on cross-country skis takes effort: try the splayed herring-bone technique and hope you can beat gravity.

After a few hours you'll be exhausted – but exhilarated. Time to refuel. As cute as Vieux-Québec is, head for the less touristy neighborhoods of Faubourg St-Jean or Nouvo St-Roch; try Le Billig (526 Rue St-Jean), a crêperie par excellence. If you've timed it right, your visit will coincide with Winter Carnival. Ice sculptures, parades, skating rinks, snow slides... the city is overcome with glacial gaiety. It's wonderful, kitschy fun – raise of glass of Caribou liquor and join in.

■ PLAN IT

Québec City's Jean Lesage International Airport is 10 miles (16km) southwest of the center. Bus 78 runs from the airport to Les Saules terminal, Monday to Friday. The Québec Winter Carnival is held for 17 days every January/February; accommodation must be booked well in advance. The ferry to Lévis runs regularly, daily. Skis, boots and poles can be hired from the Plains of Abraham Discovery Pavilion.

■ DETOUR

If all of that white stuff has made your toes tingle for some proper downhills, there are four ski resorts within a snowball's throw of the city. Le Relais, just 15 minutes from town, has 32 runs and is especially well-equipped for families. Stoneham Mountain Resort contains the country's largest night-skiing area and a lively après-ski scene. Slightly further out, Mont-Sainte-Anne has three mountain faces and one of the longest seasons, while Le Massif de Charelvoix is 45 miles (75km) from the city, but offers the highest vertical drop (2526ft; 770m), and the most snow east of the Rockies.

MARK READ | LONELY PLANET ©

NINO H. PHOTOGRAPHY | GETTY IMAGES ©

OPENING SPREAD The toboggan slide past the grand Château Frontenac hotel. **ABOVE (L)** A slice of sugar pic from the city's Café Krieghoff. **ABOVE (R)** The postcard-ready skyline of Québec City. **LEFT** Kicking up powder on the slopes of the nearby Mont-Sainte-Anne resort.

DECKCHAIR

❋ **Winter Wonderland** (Belinda Jones) Heart-warming chick lit, played out at the fairytale Québec Carnival.

❋ **To Québec and the Stars** (HP Lovecraft) The fantasy and 'weird fiction' writer loved Québec City – his novels evoke a sense of the place, while this essay collection includes musings on the province.

❋ **Shadows on the Rock** (Willa Cather) American novel about Québec, set in the early days of New France.

❋ **Where the River Narrows** (Aimée Laberge) This family saga spans from the early days of settlement to the 1970s – a thoughtful look at modern Québec.

❋ **Québec: The Story of Three Sieges** (Stephen Manning) Military history at its most readable.

❋ **I Confess** (1953) Hitchcock used Québec City as the setting for this noir-ish suspense thriller.

USA

❦

1 RAFT THE COLORADO RIVER 2 HIKE CALIFORNIA'S JOHN MUIR TRAIL

3 HEAR MOUNTAIN MUSIC IN THE APPALACHIANS 4 ENJOY HAWAII ON A DIME

5 JOURNEY THROUGH MARK TWAIN'S USA 6 PARTY HARD IN THE BIG EASY

7 WALK WITH WOLVES IN YELLOWSTONE 8 JOIN THE REVOLUTION IN BOSTON

9 FIND YOURSELF ON THE LOST COAST 10 CHECK OUT CHICAGO'S ARCHITECTURE

11 CANOE FLORIDA'S WILDERNESS WATERWAY 12 DO THE SAN JUAN ISLAND-HOP

13 CLIMB THE NOSE OF EL CAPITAN 14 TAKE A FRESH LOOK AT THE BIG APPLE

15 CRUISE THE MISSISSIPPI TO NEW ORLEANS 16 HIKE ALASKA'S CHILKOOT TRAIL

17 TAKE A BITE OF SAN FRANCISCO 18 TRACE THE LIFE OF AMELIA EARHART

19 WINDSURF THE COLUMBIA RIVER GORGE 20 RIDE THE CALIFORNIA ZEPHYR

21 LEAVE THE LAS VEGAS STRIP 22 MOUNTAIN BIKE MOAB'S SLICKROCK TRAIL

23 ROAD TRIP THE RIVER ROAD (RÍO GRANDE) 24 CANYONEER UTAH'S PARIA CANYON

25 TAKE A SPIN DOWN ROUTE 66 26 MOUNTAIN BIKE THE GREAT DIVIDE

EXPLORE THE AMERICAS

RAFT THE COLORADO RIVER

TO FLOAT THROUGH THE GRANDEST CANYON OF THEM ALL IS TO TRAVEL ACROSS MILLENNIA. BUT AS WELL AS AWESOMELY ANCIENT ROCK WALLS, THERE ARE QUIET BEACHES, TUMBLING FALLS AND THE CHANCE TO PIT YOURSELF AGAINST SOME OF THE WILDEST WATER IN THE WORLD.

That the first person to successfully navigate the length of the Colorado River had only one arm says more about the man than the undertaking. Civil War veteran John Wesley Powell's 10-strong team set off on their mission to chart the then-uncharted river in June 1869, in four heavy (and quite unfit for purpose) oak rowing boats. It was a fearful voyage, haunted by the prospect that the next meander might plunge them over an unknown waterfall. But on 29 August, Powell emerged from the Grand Canyon – his crew bedraggled and depleted – as an American hero.

Powell put-in at Green River Station, Wyoming and floated some 870 miles (1400km) to Arizona's Grand Wash Cliffs. Today's rafters don't travel so far. The official launch point is Lees Ferry (Mile 0), at the northeast edge of Grand Canyon National Park; the Colorado empties into Lake Mead at Mile 277 (446km later).

It's still an epic ride, however. There are 160-plus rapids to negotiate, ranging from mere ripples to rip-roaring rides. There are side canyons to hike into and rock pools to swim in. And then there's the geology: the red-orange-yellow-black walls that flank your progress are up to two billion years old.

A full run, Lees Ferry to Pearce Ferry (on Lake Mead), can take just under three weeks in an oar-powered boat. Those with less time can do sections: an Upper Canyon expedition, from Lees to Phantom Ranch (Mile 87), takes around four days, ending in a hike up to the rim – there's no road out from the bottom. A Lower Canyon stretch, say from Phantom to Diamond Creek (Mile 226), starts with a trek down, and takes five or six days. Every inch of the ride is fascinating. The Upper realms allow a gentler introduction, but have more white water overall, and highlights such as Vasey's Paradise, a fecund garden at Mile 31. The Lower run has the biggest rapids, and access to the narrow and falls-filled Olo and Matkatamiba slot canyons. Undecided? Do the lot.

ESSENTIAL EXPERIENCES

✳ **Camping out on a sandbar by the riverside, and waking to watch the sun gradually seep down the canyon walls.**

✳ Tackling some gnarly white water, such as boulder-strewn Hance Rapid and the big waves of Hermit.

✳ **Mooring up for a trek into a side canyon, to find swimming pools, cascades and ancient petroglyphs.**

✳ Relishing the quiet bits, where you glide in calm waters just shooting the breeze.

✳ **Getting into geology, studying two-billion-year-old rock striations as you float by.**

✳ Hitting iconic canyon hikes (perhaps Bright Angel Trail or the walk to Tapeats Creek) early, before the sun gets too fierce.

DISTANCE 275 MILES (443KM) | **LOCATION** ARIZONA, USA | **IDEAL TIME COMMITMENT** 5 TO 18 DAYS | **BEST TIME OF YEAR** MAY TO OCTOBER | **ESSENTIAL TIP** PREPARE FOR VERY HOT AND VERY COLD WEATHER, YEAR-ROUND.

COMMUNITIES OF THE CANYON

The earliest traces of human life in the Grand Canyon date back to 10,000 BC, when nomadic hunters chased game through the gorge. Later, hunter-gatherers appeared, leaving small animal-shaped trinkets made of willow twigs; examples found in Marble Canyon are up to 4000 years old. The Basketmakers moved in to grow corn from around 100 BC. By AD 700, the Ancestral Puebloans had set up villages (pueblos) here; remains can be seen near Phantom Ranch, at Tusayan Ruin (South Rim) and Walhalla Glades (North Rim). The Havasupai, descendants of the Puebloans, still live largely traditional lives in Havasu Canyon today.

■ THE ADVENTURE UNFOLDS

As you float along the green-tinged Colorado – which is currently taking a breather between contractions of white-water fury – you gaze at the canyon wall: layer upon layer of geological history stacked like a club sandwich. The smooth black stuff at the bottom – Vishnu schist, so your guide says – is older than the dinosaurs; above that sit strata of blood-orange, purple, ochre, and gold.

Uh oh, something's afoot. The walls narrow, the water picks up pace... there's a rapid upcoming. You and your boat-mates adopt the ready position, paddles raised to row like billy-o, and prepare to be tumbled like a sock in a washing machine. Your guide hollers instructions you can barely hear as the inflatable pitches amid majestic chaos. Then all is still. Another torrent conquered.

Life's rhythm on the river is sublime. Days are spent gliding serenely or being bucked ferociously (dependent on the Colorado's whim). But you also take breaks. The beauty of being at the canyon bottom is the exclusive access to sandy beaches and hidden caverns, to side streams with sun-warmed swimming holes and to ancient Puebloan sites hidden amid the cliffs. Each evening you haul up at a shore-side camp, to toss a frisbee, cook over a campfire and watch as the light is sucked out of your awesome abyss – but not before it sets all that red rock on fire. Then the stars are spectacular.

Amenities are basic: bush toilets lurk amid the tamarisk trees, 'showers' are dips in the side canyons' pools (the river itself is way too chilly). But that's half the pleasure – adjusting yourself to Colorado living, just you, your boat and millions of years of Mother Nature in very top form.

■ MAKING IT HAPPEN

On commercial trips, an accredited operator will arrange all the guiding and logistics; options range from day-long to three-week floats, on either motorized or oar-powered boats. Noncommercial private trips are for very experienced rafters who want to organize their own river-run; rafters must apply for permits via the 'weighted lottery' system, which is massively oversubscribed (there's a waiting list of several years).

■ AN ALTERNATIVE CHALLENGE

There is fine hiking around the Grand Canyon, but short walks here are made punishing by extreme temperatures, thin air and steep climbs. A great multiday option is to combine the South and North Kaibab trails; this 20.5-mile (33km) route, from Yaqui Point (South Rim) down to the canyon floor then up to the North Rim, takes three days (stop at Bright Angel camp and Cottonwood camp or Phantom Ranch). You need a Backcountry Permit, which you can apply for up to four months in advance from the National Parks Service.

KRIS DAVIDSON | LONELY PLANET ©

OPENING SPREAD The Colorado River snakes its way through the Grand Canyon. **ABOVE** A guide gathers visitors' kayaks during an expedition through Black Canyon. **LEFT** White-water thrills while paddle rafting the turbulent rapids of the Colorado River.

ARMCHAIR

* ***The Exploration of the Colorado River and its Canyons*** (John Wesley Powell) True tale of adventure in the unmapped southwest in 1869 – an American classic.

* ***Over the Edge: Death in Grand Canyon*** (Michael P Ghiglieri & Thomas M Myers) Accounts of the 550 unfortunates to have died hereabouts, from Powell's expedition up to the book's publication in 2001; includes safety tips too.

* ***Grand Canyon National Park*** (Lonely Planet) Inspirational guide containing planning advice, itineraries and insider tips.

* ***Lasting Light: 125 Years of Grand Canyon Photography*** (Stephen Trimble) A compilation of the best historic shots and the stories behind them.

* ***The River Wild*** (1995) Meryl Streep is the plucky rafter in this formulaic thriller that's full of white-water action.

HIKE CALIFORNIA'S JOHN MUIR TRAIL

STEP OUT INTO A WILDERNESS THAT INSPIRED OVER A CENTURY OF CONSERVATION, FOLLOWING A HISTORIC TRAIL THROUGH THE LOFTY RANGES, PEACEFUL MEADOWS, BEAR-GRAZED FORESTS, AND FRESH-AIR SPLENDOR OF CALIFORNIA'S SIERRA NEVADA.

John Muir: inventor, conservationist, writer, tramp – and one of the most important men of the past millennium. Yet most people outside the US have never heard of him, and might wonder what his claim is on one of that country's best-known hikes. The answer's simple: without Muir there'd likely be no trail, and no wilderness here worth walking through. This eccentric Scot, who immigrated to the States at the age of 11, was at the forefront of the national parks movement. He spent years walking across backwoods America, living off the land, living for the land, getting 'as near to the heart of the world' as he could. His passions stoked, he focused them on persuading presidents to safekeep the country's wildest places. We owe him much.

Fitting, then, that this 214-mile (344km) hike across Muir's beloved Sierra Nevada, from the great granite valley of Yosemite to 14,505ft (4421m) Mt Whitney, bears his name. The trail was advocated by the Sierra Club, the environmental organization Muir founded; construction began in 1914, the year he died. It was 1938 before the route was finished, having forded rivers and surmounted high-altitude passes. It is the ultimate access to the land that Muir so loved.

There's lots of up and down (walk the entire route, north to south, and the total ascent is 42,000ft (12,800m); walk south–north and it's 46,700ft (14,234m)). But, despite this, the trail seldom feels tough – gradients are mostly gentle, the way largely sheltered. The toughest part is being self-sufficient. There are no real towns or shops en route, and hikers must carry much of what they need, meaning weeks of dried food and watery porridge.

But the trail compensates for this culinary fatigue with sheer wow. This is magnificent countryside, where every step seems to reward with yet another deer-nibbled valley or lake-reflected mountain range; where every night's camp, even if busy with other hikers, makes you feel a bit like a pioneer.

ESSENTIAL EXPERIENCES

✳ **Watching the sun set and rise over Thousand Island Lake.**

✳ Marveling at the basalt columns of the Devil's Postpile – and nipping to nearby Red Meadows Resort for a hot-spring-powered shower.

✳ **Looking out for lupines, Indian paintbrush and other wildflowers, as well as mule deer, marmots and black bears.**

✳ Camping beside mountain-hugged Evolution Lake, one of the JMT's remoter reaches.

✳ **Casting a line (if you have a fishing permit) into the five serene pools of Rae Lakes.**

✳ Standing atop Mt Whitney, gazing over the rugged wilderness you've just traversed.

DISTANCE 214 MILES (344KM) | **LOCATION** SIERRA NEVADA, CALIFORNIA, USA | **IDEAL TIME COMMITMENT** THREE WEEKS
BEST TIME OF YEAR MID-JULY TO EARLY SEPTEMBER | **ESSENTIAL TIP** NEVER APPROACH OR RUN FROM A BEAR, BACK OFF SLOWLY.

THE GRAND TRAVERSE

John Muir Trail too tiny? The Pacific Crest Trail follows the JMT through southern Yosemite – though this is merely one small step on its 2635-mile (4240km) journey from the Mexican border (near the small town of Campo) to the Canadian border at Manning Park. This epic hike across California, Oregon and Washington traverses old-growth rainforests, deserts and all the major western mountain ranges. Every year around 300 'thru-hikers' attempt it in one go; tramping an average of 20 miles (32km) a day, and allowing for plenty of rest days, it generally takes five or six months.

THE WILD WEST

There's a wealth of wildlife in the Sierra Nevada. More than 1500 types of flower fleck the region: blooms such as mountain violet, azaleas, and red columbine color lower elevations, while orchids, mariposa lilies, and alpine monkey flowers grow higher. Easily spotted birds include red-tailed hawks, turkey vultures and bold Steller's jays; listen for owls after dark. Ground squirrels, raccoons and marmots are the mammals most commonly seen; mule deer thrive, as hunting is not permitted in protected areas. Black bears might be seen, and often raid camping grounds at night – keep your food stored in a bear barrel.

■ THE ADVENTURE UNFOLDS

Your legs ache. Your armpits smell. And your shoulders burn from the weight of your backpack. But you've never felt more alive. It's that blissful hour, when the day's walk is done and memories are flashbacking in your brain as you rest by the glow of your stove. The sun has dipped, rendering the cold gray mountains a warmer hue; the lake by your tent glitters as a breeze riffles its surface.

Dinner is uninspiring – mush with dried something – but you're famished so it tastes fantastic, especially when gulped down with those views. There are others camped here too, some in groups, some hiking solo. One starts to play a harmonica. You lie back and feel the last of the earth's warmth seep into your tired but contented bones. Later, stars sprinkle the sky like fairy dust. Inside your tent you lay awake, listening for snuffles – is that a black bear?

The days adopt a rhythm: rise with the sun, brew a cuppa, pack the tent, away you go. There's little to consider other than your physical motion and the beauty of the world around. That, and when you'll meet your next food drop – three days? Five? It's easy to lose time in this world of lakes and mountains, though you're looking forward to that chocolate ration. Food is a bit of an obsession on the trail; it's the main topic when you meet fellow trekkers – which you do, frequently. The JMT is too popular to be a total step out of civilization, but it's good to know there are others around in case you have an accident – or accidentally come face to face with a bear...

You've spotted one, foraging in a far-off meadow. It paid you no mind and you carried on carefully, privileged to have entered, briefly, its domain.

■ MAKING IT HAPPEN

Most hikers tackle the JMT north–south (Yosemite–Mt Whitney); buses run from San Francisco to Yosemite, via Merced. You need a Wilderness Permit from the reservation station nearest your starting point; apply online or by post, up to 24 weeks in advance. You must be self-sufficient, carrying camp kit and filtering water. Pack plenty of food and prearrange resupplies at points en route; keep food in bear barrels. Local companies run organized full and shorter JMT hikes.

■ DETOUR

The great granite baldy of Half Dome, Yosemite's most iconic outcrop, is not officially on the John Muir Trail. However, it's only a short diversion on day one (if walking north–south). The JMT–Half Dome trail junction is just after Little Yosemite Valley Campground; allow three hours for the round trip from here. The climb is well marked but strenuous, the final section entailing a haul up bare rock with the aid of a fixed cableway. Take gloves, and don't attempt it if you suffer from vertigo.

53

OPENING SPREAD Pausing for a breather, and another peek at the view, on the John Muir Trail. **ABOVE (L)** Nevada Fall. **ABOVE (R)** View of Yosemite's Half Dome. **LEFT** Mule deer, like this magnificent buck, are frequently spotted in the Sierra Nevada mountains.

ARMCHAIR

* ***The John Muir Trail*** (Cicerone) Dedicated trekking guide that breaks the route into 21 stages and includes planning and preparation info.

* ***On the Trail of John Muir*** (Cherry Good) An investigation of the man behind the hike; looks at Muir's life and work, as well as his legacy.

* ***Sierra Nevada: The John Muir Trail*** (Ansel Adams) Iconic black-and-white images by the famed American photographer.

* ***John Muir Trail: The Essential Guide*** (Elizabeth Wenk & Kathy Morey) The latest edition of this US hiking guide contains GPS coordinates for landmarks and updated topographical maps.

* ***The Eight Wilderness Discovery Books*** (John Muir) A compendium of Muir's nature and conservation writing, including 'My First Summer in the Sierra' and 'The Yosemite'.

HEAR MOUNTAIN MUSIC IN THE APPALACHIANS

RAW. HEARTFELT. REAL. WHETHER IT'S A GRAMMY WINNER CROONING ON A MOUNTAIN STAGE OR A TRIO OF TEENS PLAYING FIDDLES ON THE SIDEWALK, MOUNTAIN MUSIC SPEAKS TO YOUR SOUL. AND THERE'S NO BETTER PLACE TO HEAR IT THAN IN THE HILLS AND HOLLERS OF THE SOUTHERN APPALACHIAN MOUNTAINS.

Catchy fiddle-and-banjo tunes ripple over the lawn at the Humpback Rocks Visitor Center, a stone cottage tucked in the shadows of the hardwoods that border the northern reaches of the Blue Ridge Parkway. Beneath the leafy branches of a lone black walnut tree, you'll find the source of the mesmerizing music: an old-time band playing like it's juiced by the devil himself.

In the distance, the jagged profile of Humpback Rocks overlooks the concert. A 19th-century log cabin and a simple garden are a few steps away, part of the sprawling farm museum here. The entire scene encapsulates what lies ahead along the Blue Ridge Parkway, which twists across the Blue Ridge Mountains for 469 miles (755km). Part of the national park system, it celebrates its Appalachian heritage with music jams and history exhibits.

Mountain music traces its roots to the earliest days of America. European settlers brought their violins, also called fiddles, to the Virginia coast in the 1600s. Soon after, African slaves were creating music with their own banjo-like instruments. The fiddle and banjo joined forces, and their combined sound migrated west. In the southern Appalachians this music marinated with the songs and stories carried south from Pennsylvania by Scots-Irish and German immigrants, who established farms in the mid-1700s.

The music met a wider audience after the historic 1927 Bristol Sessions, when the old-time songs of the Carter Family, Jimmie Rodgers, and other regional musicians were studio-recorded in Bristol, Virginia. Their subsequent success earned Bristol the nickname 'The Birthplace of Country Music'. Today, mountain music is an umbrella term covering traditional old-time music and the more modern sounds of bluegrass. Stereotypes persist about the residents of Appalachia: stubborn, suspicious, insular. But listen to the lyrics and you'll understand that the music speaks to essential shared truths. It's the music of family and community. And usually a lot of fun.

54

ESSENTIAL EXPERIENCES

✻ **Catching a sunset from a viewpoint overlooking the Shenandoah Valley.**

✻ Exploring the historic charms of downtown Staunton and Lexington.

✻ **Paddling through the mountain foothills on the Upper James River Water Trail.**

✻ Hiking to the summit of Sharp Top at the Peaks of Otter for 360° views.

✻ **Joining Appalachian Trail hikers for fried chicken, ham and biscuits served family-style at the Homeplace (4968 Catawba Valley Dr) in Catawba.**

✻ Busting a move on the dance floor at the Floyd Country Store.

✻ **Appreciating the daily musical wizardry at the Blue Ridge Music Center.**

DISTANCE 213 MILES (343KM) | **LOCATION** VIRGINIA, USA | **IDEAL TIME COMMITMENT** FOUR DAYS
BEST TIME OF YEAR JUNE–MID-OCTOBER | **ESSENTIAL TIP** BRING HIKING SHOES. TRAILS LEAD TO WATERFALLS AND BIG VIEWS.

THE APPALACHIAN TRAIL

Outdoor adventurers who want to add hiking to their concert-going can explore the Appalachian Trail (AT) in the northern section of the Blue Ridge Parkway. The 2190-mile (3524km) trail starts at Springer Mountain in Georgia and ends atop Mt Katahdin in Maine, crossing 14 states along the way. In Virginia, the AT runs close to the Blue Ridge Parkway from milepost 0 to about milepost 100, where it swings west across the Roanoke Valley. For mountain music fans, the AT passes close to Humpback Rocks Visitor Center and the Peaks of Otter.

THE CROOKED ROAD

The Blue Ridge Parkway occasionally overlaps
with the Crooked Road, a 330-mile (531km)
driving route that passes nine major venues for
mountain music and more than 60 affiliated
music and cultural sites across southwest
Virginia. As its name suggests, the Crooked
Road zigzags through the surrounding scenery.
Signs emblazoned with banjos mark the route.
The phrase 'taking the crooked road' can also
describe a twisty and unpredictable solo run
by a fiddler during a song. Three key stops on
the Crooked Road are the Floyd Country Store,
the Blue Ridge Music Center and the Carter
Family Fold. The eight-day Mountains of Music
Homecoming in mid-June is a multi-venue
celebration of Crooked Road music and culture.

THE ADVENTURE UNFOLDS

The final scramble up Humpback Rocks at milepost 5.8 will give you pause – you can't quite see what's ahead as you find your footing and clamber up the rock ledge. But the reward at the end of this one-mile (1.6km) climb is sweeping views of the forested spine of the Blue Ridge Mountains. The Blue Ridge Parkway crosses these peaks, linking Shenandoah National Park in Virginia with Great Smoky Mountains National Park in North Carolina. There are no stoplights or billboards along the way. Just trees, trailheads and scenic overlooks. Mileposts mark your progress.

Step into the white-clapboard Johnson Farm at milepost 86 for a glimpse into the life of a hard-working mountain family in the 1930s. This former apple farm lies at the foot of the Peaks of Otter. For a more sonorous diversion, old-time and bluegrass bands play on Sunday nights from late May until mid-October at the Roanoke Music Picnic Area near milepost 120. Drive into Roanoke from here for the pimento-and-bacon-topped burger and other farm-to-table fare at the Local Roots restaurant.

The clack-clack-clack of tap shoes against the wooden floor signals that dancers are approaching the stage at the century-old Floyd Country Store. Anchoring the tiny town of Floyd, the store is the liveliest music venue in the Blue Ridge during its Friday Night Jamboree. The evening always ends with an old-time band getting the crowd truly moving.

Musicians play daily during the Midday Music Sessions (noon-4pm May-Oct) at the Blue Ridge Music Center at milepost 213 near the North Carolina border. The adjacent museum traces the history of mountain music. On most Saturday nights from late May to early October, bands perform at the outdoor amphitheater where the Blue Ridge Mountains are the backdrop. Settle in for mountain magic.

MAKING IT HAPPEN

The Friday Night Jamboree in Floyd occurs year-round, but for a full slate of live music, visit between June and mid-October. Most parkway attractions close in winter. The Peaks of Otter Lodge is the only accommodation along the parkway in Virginia, but there are several campgrounds. B&Bs and indie hotels in nearby towns are plentiful. From northern Virginia, follow I-81 south to I-64 east, which leads to Afton, VA and the start of the parkway.

DETOUR

The Carter family recorded songs for the 1927 Bristol Sessions, to international renown. Today, descendants of band members AP, Sara, and Maybelle Carter oversee Saturday night old-time shows at the Carter Family Fold in Hiltons. June Carter, daughter of Maybelle, married Johnny Cash, whose last performance was at the Fold in 2003.

MYLES NEW | LONELY PLANET ©

MATT MUNRO | LONELY PLANET ©

OPENING SPREAD Fall sets the Linn Cove Viaduct ablaze on the Blue Ridge Parkway. **ABOVE (L)** A fiddle-maker at work in his Floyd store.
ABOVE (R) A typically scenic setting in the Blue Ridge Mountains. **LEFT** An old-time band rip it up on Friday night at the Floyd Country Store.

ARMCHAIR

✳ *Guide to the Crooked Road: Virginia's Heritage Music Trail* (Joe Wilson) This informative book by the National Heritage Award recipient explores the origins of mountain music and describes key sights along the music trail.

✳ *The Ballad Novels* (Sharyn McCrumb) A series of novels set in the southern Appalachians telling tales of adultery, murder and star-crossed lovers.

✳ *Factory Man* (Beth Macy) The real-life fight of a southwest Virginia furniture store owner against the global forces destroying the region's deep-rooted furniture-making industry.

✳ *Folk Songs from the West Virgina Hills* (Patrick Ward Gainer) Learn the words and stories behind those tunes you're whistlin'.

✳ *The Winding Stream* (2014) This documentary spotlights the impact of the Carter Family on country music.

ENJOY HAWAII ON A DIME

THE USA'S ISLAND GETAWAY DOESN'T HAVE TO BE EXPENSIVE – FROM SHRIMP TRUCK LUNCHES TO HOURS OF BEACHSIDE IDYLL AND ENCOUNTERS WITH THE LOCALS ON 'THE BUS', IT'S POSSIBLE TO DO O'AHU ON LITTLE MORE THAN SPARE CHANGE.

The guy across the aisle looks like Nick Nolte. Not the polished Nick Nolte from films, but the Nick Nolte from that infamous drunken mugshot – the one with the Hawaiian shirt and the leathery, sun-creased skin, the electric-shock hair, and the dazed expression. His lookalike glances up now, locks eyes and breaks into a lopsided smile: 'What's happenin', man?'

You meet your fair share of characters – friendly ones, too – on 'The Bus', O'ahu's sole form of public transport and the savior of budget travelers. It's also popular with the occasional frazzled local, which is why Nick Nolte's doppelgänger is sitting red-eyed across the way. He's on his way to the North Shore, the same as everyone else on board.

O'ahu might conjure images of fancy hotels and overpriced mai tais, but Hawaii's main island doesn't have to be an expensive destination. Start with transport. Most visitors with cash to splash hire a car if they want to get around, but a mere US$25 buys you four days of sights, sounds and local characters on The Bus. Surfing Nick Nolte is just one of them.

It's people like him that you'll remember after taking a budget tour of O'ahu, more so than the beaches and the palm trees and the cheap drinks. There are plenty of characters, for instance, down at Rainbow Drive-In, a classic O'ahuan plate-lunch joint close to Waikiki. This fixed-plate meal consists of 'two scoop' rice, macaroni or potato salad and a hot protein dish reflecting Hawaiian polyglot food heritage, such as mahi-mahi, teriyaki chicken or Korean-style short ribs. Wrapped in rainbow-colored neon, this famous drive-in was started by an island-born US army cook after WWII and has been doling out down-home favorites to construction workers, surfers, and gangly teenagers ever since. It's different and delicious. Wipe your plate clean, pay the bill, and jump back on The Bus with its whacked-out celebrity lookalikes. It's time for another adventure.

ESSENTIAL EXPERIENCES

* **Eating fried seafood while sitting in the sun at one of the North Shore's famous shrimp trucks.**

* Drinking rum cocktails at La Mariana Sailing Club, one of Hawaii's last authentic tiki bars.

* **Going Hawaiian-shirt shopping at Bailey's Antiques and Aloha Shirts, which has thousands upon thousands of colorful garments, ranging from US$5 to US$5000.**

* **Learning to play the ukulele for free at Ukulele Puapua, a shop that's part of the Sheraton in Waikiki.**

* Getting a 'shave ice' from Matsumoto – it's just crushed ice and sugary syrup, but it's worth queuing for.

LOCATION O'AHU, HAWAII, USA | **BEST TIME OF YEAR** YEAR-ROUND | **IDEAL TIME COMMITMENT** ONE WEEK
ESSENTIAL TIP DON'T EXPECT TO SEE THE FAMED BIG WAVES IN SUMMER; EVEN WAIMEA BAY IS LIKELY TO BE DEAD FLAT
PACK BOARDSHORTS AND SUNSCREEN – THAT'S IT.

ALOHA, GOOD-LOOKING!

It's not just a tourist thing — Hawaiians really do love their brightly colored, patterned shirts, referred to as 'aloha shirts'. The gaudy garments were popularised in the 1930s by a local called Ellery Chun, who turned his Chinese grocery store into a producer of ridiculously colorful tops and coined the popular term. Pretty soon the local surfers started buying aloha shirts, and then the tourists, and before Chun knew it he had a full-scale craze on his hands. That craze has lasted some 80-odd years — vintage aloha shirts now sell for as much as US$5000, and there's a thriving trade in new and secondhand numbers.

HOLLYWOOD IN HAWAII

It's the question so often asked in Hawaii: where did they shoot *Lost*? And what about *Jurassic Park*? The good news is the filming locations are easy to scout out if you know where you're looking. The initial plane crash in *Lost* and much of the first season of the hit TV show were filmed at Mokule'ia Beach on the North Shore of O'ahu. Nearby is Police Beach, where the bulk of season two was shot. The Ka'a'awa Valley, meanwhile, has been in more movies than Tom Cruise. OK, not quite. But a large amount of *Jurassic Park* was shot there, as well as scenes from *50 First Dates, Pearl Harbor, Mighty Joe Young*, and plenty of action from *Lost*.

■ THE PERFECT GETAWAY

The cliché that the best things in life are free rings true in O'ahu. Take ukulele lessons: a tutorial in the quintessential Hawaiian instrument costs nothing at Ukulele Puapua, a store in Waikiki. There you can spend an hour learning the basics – how to hold, how to strum – with no pressure to buy. Of course, once you realize your own awesomeness you might not need any more encouragement.

Another free activity is a trip to Bailey's Antiques and Aloha Shirts, which is ostensibly a shop, but feels more like a museum dedicated to those colorful shirts as well as kitsch souvenirs. The store bulges with vintage and new shirts and knick-knacks.

For a day away from the touristy buzz of Waikiki, jump on The Bus to the old town of Hale'iwa on the North Shore. This is where the famous shrimp trucks dish up huge plates of fried shrimp for a very reasonable price. It's all pretty rough-and-ready – collect your plastic plate and then take a seat at a wooden bench. Want dessert? Just down the road you'll find Matsumoto's, where locals queue down the street for the island's best shave ice (crushed ice with syrup). The North Shore's best attraction, of course, is at Waimea Bay. There you won't pay a cent to just lie on the sand and watch the world go by.

There is one final stop on your shoestring tour of Hawaii: Hank's Cafe in Chinatown. One of Honolulu's few 'dive' bars, what Hank's lacks in fancy decor it certainly makes up for in drinks prices, and a friendly atmosphere. Live music rolls in some nights and regulars practically call it home. It mightn't be beachy or kitsch, but it sure is affordable.

■ PLAN IT

Winter (November to April) is the perfect time to visit O'ahu for big-wave viewing. If lying on the sand is more your thing, Hawaii is a year-round destination. Los Angeles and Sydney provide the easiest access but flights also operate from Japan and Korea. Honolulu Airport is a short bus transfer from Waikiki, where most hostels and hotels are located, or a two-hour bus ride to the less touristy North Shore, where accommodation is harder to come by in November and December.

■ DETOUR

Hawaii doesn't have to be done on a strict budget. Start with lunch at Alan Wong's for Hawaiian haute cuisine, where traditional dishes are reinterpreted with serious skill. Next, pick up your rented convertible and go for a lap around the island before parking it at Halekulani Resort, one of Waikiki's finest and therefore most expensive beachfront hotels. To finish things off, grab a cocktail and a bite to eat at Nobu, every celebrity's favorite Honolulu watering hole.

MATT MUNRO | LONELY PLANET ©

OPENING SPREAD A local treat, shave ice is served. **ABOVE (L)** Paddling out to catch the surf at Waikiki Beach. **ABOVE (R)** Tempting bowls of traditional Hawaiian food. **LEFT** The paradisiacal scenery of Kalalau Valley provides one of Hawaii's many photogenic settings.

ARMCHAIR

* ***Honolulu*** (Alan Brennert) This 20th-century tale of a Korean immigrant in Hawaii's capital provides a window into a surprisingly complex culture.

* ***Diamond Head*** (Charles Knief) This murder mystery set among the palm trees of the Aloha State makes perfect airplane reading.

* ***Hawaii*** (James A Michener) Michener's novel tackles Hawaiian history, from the volcanic formation of the islands onward.

* ***Moana*** (2016) Controversial yet popular, this animated Disney film weaves a tale about ancient Polynesia.

* ***Big Wednesday*** (1978) Granted, it's set in California, but this cult film's most important scenes – the ones in the huge surf – were shot in Hawaii, mostly around Waimea Bay.

* ***Point Break*** (1991) Another cult surf classic, featuring Keanu Reeves in all his Johnny Utah glory.

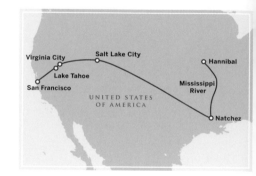

JOURNEY THROUGH MARK TWAIN'S USA

HOP ABOARD A MISSISSIPPI RIVERBOAT, BUNK IN THE VERY ROOM ABOVE THE VERY SALOON THE ONE-TIME STEAMBOAT PILOT PATRONIZED. NAVIGATE THE WESTERN USA TO EXPERIENCE THE CHILL OF A SAN FRANCISCO SUMMER FOG, AND GET INTO THE HEAD OF THE OFT-QUOTED GENIUS, MARK TWAIN.

To follow in Mark Twain's footsteps is to journey south and west from his home state of Missouri with spurs floating down the Mississippi River into America's deep south, and another rambling to San Francisco, California's first great, and most beautiful, city. Armed with the proper reading material, your mind will be opened and your point of view sharpened by the very same land and waters that moulded Twain's humor and insight, and inspired within him a literary mischief that bottled a still young and wild America back in the 19th century.

Whether he was writing about the small towns and thick wilderness along the Big Muddy from Missouri to New Orleans, hopping the first steamship to the Sandwich Islands or wandering the streets of San Francisco, Twain made his adventures, real and imagined, leap from the page and take anchor in a reader's mind and heart, as well as America's cultural zeitgeist forever.

Born Samuel Clemens, in Florida, Missouri in 1835, Twain moved to Hannibal when he was four. Missouri was a slave state and Hannibal's characters, scenery and politics would later inspire the fictional town of St Petersburg, home of Tom Sawyer and the mischievous orphan hero, Huckleberry Finn. After a stint as a printers' apprentice, Twain became a riverboat pilot and made dozens of trips up and down the Mississippi River before heading west into the Nevada Territory in 1861.

He spent two weeks in a stagecoach rolling through the Great Plains, and over the Rocky Mountains, before stopping briefly in the new Mormon community of Salt Lake City. After trying his hand at gold mining in Virginia City, Nevada, he became a journalist and moved to San Francisco in 1864. From here, local newspapers funded his sojourn to the Sandwich Islands (now Hawaii) and Europe. His most creative period was the 17 years he lived in Hartford, Connecticut with his family.

ESSENTIAL EXPERIENCES

* **Exploring Twain's own Hannibal, MO, and mingling with other Twain devotees.**

* Listening to a banjo strumming, and the Big Muddy sloshing against the bow, on a ride on a real Mississippi riverboat.

* **Surveying the Mississippi River from the atmospheric Under-The-Hill Saloon, a glorious dive with bluegrass bands jamming on weekends.**

* Setting out on one of the most beautiful drives in the American West, following the route Twain took through the Utah high desert, up and over the Sierra Nevada, past Lake Tahoe to the San Francisco Bay.

DISTANCE 1430 MILES (2303KM) | **COUNTRIES COVERED** USA | **IDEAL TIME COMMITMENT** ONE WEEK | **BEST TIME OF THE YEAR** JUNE TO AUGUST | **ESSENTIAL TIP** DO THIS TRIP IN ONE SHOT BY DRIVING FROM NATCHEZ TO NEW ORLEANS THEN FLYING TO SALT LAKE.

The former Hartford, Connecticut home of the legendary author is now the Mark Twain House & Museum. It was here that Twain penned many of his greatest works, including *Tom Sawyer*, *Huckleberry Finn* and *A Connecticut Yankee in King Arthur's Court*. The house itself, a Victorian Gothic with fanciful turrets and gables, reflects Twain's quirky character. Inside you'll find 25 rooms in all including a glass conservatory, a grand library, and billiards room. The house was built in 1873–74, but financial issues demanded a move across the Atlantic to Europe in 1891 and they never lived in the Hartford house, Twain's all-time favorite nest, ever again.

■ THE JOURNEY TODAY

The first leg of your journey begins in Hannibal, MO, where you can visit the Mark Twain Boyhood Home & Museum, a complex of seven buildings including two houses Twain lived in, and the home of Laura Hawkins, the true-life inspiration for Tom's great love, Becky Thatcher. In his twenties, Twain was a commercial steamboat pilot on the Big Muddy, and he got to know all the bends and eddies, towns and outlaws, islands and sandbars that made Huck's grand escape with Jim, the runaway slave, so true to life. You don't have to pilot a driftwood raft to honor that legacy, just join a dinner cruise aboard the Mark Twain Riverboat. Further downriver, historic antebellum mansions will greet you in Natchez, MS. In the 1840s, there were more millionaires per capita here than anywhere in the world. When Twain passed through, he crashed in a room above the Under-The-Hill Saloon, which remains the best bar in town, with terrific live music on weekends. You can still sleep upstairs at what is now called Mark Twain Guest House. Reserve your bed at the bar.

It would be unreasonable to recreate the entire overland stagecoach journey he depicted in his 1872 tome, *Roughing It*. Instead, pick up the Mark Twain trail in Salt Lake City. Once a Mormon camp and homestead, Utah's largest city remains one of the American West's best-kept secrets. From here, drive I-80 to the foot of the Sierra Nevada and Virginia City, where you can tour the Mark Twain Museum, set in the offices of the Territorial Enterprise where Twain honed his skills as a journalist.

Stay on I-80 and wind your way into the Sierra Nevada and Lake Tahoe. Tahoe trout was one of Mark Twain's favorite foods, and you can still fish here in a deep cobalt lake ringed with jagged granite peaks, but it's all catch and

ARMCHAIR

* *The Celebrated Jumping Frog of Calaveras County* (Mark Twain) His first important work, originally published in the *New York Saturday Press* in 1865, is about a gold-rush gambler named Jim Smiley.

* *A Connecticut Yankee in King Arthur's Court* (Mark Twain) In one of the original time travel tales, a 19th-century Yankee meddles in the lives of King Arthur, Sir Lancelot and Guinevere.

* *The Adventures of Tom Sawyer* (Mark Twain) This American classic drew upon Twain's experience growing up along the Mississippi River.

* *Adventures of Huckleberry Finn* (Mark Twain) Considered Twain's greatest work, Huck Finn, a poor orphan teen, slips from the 'sivilizing' confines of St Petersburg and escapes his violent father to float down the Mississippi with runaway slave, Jim.

STILL MAKING WAVES

Twain is still making waves. First came the publication of his autobiography in November 2010, which despite middling reviews became an unexpected bestseller, making Twain the only author ever to publish bestsellers in the 19th, 20th and 21st centuries. Then, in 2012, NewSouth Books released a new edition of *Huckleberry Finn*, in which the 200-plus mentions of the 'n-word' were replaced with 'slave'. NewSouth's argument was that *Huckleberry Finn* and *Tom Sawyer* have been disappearing from school curricula in the US due to their offensive language. This is by no means the first attempt to cleanse Twain. *Huckleberry Finn* was banned or altered by institutions and media outlets across the country in 1885, 1905, 1955, 1998 and 2015.

release. San Francisco bay oysters were another favorite of Twain's. Although they still exist, bay pollution is far too severe to consider them a viable protein. But you can slurp safely at Hog Island Oyster Bar in the Ferry Building.

◼ SHORTCUT

Mark Twain will always be synonymous with the mighty Mississippi River. Start in Hannibal at the Mark Twain Boyhood Museum, hop on the Mark Twain Riverboat, and if you crave more road miles, follow the river down to Memphis and over to the Natchez Trace Parkway, which will lead you to the Under-The-Hill Saloon, an old Twain haunt in Natchez, Mississippi.

◼ DETOUR

Twain cut his teeth as a journeyman writer on a nine month sojourn through the Hawaiian Islands (then known as the Sandwich Islands) in 1966 for the Sacramento Union. Twain-era Honolulu is long gone, but you can still taste wild 19th-century Hawaii on the Big Island, which the 31-year-old explored on horseback. He also paddled with local surfers and rode to the edge of the Kilauea caldera, its lava flowing then as now

T. MALACHI DUNWORTH | 500PX ©

OPENING SPREAD Onboard a ferry voyage along Twain's beloved Mississippi River. **ABOVE** A cable-car crests one of the precipitous streets of San Francisco, where Twain worked as a journalist. **BELOW** Lake Tahoe, on the border with California and Nevada.

PARTY HARD IN THE BIG EASY

NEW ORLEANS IS ONE OF THE GREATEST MUSIC CITIES ON EARTH. AND EVERY FEBRUARY THE WHOLE PLACE SHUTS DOWN TO CELEBRATE MARDI GRAS – THE WILDEST PARTY FESTIVITIES IN ALL OF NORTH AMERICA.

Here they come! All feathers and finery, dancing and chanting, and surrounded by their followers. Hey, hey, it's the Mardi Gras Indians. 'Iko! Iko!' they chant while dancing in the street, surrounded by revelers, everyone caught up in the joy and excitement of Fat Tuesday, the final day of the craziness that is Mardi Gras in the city of New Orleans.

The Mardi Gras Indians are African American men who every year sew strikingly original, outrageously colorful 'suits' – suits that make Lady Gaga's stage costumes look conservative – then come out and parade in their 'tribes' on Fat Tuesday, Mardi Gras' climax. Also taking to the streets on Fat Tuesday is the Zulu Parade, when black New Orleans comes out to strut and celebrate. This parade starts early – be out on the streets by 8am to catch it – and moves across the central city. It is a feast of brass bands, marching girls, and elaborate floats, as 'krewes' toss beads and gifts (try to catch a painted coconut – exclusive to Zulu!), and huge fun. Follow the parade as it moves across downtown and you will get a real feeling for the city.

Great live music can be heard year-round in this humid, sensual city. There are bars and clubs and the best buskers on earth around the French Quarter, from funky brass bands and jazz musicians to crusty young folkies and blues singers and rockers – and myriad music festivals.

However, Mardi Gras is when the whole city comes out to play. It precedes the Catholic celebration of Lent: Louisiana was, firstly, a Spanish and then a French colony (until 1803). The French allowed their slaves a certain degree of freedom to dance and perform music – providing the foundations for New Orleans as a hotbed of music-making. These days, Fat Tuesday's party is about witnessing a city, which has been through and survived hard times, get up and shake its tail feathers.

ESSENTIAL EXPERIENCES

* **Riding the streetcar through the Garden District – a glorious way of experiencing New Orleans' architectural glory.**

* Wandering around lively Frenchmen St: dive bars, superb clubs, buskers, beggars, eccentrics, and a very fine bookshop. Never a dull moment.

* **Following a street parade with brass band and dancers during Mardi Gras – part of black New Orleans tradition.**

* Attending concerts by local artists: Dr John, Irma Thomas, Jon Cleary, The Wild Magnolias, Hurray for the Riff Raff, Little Freddie King, Aaron Neville, Chuck Perkins, Walter 'Wolfman' Washington, Kermit Ruffins, George Porter Jr, the Hot 8 Brass Band and others.

* **Sinking happily into a Cajun-Creole food-induced coma.**

LOCATION NEW ORLEANS, LOUISIANA, USA | **BEST TIME OF YEAR** SEPTEMBER TO NOVEMBER; MARDI GRAS TAKES PLACE ACROSS FEBRUARY OR EARLY MARCH | **IDEAL TIME COMMITMENT** ONE WEEK | **ESSENTIAL TIP** TO CATCH THE MARDI GRAS INDIANS HEAD TO TREMÉ ON FAT TUESDAY AFTERNOON | **PACK** GOOD SHOES (YOU'LL BE ON YOUR FEET ALL DAY).

THE MARDI GRAS INDIANS

The Mardi Gras Indians' historic tradition dates back to the late 19th century and is thought to possibly reflect the kinship of recently freed African slaves and Native Americans. For decades they were an underground movement who often fought pitched battles (between the tribes) on the street. But in recent decades several of the Mardi Gras Indian tribes (The Wild Tchoupitoulas, The Wild Magnolias) have embraced the wider world, making seminal albums and joining the likes of Dr John on stage while also becoming a popular part of New Orleans folklore.

BRASS BANDS

New Orleans is full of funky brass bands: the Treme Brass Band play old-school style; the Dirty Dozen Brass Band bring fine jazz flavors in, and the Stooges Brass Band are young and tough. The most well known of these brass blasters is the Hot 8 Brass Band, who bring a swaggering, rap-influenced groove to their music. The Hot 8 have released several fine albums and often play concerts and parades across the city (find them at their Sunday night residency at the Howlin' Wolf). This is party music with funky chops. Watch the locals dance!

■ THE PERFECT GETAWAY

While Mardi Gras may be when New Orleans becomes one big party, the city is open for those wanting a good time all year round. From when jazz first flowered in the city's brothels a century ago, through New Orleans' finest blues and soul, R&B and funk, rap and rock, it is *the* US music metropolis, a city rich with talent. The French Quarter, with its historic buildings, faded grandeur, and wrought-iron balconies, is what visitors initially discover. In the Quarter there is Bourbon St, home to bars and clubs, fast-food joints, and strip joints, the place where, every weekend, young Americans head to party and get very drunk. But beyond such hedonism the French Quarter does offer more refined experiences, including Preservation Hall, a venue dedicated to trad Dixieland jazz.

The city spreads beyond the French Quarter's narrow warren of streets. On Frenchmen St in the 7th Ward there are considerable music venues. This is where the young and hip come out to party. Legendary music venues such as the Howlin' Wolf, Tipitina's, and the Maple Leaf Bar are spread across the city and require a car to get to.

Let your tastebuds join the fun: alongside Louisiana's gumbo and jambalaya, there's superb *beignets* (doughnuts) and coffee. The city also has excellent museums, while its gothic cemeteries are fascinating to explore. Take a streetcar out to the Garden District, where huge antebellum-era mansions offer a vision of an old South, one of luxury and servitude. New Orleans gave the world jazz and blues, gumbo and voodoo, Louis Armstrong and Lil' Wayne. This is where music, magic and an ever-present hint of madness come together to party.

■ PLAN IT

Louis Armstrong Airport only receives a handful of international flights: you might change planes in Atlanta, Georgia, or Houston, Texas. Amtrak trains provide a pleasant overnight journey from Chicago. New Orleans is popular year-round (although it is hot and sticky in summer), but Mardi Gras is when the city swells in size – book at least two months in advance. A car is not necessary – streetcars, buses, and taxis are plentiful and should be used (after dark the city can be dangerous).

■ DETOUR

Had enough of the Crescent City? Drive 90 minutes north to Lafayette, the capital of Cajun Country – a good place to learn about Cajun history and praised as a top food destination in the South. Here, French is still widely spoken and violins and accordions get everyone dancing. Restaurants serve great gumbo while dance halls host rocking Cajun and zydeco bands. Swamp tours allow you to observe bird life and feed alligators. After being in New Orleans, you'll find Lafayette laid-back.

LAJRI PATTERSON | GETTY IMAGES ©

KRIS DAVIDSON | LONELY PLANET ©

OPENING SPREAD A marching band celebrate Mardi Gras. **ABOVE (L)** Shrimp and sausage simmer in a pot of Louisiana gumbo. **ABOVE (R)** Music can be found on every corner in the French Quarter. **LEFT** Daniel 'Weenie' Farrow, saxophonist and band leader, at Preservation Hall.

ARMCHAIR

* *Mister Jelly Roll* (Alan Lomax) Brilliant oral autobiography of jazz piano pioneer Jelly Roll Morton, rich with detail on New Orleans in the early 20th century.

* *Mardi Gras Indians* (Michael P Smith) The late Smith was the great photographer of New Orleans vernacular culture.

* *Treme* (2010–13) This HBO TV series by David Simon is about the renewal of New Orleans after Hurricane Katrina.

* *A Streetcar Named Desire* (1951) Film of Tennessee Williams' New Orleans drama, starring Marlon Brando and Vivien Leigh.

* *All On A Mardi Gras Day* (2003) Royce Osborn's fascinating documentary on black New Orleans' Mardi Gras traditions.

* *Heaven Before I Die: A Journey to the Heart of New Orleans* (Michael Oliver-Goodwin) This collection of journalism covers local music-making in all its facets.

WALK WITH WOLVES IN YELLOWSTONE

UNKNOWN TO THE MAJORITY OF ITS THREE MILLION ANNUAL VISITORS, YELLOWSTONE NATIONAL PARK HIDES SOME OF THE WILDEST CORNERS OF THE WEST. BED DOWN WITH GRIZZLIES, ELK AND WOLVES ON THIS TREK THROUGH THE MOST REMOTE WILDERNESS IN THE LOWER 48 STATES.

Yellowstone National Park boasts true marvels: exploding geysers, thundering waterfalls, and some of the largest herds of bison and elk on the whole continent. It's also one of the USA's most popular parks, visited by more than 30,000 people per day in the peak summer months of July and August. Hike a mile from the road, however, and you'll lose 99% of the tourists. Trek into the park's remote southeastern corner, known as the Thorofare, and you'll lose pretty much everybody.

The spectacular valley is bordered to the north by huge Yellowstone Lake, to the east by the brooding, volcanic Absaroka Mountains, and to the south by the Bridger-Teton Wilderness. Apart from the odd ranger's cabin, the land is home only to populations of grizzly bears, wolves and elk.

Trappers, hunters and Native Americans have long used the broad valley, following game trails and the migration routes of the local wapiti elk herds. The Hayden Survey visited in 1871 and their reports led to the creation of the world's first national park the following year.

A trek into the Thorofare is a physical and logistical challenge, involving at least a week-long journey into the heart of nowhere, so you need excellent wilderness skills, including experience of fording rivers and camping safely in grizzly country. There are no easy escape routes if you run into trouble.

You can make life easier by employing a local outfitter to arrange a horse trek through the region. Or you could use a boat shuttle to deposit you and a kayak or canoe at the southwestern branch of the lake, using the many backcountry lakeshore sites to explore the region around Trail Creek Trail before being picked up again a few days later.

Whichever way you do it, for sheer primeval wildness and immersion in the natural world, with the right preparation and back up, there's not an adventure for a thousand miles that can beat it.

ESSENTIAL EXPERIENCES

✳ **Watching the sun set crimson and gold over the silvery waters of Yellowstone Lake.**

✳ Staying awake through the night as you imagine all the bloodthirsty animals that could be the source of that tiny scratching at the corner of your tent.

✳ **Feeling the hair stand up at the back of your neck as you spot your first wolf in the wild.**

✳ Listening to the silence and the solitude, knowing that you are as far away from a road as you can get in the lower 48 states.

✳ **Gulping your first burger or cold beer after a week dining on ramen noodles and marshmallows.**

DISTANCE 70 MILES (113KM) | **LOCATION** YELLOWSTONE NATIONAL PARK, WYOMING, USA | **IDEAL TIME COMMITMENT** ONE WEEK
BEST TIME OF YEAR AUGUST TO SEPTEMBER | **ESSENTIAL TIP** BRING MOSQUITO REPELLENT, BINOCULARS AND AN EMERGENCY BEACON.

SUPERVOLCANO!

Few campers in Yellowstone realize that they have decided to pitch their tent atop one of the world's largest supervolcanoes. Much of the park is in fact floating above a giant hot spot of magma 124 miles (200km) deep, which provides the fuel for the world's most dense collection of geysers and hot springs. Scientists estimate that the last major eruption was 600,000 years ago, when Yellowstone's mountains were blown away and superheated ash blocked out the sun, creating a global volcanic winter. The next eruption? Well, that's due any time in the next 10,000 years or so...

■ THE ADVENTURE UNFOLDS

The week-long trek starts with a two-day walk down the eastern shore of Yellowstone Lake, North America's largest mountain lake, whose outline traces the caldera of the Yellowstone supervolcano. Campgrounds offer fine dusk views of the lake and the chance to spot pelicans, otters and ospreys.

By the end of the second day you reach the wide, flat, open valley of the meandering Upper Yellowstone River, its creeks thick with cutthroat trout (and merciless clouds of mosquitoes in early summer – bring repellent). All around lie burned and fallen trees from the huge wildfires of 1988.

The valley is a great place to spot moose, elk and grizzlies as well as summer wildflower blooms. For the next day or two, listen for the howling of the Delta wolf pack, the most remote and least studied of Yellowstone's wolf populations. Packs constantly shift numbers, strength, and territory, so check the latest locations with rangers. In this primeval land of grizzlies and wolves, it comes as quite a shock to realize that you are now firmly part of the local food chain, so bring bear spray for some peace of mind.

As you continue south, the Thorofare Trail follows the Upper Yellowstone River (the longest undammed river in the US) to reach the Thorofare Patrol Cabin at the park's southernmost extent. Just across the border by the headwaters of the Yellowstone lies a geographical curiosity. Here, high on Two Ocean Plateau, a creek of the same name branches into two streams; one is headed east for the Atlantic Ocean, the other west to reach the Pacific – truly a continental divide. At this furthest point you are perhaps 30 miles (50km) from the nearest road, about as far from the modern world as you can get. There are a couple of choices back to civilization. Head straight east via the South Boundary Trail all the way to the South Entrance, or branch northwest following the Continental Divide Trail to lovely Heart Lake, a worthy destination in its own right.

■ MAKING IT HAPPEN

Backcountry campgrounds need to be booked in advance, and you need to pick up permits in person. Bridge Bay Marina offers boat shuttles to the northern point of the lake's Southeast Arm. Outfitters can arrange horse trips into the Thorofare, mostly from the Bridger-Teton Wilderness to the south, and companies such as Wildland Trekking offer guided trips.

■ AN ALTERNATIVE CHALLENGE

If you don't have time for a long backpacking trip, consider a guided wolf-watching tour. The highly regarded Yellowstone Forever Institute offers packages that take you to the best locations and teach you about wolf behavior, communication and restoration efforts. Other courses range from backpacking trips to photography and bird-watching seminars.

THANKS! STEVE MCKINZIE | GETTY IMAGES ©

PETE SEAWARD | LONELY PLANET ©

OPENING SPREAD Yellowstone's Grand Prismatic Spring is the largest hot spring in the US. **ABOVE (L)** A gray wolf; the animals were released back into the park in 1995. **ABOVE (R)** Steam rises from a thermal spring. **LEFT** A bison grazes in front of the Old Faithful geyser.

ARMCHAIR

✳ **Hawk's Rest** (Gary Ferguson) Lyrical account of a season spent at the Hawk's Rest ranger's cabin deep in the Thorofare.

✳ **Lost in My Own Backyard** (Tim Cahill) Witty and engaging series of Yellowstone-related essays from the American travel writer.

✳ **Decade of the Wolf** (Douglas W Smith & Gary Ferguson) Chronicles the politics and science behind the reintroduction of wolves to Yellowstone.

✳ **Back of Beyond** (CJ Box) Murder mystery set among outfitters in the park's remotest corner, from the Wyoming-based author.

✳ **The Yellowstone Story** (Aubrey L Haines) The definitive account of the founding of America's first national park, written by a former park ranger.

✳ **Yellowstone** Imax big-screen film that shows daily in West Yellowstone.

JOIN THE REVOLUTION IN BOSTON

TAKE THE FAMILY TO BOSTON TO DISCOVER THE DARING AND DEFIANCE OF AMERICA'S FIERY FOREBEARS. JUST DON'T BE SURPRISED IF YOUR CHILDREN START TO MAKE DEMANDS LIKE 'GIVE ME LIBERTY OR GIVE ME DEATH!'

'Dump the tea!' shouts the rabble-rousing patriot, as he storms down the gangway to Griffin's Wharf.

'Into the sea!' responds the frenzied crowd, following close on his heels.

The raving mob has come straight from the meeting house at the Boston Tea Party Museum, where Sam Adams and other Sons of Liberty have been stirring up trouble. Cries of 'Boo!' and 'Fie!' can be heard when the rebels remind the assembled townsfolk of the injustices they have suffered at the hands of the British Crown. 'Huzzah!' rings forth when the decision is made to take a stand against taxation without representation.

The Boston Tea Party Museum is one of many destinations in the city where children can immerse themselves in the events that led to the birth of a nation, but also to experience the peril and passion that the early patriots knew. As the town where the American Revolution started, Boston is a living history museum. You can hardly walk a step on these cobblestone sidewalks without stumbling over a historic spot. Tour guides don colonial dress and share their 'personal' experiences, imbuing the stories with the energy and the excitement of revolution.

It may give parents pause to think that a visit to Boston will encourage their children to be rebellious. But the take-away message is that principles such as freedom and fairness are more important than order and obedience. As John Adams so eloquently put it, 'Let justice be done though the heavens may fall.'

With that sentiment in mind, the patriots on Griffin's Wharf hoist crates of tea high over their heads and hurl them into Boston Harbor. The crowd cheers, holding cameras and phones aloft all around. Then the enthusiastic participants pull the crates out of the water by their tethers, and throw them overboard again. 'Boston Harbor a teapot tonight! Huzzah!'

ESSENTIAL EXPERIENCES

✳ **Donning a Mohawk disguise and tossing crates of tea into the harbor at the Boston Tea Party Ships & Museum.**

✳ Investigating the bronze plaque that commemorates the Boston Massacre, the first violent encounter of the American Revolution.

✳ **Spotting the iconic grasshopper weathervane that tops Faneuil Hall.**

✳ Sampling the sweet colonial treat known as 'Indian pudding' at Durgin-Park in Faneuil Hall.

✳ **Discovering the headstone of Captain Daniel Malcom in Copp's Hill Burying Ground – his epitaph apparently provoked British soldiers to use the headstone for target practice.**

✳ Getting the bird's-eye view of Boston from high atop the Bunker Hill Monument.

LOCATION BOSTON, MASSACHUSETTS, USA | **BEST TIME OF YEAR** APRIL TO OCTOBER | **IDEAL TIME COMMITMENT** TWO DAYS
ESSENTIAL TIP MOST OF THE FREEDOM TRAIL SITES HAVE WEBSITES THAT OFFER GAMES, TRIVIA, AND ACTIVITIES TO GET YOUR KIDS EXCITED ABOUT WHAT THEY WILL SEE | **PACK** WALKING SHOES, RAIN GEAR AND SUNSCREEN.

A TRUE SON OF LIBERTY

History has it that British soldiers in Boston occasionally exhibited their aggression by taking aim at headstones in local cemeteries. They were, perhaps, particularly irked by one Daniel Malcom, whose final resting place is in Copp's Hill Burying Ground. Malcom's epitaph calls him 'A true son of Liberty... an Enemy to oppression and one of the foremost in opposing the Revenue Acts on America.' The headstone is marred by pockmarks, apparently caused by muskets shot at close range. Not much is known about this great patriot Daniel Malcom, except that he was a local merchant who was arrested for smuggling 60 kegs of wine and brandy into Boston. True Son of Liberty, indeed.

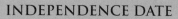

INDEPENDENCE DATE

Encircled by cobblestones, the Boston Massacre site marks the spot where the first blood was shed for American Independence. On March 5, 1770, an angry mob of colonists swarmed the British soldiers guarding the State House. About 40 protesters hurled insults, snowballs and rocks. Thus provoked, the soldiers fired into the crowd and killed five townspeople. The incident sparked enormous anti-British sentiment; Paul Revere fanned the flames by widely disseminating an engraving that depicted the scene as an unmitigated slaughter. Interestingly, John Adams and Josiah Quincy defended the accused soldiers in court, and seven of the nine were acquitted.

■ THE PERFECT GETAWAY

Boston isn't called the Cradle of Liberty for nothing. To see where the action went down, follow the Freedom Trail. This 2.5-mile (4km) walking path winds around the city center, connecting 16 of the most significant spots. Your children can download an activity-packed *Junior Ranger Activity Book* (or pick one up from the visitor center in Faneuil Hall) before starting out. The Freedom Trail is a lot to take in, especially for the younger set, so stick to the highlights. And if things start to fall apart, the Boston Common – America's oldest public park – has a huge playscape, a spray pool and plenty of wide open spaces where kids can run free.

The Old South Meeting House is the location of the rally that led to the Boston Tea Party. Listen to a re-enactment and let your kids explore the building on a scavenger hunt. For years, Faneuil Hall and Quincy Market were the community's market place – and they still are, with shops, restaurants, and street performers. Visiting them is less of a history lesson and more of a lunch break. Durgin Park is an atmospheric option for old-fashioned Boston fare, such as roast beef or fish cakes.

After lunch, stroll to Long Wharf and catch the ferry to Charlestown, on the Charles River's north bank. It will drop you at Pier 3, near the USS *Constitution*. The country's oldest warship, it was launched during the War of 1812. Today, you can take a tour of its decks for a glimpse of life at sea. Your kids can try their hands at firing a cannon or furling a sail at the museum. If they still have energy, head to the Bunker Hill Monument. The young and spry can end their tour by climbing 294 steps to the top of the obelisk for a 360-degree vista of Boston.

■ PLAN IT

Boston is an easy escape. Logan International Airport is easy to reach by public transport. Accommodations tend to be pricey, but options are plentiful so it's often possible to score high-quality, centrally located hotels for a bargain online. Many companies offer guided tours of the Freedom Trail, some of which are designed for children: try the National Park Service, Boston by Foot, and the Freedom Trail Foundation.

■ DETOUR

When your kids are historied out, explore Boston's connection to the sea. The New England Aquarium (NEAQ) is home to 600 species of sea creatures, from ethereal jellyfish to playful penguins. The main highlight is the three-story Great Ocean Tank, which swirls with thousands of creatures great and small, including turtles, sharks and eels. Most of the first floor is occupied by an enormous penguin exhibit. NEAQ also takes whale-watching cruises out to Stellwagen Bank, a rich feeding ground for whales, dolphins and sea birds.

RICHARD CAVALLERI | SHUTTERSTOCK ©

OPENING SPREAD In Boston's Public Garden visitors are met by Revolutionary War hero George Washington nobly sitting on a horse. **ABOVE** The Charles River esplanade offers excellent walking. **LEFT** Tourists explore Beacon Hill, one of the oldest neighborhoods in the US.

ARMCHAIR

✳ *Paul Revere's Ride* (Henry Wadsworth Longfellow, Ted Rand) Longfellow's famous poem is dramatized by Rand's vivid illustrations, making it a perfect introduction for children.

✳ *George vs George* (Rosalyn Schanzer) Tells both sides of the story, with great illustrations and text.

✳ *Willow's Walkabout* (Sheila S Cunningham) An Australian wallaby escapes from the zoo and explores Boston.

✳ *Sam the Minuteman/George the Drummer Boy* (Nathaniel Benchley) Chronicle of the Revolutionary War from the point of view of a colonial boy and a British boy, respectively.

✳ *Johnny Tremain* (Esther Hoskins Forbes) A colonial-era teenager is swept up in the excitement of the Boston Tea Party.

✳ *Make Way for Ducklings* (Robert McCloskey) The adventures of a mother duck and her ducklings in Boston.

FIND YOURSELF ON THE LOST COAST

A TRIP TO CALIFORNIA'S LOST COAST BRINGS VISITORS TO THE RUGGED, REMOTE, AND UTTERLY UNTAMED EDGE OF THE CONTINENT, WITH SCANT TRACES OF HUMAN IMPACT. WHEN THE FOG LIFTS, THE COASTAL EPIC REVEALS BEACHES OF GNARLED DRIFTWOOD, RUSTING SHIPWRECKS AND WILD SURF.

If you find yourself on a trail penetrating California's Lost Coast, congratulate yourself. As one of the superlative hiking and backpacking destinations in Northern California, the Lost Coast is a rugged, mystifying stretch of coastline where narrow trails ascend imposing coastal jags, cross empty volcanic beaches and traverse forests of mist-shrouded redwood. It's the provenance of majestic Roosevelt elk, lording redwood giants and ethereal banks of fog. During the three-day hike along its length, the scale of your surroundings might just spark an existential crisis, set to the powerful heartbeat of pounding waves: visitors tend to feel like an infinitesimal speck in a great big universe as they inch along between the 3937ft (1200m) peaks of the Kings Range and the icy rage of the Pacific. The coast became 'lost' when state highway surveyors deemed it impassable in the early 20th century and cut the highways inland, where the terrain was more manageable.

The three-day hike is a chance to connect with Northern California's flora and fauna – including some 300 species of birds, sea lions, seals, elk, river otter, and migrating whales. It's also the perfect chance for Silicon Valley execs and the rest of us to unplug from the frantic pace of modern life: cell phone reception around these parts is virtually nonexistent.

After cutting ties to the outside world, your experience on the Lost Coast will be one of rich rewards, filled with days of meditative hiking and cool nights where you'll zip into your sleeping bag and drift off to the rhythm of the waves. The hike encounters some challenging terrain, with boulder-hopping, stretches that need to be timed with the tide, and a fair bit of slow-going sand. But when you set up camp to enjoy the spoils of your effort, it's more than worth it: a beachfront view of a deep-orange sunset and a brilliant display of stars.

ESSENTIAL EXPERIENCES

* **Wandering around the Punta Gorda Lighthouse, a retired relic of the early 20th-century California coast, and scanning the horizon for migrating whales.**

* Climbing Kings Peak, a detour that takes some effort but rewards with a 360-degree view.

* **Scouring the beaches for treasures of all sizes – from tiny shells to the rusting hulks of abandoned fishing vessels.**

* Devouring a basket of fish and chips at Shelter Cove's Airport Deli, a place with 'World Famous' fried goodies that taste like heaven after the hike.

* **Finding one of the area's 'drive-thru' trees, mid-century roadside attractions that allow drivers to navigate through the carved-out belly of a living redwood.**

78

LOCATION CALIFORNIA, USA | **BEST TIME OF YEAR** JUNE, OR LATE AUGUST THROUGH EARLY OCTOBER
IDEAL TIME COMMITMENT FIVE DAYS | **ESSENTIAL TIP** REFER TO A TIDE TABLE FOR CROSSING CREEKS | **PACK** A DECENT TOPOGRAPHICAL MAP IS A MUST FOR KNOWING WHICH SIDE TRAILS TO NAVIGATE.

THE LOST COAST'S SHIPWRECKS

With lots of thick fog and churning tides, the waters off the Lost Coast were fearsome during California's settlement. A state database lists 350 ships along this stretch that were wrecked, stranded or severely damaged between the 1850s and the 1950s. Many of them were shipping lumber up and down the coast, but the most notorious was the SS *Brother Jonathan*. Carrying 244 passengers and a full load of gold – payments to honor local treaties with Native American tribes – the ship plowed into a rock near Crescent City. Divers didn't find the wreck until 1993, 125 years after it sank.

THE PERFECT GETAWAY

This getaway starts with the leisurely drive north from San Francisco to the trailhead. Passing larger and larger stands of redwood, the drive is dotted by historic logging towns. A favorite among these is tiny Garberville, the last town with any real services in the area. It's a place where the longstanding rivalry between loggers, environmentalists, and cannabis farmers is palpable. It also has a couple of excellent restaurants and a string of comfortable family-run motels.

After stocking up in Garberville, find your way to the start of the hike at the Mattole Campground, 1½ hours northwest at the mouth of the Mattole River. It's at the ocean end of Lighthouse Rd, about 4 miles (6.5km) from Mattole Rd (which is sometimes marked as Hwy 211), south and east of a speck of a town called Petrolia. Locals know the area and often point Patagonia-clad greenhorns in the right direction.

It's best to get to the trailhead as early as possible on the first day. The Lost Coast Trail – the main thoroughfare for foot traffic – follows 25 miles (40km) or so of coastline from Mattole Campground in the north to Black Sands Beach at Shelter Cove in the south; the best way to tackle this hike is from north to south, which takes advantage of the prevailing winds. Given the conditions of the trail, you'll want weatherproof boots with lots of foot support.

If you're not up to the three-day hike, you can get a taste of the Lost Coast on a day hike that starts from the campground at Lighthouse Rd, following a 4WD trail out to the Punta Gorda Lighthouse. Alternatively, you can use Shelter Cove, the isolated town that is the southern point of the hike, as a hub, and get your fill of the North Coast's dramatic scenery without the need for fancy outdoor gear.

PLAN IT

From San Francisco, the trailhead is a long (and particularly lovely) five-hour drive north. Book a shuttle from a licensed operator such as Lost Coast Trails or Lost Coast Adventure Tours; if you don't you'll have to take two vehicles and stash one at the end of the hike. For supplies and insider information, hit Garberville's sporting goods stores. No camping fees or overnight permits are required, but you will need a campfire permit, which can be obtained at trailheads.

DETOUR

Want to be gobsmacked by Northern California's natural splendor without breaking a sweat? Cruise the 32-mile (50km) Avenue of the Giants to see the region's redwood groves. The route passes through the Humboldt Redwoods State Park, which has the largest stand of virgin redwoods in the world. The more ambitious can navigate the well-marked network of short trails. You'll find free driving guides at roadside signboards at both the avenue's southern and northern entrances. Hungry? Good: the Avenue features roadside restaurants, several places to taste wine and lots of options for an unforgettable picnic.

SNYFEROK | GETTY IMAGES ©

OPENING SPREAD A characteristically rugged panorama along the Lost Coast.
ABOVE Camping close to the shoreline – and the local wildlife. **BELOW** Redwoods loom over the Avenue of the Giants.

ARMCHAIR

✴ *The Wild Trees: A Story of Passion and Daring* (Richard Preston) A must-read for those interested in the astounding magical life of the world's tallest trees.

✴ *California's Lost Coast* (Wilderness Press Maps) An excellent, waterproof map that covers King Range National Conservation Area and Sinkyone Wilderness State Park. It also features some great day hikes.

✴ *The Big Trees* (1952) Kirk Douglas plays an unscrupulous timber baron who meets resistance from plucky Quaker homesteaders.

✴ *Return of the Jedi* (1983) Adorable Ewoks live in the canopy of the redwoods in this *Star Wars* sequel.

✴ *ET the Extra-Terrestrial* (1982) On the subject of iconic 1980s sci-fi, several scenes in Spielberg's classic were shot in Redwoods State Park and, a little further north, Crescent City.

CHECK OUT CHICAGO'S ARCHITECTURE

CHICAGO IS AN ARCHITECTURAL MECCA, BRISTLING WITH BUILDINGS BY THE STARCHITECTS OF TODAY AND HOME TO THE WORK AND STUDIOS OF PAST MASTERS LOUIS SULLIVAN, FRANK LLOYD WRIGHT, AND MIES VAN DER ROHE.

The panorama from Chicago's Millennium Park is of world-class architecture. Start with Frank Gehry's Jay Pritzker Pavilion, with its twisting chrome segments rippling across the lawn, then turn to the right to be greeted by a glittering plane of blades: Renzo Piano's Modern Wing of the Art Institute. Turn a little further and Adler & Sullivan's 1889 Auditorium Building on South Michigan Ave is visible in the distance, as Anish Kapoor's chrome sculpture *Cloud Gate* hovers like an alien blimp waiting to show you around the city that gave birth to the skyscraper, Chicago blues, house music, the Cubs, and the *Oprah Winfrey Show*.

Chicago's pioneering skyscraper architecture, dating from the end of the 19th century, is known as the Chicago School, and architect Louis Sullivan was one of its most notable practitioners. Buildings by Sullivan reveal themselves as you stroll through downtown Chicago, with intricate explosions of ornamentation cast across monumental commercial buildings. Wander in any direction and you will come across a building or two by Ludwig Mies van der Rohe, whose work is attributed to the Second Chicago School of the mid-20th century – minimalistic black towers of glass and steel that inspired modernist architecture across the globe. However, it's not just the world's finest skyscrapers that entice the archi-tourist to Chicago. Frank Lloyd Wright, one of the 20th century's most famous architects and a pupil of Sullivan's, has given the region a suite of prairie-style homes that are furnished with his own designs and open to the public.

The city's appeal goes far beyond its buildings. From the 1940s to the 1970s Chicago was a hothouse for blues music, and then in the 1980s it became the crucible for house music, thanks to local radio stations, DJs and artists such as Larry Heard. Music is still at the heart of Chicago and no escape would be complete without a nocturnal adventure in sound.

ESSENTIAL EXPERIENCES

❋ **Immersing yourself in the Art Institute of Chicago's renowned collections of Impressionist, post-Impressionist, American and contemporary art.**

❋ Touring Frank Lloyd Wright's home and studio – a fascinating place filled with the details that made the architect's style distinctive.

❋ **Catching a Cubs baseball game at home stadium Wrigley Field.**

❋ Strolling the campus of the Illinois Institute of Technology's College of Architecture in Bronzeville, studded with architectural gems by the likes of Rem Koolhaas, Helmut Jahn and Mies van der Rohe.

❋ **Dining with a live blues act in Rosa's Lounge, or tapping your toe at a blues gig on revitalized Motor Row (South Michigan Ave).**

LOCATION CHICAGO, ILLINOIS, USA | **BEST TIME OF YEAR** APRIL THROUGH OCTOBER | **IDEAL TIME COMMITMENT** A WEEKEND OR A WEEK | **ESSENTIAL TIP** DON'T MISS THE CHICAGO-STYLE BEEF SANDWICH (AND THE VIEW!) AT THE SIGNATURE LOUNGE ATOP THE JOHN HANCOCK CENTER | **PACK** SOMETHING SMART TO WEAR OUT AT NIGHT: CHICAGOANS ARE VERY STYLISH.

AL CAPONE, KING OF CHICAGO

Al Capone, history's most renowned mobster, may have been born in New York City, but it was after moving to Chicago that the young criminal made his mark. Exploiting the Prohibition Era of the 1920s to smuggle and bootleg alcohol, while also involved in other illegal ventures such as gambling and prostitution, Capone was able to lead the crime empire known as 'the Outfit' to great success, generating hundreds of millions of dollars in revenue annually. Capone's support of charities made him a popular figure in Chicago, but his involvement in a mob-related shooting in 1929 tarnished his image. Capone was eventually convicted on tax offences and languished in Alcatraz prison from 1931 to 1939, before dying at home in 1947.

GOT THOSE CHICAGO BLUES?

Blues music made it to Chicago from its southern origins in the Mississippi River Delta as a result of the Great Migration, when more than one million African Americans moved north in search of work in the industrialized cities. The genre, inspired by African music and the highs and lows of daily life, flourished in Chicago and developed a regional dialect, characterized by an amplified harmonica and bass guitar, known as Chicago blues. The sound was centered on the Chess Records studio on South Michigan Ave. Now known as Motor Row, the strip of derelict car showrooms is being revitalized as an entertainment district, with a new L transit station, a craft brewery and live-music venues.

■ THE PERFECT GETAWAY

Arriving at the Art Institute of Chicago on South Michigan Ave with coffee in hand, a takeaway from Così a block north, you decide to leave the Impressionists for tomorrow and focus on the most unexpected permanent collection you could imagine in a city with the largest buildings in the Midwest. The exquisite Thorne Miniature Rooms, of which there are 68, are delicately crafted interiors at 1:12 scale, covering European design from the 13th century and American design from the 17th century through until the 1930s, when the models were made.

Before heading north for lunch in one of the steakhouses by Mariano Park, you cross the road to the Chicago Architecture Foundation. Here you find architecture enthusiasts who can sell you Gehry fridge magnets, and organize tickets for the architecture cruise on the Chicago River. Grab a ticket for tomorrow's bus trip to the neighborhood where Frank Lloyd Wright lived and worked from 1889 to 1909; opt for the tour that takes in Wright's own home and studio and includes a walking tour of Oak Park – a picturesque residential area with many prairie-style homes by Wright – culminating in a tour of his charmingly detailed Unity Temple.

As light fades you jump on the L, the rail network elevated above the streets of Chicago's inner Loop district, and travel on the red line north to Addison station; it's only a short walk to Wrigley Field. While watching a Cubs baseball game you notice the scoreboard being operated by hand, the numbered plates carefully interchanged, and it becomes apparent the effort Chicagoans have invested, both today and in the many years past, in building their city and making it work.

■ PLAN IT

Chicago's O'Hare International Airport is 18 miles (30km) from downtown Chicago; catch a cab, train or bus into the city center. Consider renting an apartment in one of Chicago's elegant inner suburbs, such as Lakeview or Oak Park; good public transport allows you to expand your accommodation search beyond downtown. The Chicago Architecture Foundation is open daily until 9pm; the river cruise is offered in the warmer months. The Cubs play at Wrigley Field from April to September; book tickets well ahead.

■ DETOUR

Mies van der Rohe's seminal work, Farnsworth House, is considered to be one of modernism's masterpieces. Completed in 1951, the home is a perfect expression of Mies' modernist ideal of architecture reduced to its straight-lined essence. Located near Plano, just over an hour's drive west of Chicago, Farnsworth House can be reached by car or by train, or on organized bus tours such as those run by the Chicago Architecture Foundation.

NAGEL PHOTOGRAPHY | SHUTTERSTOCK ©

THOMAS BARRAT | SHUTTERSTOCK ©

OPENING SPREAD The Windy City's unmistakable skyline rises above North Ave Beach. **ABOVE (L)** The Museum of Contemporary Art's dizzying staircase. **ABOVE (R)** One of Frank Lloyd Wright's constructions in Oak Park. **LEFT** A band strikes up at the Green Mill jazz club.

ARMCHAIR

* ***Grand Obsessions*** (Alastair McGregor) Follow the journey of two of Frank Lloyd Wright's finest protégés, Walter Burley Griffin and Marion Mahony, in this epic biography.

* ***Chicago: A Novel*** (Brian Doyle) A young writer chronicles his time in the 'real Chicago', with a colorful cast of characters.

* ***The Blues Brothers*** (1980) Seek out the film locations for this classic in the Loop district. The soundtrack is pure Chicago.

* ***Ferris Bueller's Day Off*** (1986) This 1980s teen flick takes it to the streets of Chicago.

* ***High Fidelity*** (2000) One of the most popular movies set in the Windy City is actually based on a book set in London.

* ***The Untouchables*** (1987) Native son David Mamet wrote the screenplay for this nail-biter focusing on Eliot Ness's takedown of Al Capone.

CANOE FLORIDA'S WILDERNESS WATERWAY

MARVEL AT THE SPLENDOR OF ONE OF THE WORLD'S LARGEST AND MOST VIBRANT SMALL-CRAFT WATERWAYS: A NETWORK OF INTERCONNECTED MARSHLANDS, MANGROVES, RIVERS, AND STREAMS TEEMING WITH WILDLIFE. THE ROAD LESS TRAVELED IS OFTEN BEST WHEN IT ISN'T A ROAD AT ALL.

The Wilderness Waterway is to paddlers what the Appalachian Trail is to hikers: 99 miles (159km) – a minimum seven days of hard paddling – that snakes through one of America's most beautiful and least understood national parks, offering unparalleled wildlife close-ups and stunning scenery at every turn. The journey is like paddling back in time through American history – most of Florida used to look like this before the invention of bulldozers and backhoes enabled the destruction of swampland on an epic scale.

As recently as the early 1900s, a thin sheet of water covered as much as 11,004 sq miles (28,500 sq km), creating one of the country's most unique habitats and harboring native animals and plants. Bromeliads, orchids, palms, and even hardwood forests thrived, providing habitats for all sorts of animals that nowadays are on the brink of extinction, such as the American crocodile and Florida panthers, which currently number about one hundred. The now-ubiquitous alligator reigns over this amazing 'River of Grass'.

The area was first written about by Hugh L Willoughby in 1898, after he made a west–east crossing of the vast sawgrass prairies in 1897. Save for the chickees (raised wooden platforms for camping), the Wilderness Waterway looks much as it did then. The communities of 'Gladesmen' and indigenous tribes may have gone, but wildlife still rules and the only form of transportation in this roadless expanse remains watercraft: boat, skiff, kayak or canoe.

The Everglades National Park was established in 1947 to protect this serene and wild ecosystem. Interestingly, the park's creation was due in large part to the efforts of a developer, Ernest F Coe. He envisioned an expanse of 2,000,000 acres (approximately 810,000 hectares) and was so adamant about these boundaries (which even included Key Largo!) that the creation of the park was almost scuttled completely. Even so, it remains the largest protected area east of the Mississippi River.

ESSENTIAL EXPERIENCES

* **Marveling at unbroken vistas of sawgrass prairie as you glide through mangrove channels, lakes, and lagoons.**

* Encountering close up a host of birds and animals that many people never see.

* **Enjoying the utter stillness that comes from being as far away from motorized vehicle traffic as one can be.**

* Paddling around Florida's Ten Thousand Islands, all but a handful uninhabited.

* **Camping on chickee stilt platforms at nightfall beneath a canopy of glittering stars.**

* Traveling one of America's most epic waterways that – thankfully – has been pristinely preserved, affording a view of what most of Florida looked like for millennia.

DISTANCE 99 MILES (159KM) | **LOCATION** EVERGLADES NATIONAL PARK, FLORIDA, USA | **IDEAL TIME COMMITMENT** ONE WEEK
BEST TIME OF YEAR JANUARY | **ESSENTIAL TIP** WATCH OUT FOR ALLIGATORS.

HUGH L WILLOUGHBY

While Native Americans lived in and around the area for centuries, the Everglades, America's largest freshwater swamp, was not written about in any depth until Hugh L Willoughby of the University of Pennsylvania traversed the region in 1897. His journal entries became the still available title *Across the Everglades* and while the writing is dry (pun intended), the voyage was not: portages across the mud and shallows were common, and dry places to sleep were few and far between. His experiences and flora and fauna finds provide a fascinating glimpse back at the history of this 'River of Grass'.

THE FLORIDA PANTHER

Sadly, most people's only glimpse of these animals in the wild is on the side of the road: impacts by vehicles are the number one threat to the wild populations. While habitat loss (male Florida panthers require approximately 200 sq miles (518 sq km) of territory per cat) is the prime reason they're on the endangered species list, the few animals left need all the help they can get. Protect them (and yourself!) by minimizing the chances of an accident. Observe posted road signs and be alert — especially during the dawn, dusk, and night-time hours — for anything crossing the road.

THE ADVENTURE UNFOLDS

The put-in for a west–east journey starts at the Gulf Coast Visitors Center in Everglades City. Clearly marked signs then guide paddlers across the waterways, lagoons, inlets, and sawgrass prairies, with camping on beaches or chickees. The journey goes through almost all the ecosystems the park has to offer, starting with miles of mangroves and tannin-stained water. Little blue herons and snowy egrets erupt with squawks from the shallows as your vessel slips by, the verdant mangroves subduing the sounds of paddling. The mangroves slowly melt into coastal estuary, where salt and brackish water mix, and manatee and sea turtle sightings are common. Here one can look out across Florida Bay at the Ten Thousand Islands. All but a handful of these islands are uninhabited. While many are open to campers, it's vital to obtain park permission prior to embarking on your trip and to stick to designated areas.

Gradually you'll trade the bay for sawgrass prairie: seemingly never-ending stretches of waist- to head-high grass like the prairies out west, except here they grow out of a paddy that's only dry in certain areas and at certain times of the year. At the highest points you'll find tropical hardwood 'hammocks' (stands of trees) which support larger mammals – look for deer, feral pigs, raccoons, and (for the very lucky) a glimpse of the endangered Florida panther.

During the last days of the journey, camping is on chickees, which require some careful maneuvering and preparation for tide, wind and current so as to not damage the canoes. Capable and experienced paddlers will find the seven to eight days as rewarding as a canoe trip can be.

MAKING IT HAPPEN

Bring gear as for any canoe trip, plus ample drinking water – factoring in delays due to inclement weather, navigational mistakes, or accidents. Though mosquitoes and no-see-ums aren't as bad in winter, they're present year-round, and it's worth remembering that most of those submerged 'logs' are alligators. GPS, appropriate nautical charts and night-time navigation skills are vital. Everglades Adventure offers a variety of packages and full or partial guided tours.

DETOUR

A worthwhile side trip is to Big Cypress National Preserve, which borders part of Everglades National Park. One quick peek and you'll see why there's a line between the two: massive cypress trees blanketed with Spanish moss (a kind of lichen) create a totally different ecosystem from the sawgrass prairies and low-lying Keys, yet this too is primarily swampland. Canoe any of the five NPS Big Cypress day trips or ask at the ranger station if you plan on staying a little longer.

JUSTIN FOULKES | LONELY PLANET ©

JUSTIN FOULKES | LONELY PLANET ©

OPENING SPREAD The sun sets over the Everglades wetlands. **ABOVE (L)** Alligators are the region's primary predator. **ABOVE (R)** The Wilderness Waterway offers canoeists myriad pools and channels. **LEFT** An Everglades guide assesses the surroundings.

ARMCHAIR

* ***Field Guide to Birds of North America*** (Roger Tory Peterson) An invaluable asset to identifying the numerous waterfowl.

* ***Paddler's Guide to Everglades National Park*** (Johnny Molloy) Useful insights for first-timers as well as Glades veterans.

* ***Across the Everglades*** (Hugh L Willoughby) Details his 1897 trip along the waterway.

* ***Double Whammy / Tourist Season*** (Carl Hiaasen) Hiaasen's riotously funny works of fiction (which blend mystery, adventure and comedy as only Hiaasen can) center on Florida, and should be required reading.

* ***The Orchid Thief*** (Susan Orlean) An evocative, literary look at the area, which became the movie *Adaptation* starring Nicolas Cage.

DO THE SAN JUAN ISLAND-HOP

KAYAKING BLUE COVES AND SCANNING THE HORIZON FOR ORCAS, CYCLING COUNTRY ROADS PAST BUCOLIC FARMS, AND BREATHING AIR SCENTED WITH SALT AND CEDAR. THE SAN JUAN ISLANDS OFFER TIMELESS ADVENTURES AT A LAID-BACK PACE IN THE AMERICAN NORTHWEST.

The escape begins as soon as the ferry pushes away from the dock. As it starts to parade between the scattered emerald-green islands off the northwest tip of the United States, move out onto the deck and take a deep breath. In that air – cool, humid, strangely fresh – you'll be introduced to the San Juan Islands. This trip is a chance to leave behind day-to-day concerns, sink into the easygoing pace of the Pacific Northwest and recharge. But there's something else in the air here that inspires people to get outdoors. With a plethora of options for cycling, hiking, birding and kayaking, the escape is ideal for people who like relaxing adventures.

Situated within sight of Canadian land, the islands were the subject of some dispute throughout the 1850s, when both countries wanted to claim them. This brought about the colorfully named but casualty-free Pig War in 1859, the remnants of which are still visible in two historic sights on San Juan Island, English Camp and American Camp.

Four of the 172 named islands off the Washington coast – San Juan, Orcas, Lopez and Shaw Islands – are served by ferries. Spend an afternoon cruising around San Juan Island, the second-largest and most populated of the islands, and it's easy to see what all the fuss was about. By car or by bike, you'll roll past gentle green hills dotted with sheep, cattle and alpaca, tidy rows of grape vines or lavender plants, sun-dappled forests, and sparkling ocean views. Bring binoculars for the visit to the island's pair of historic lighthouses to search for the resident pods of orca whales. Better yet, rent a kayak to join them on the water. After you've paddled the last stroke and the bikes are put away, make for the adorable downtown of Friday Harbor for a nightcap. By the time you retreat back to your B&B for some shut-eye, you might just dream of staying here forever.

ESSENTIAL EXPERIENCES

* **Hugging the adorable and inquisitive creatures at Krystal Acres Alpaca Farm.**

* Visiting the lighthouse at Lime Kiln Point State Park, a great place to spot orcas.

* **Breathing deeply at Pelindaba Lavender Farm, where all manner of lavender products are made on-site.**

* Hunting for antiques in the island's excellent antique shops, galleries, and boutiques – most are found in downtown Friday Harbor.

* **Cruising the country on a rental bike and pedaling out to the ocean for a picnic.**

* Paddling out through one of the protected harbors to join the local orcas.

LOCATION BETWEEN MAINLAND WASHINGTON, USA, AND VANCOUVER ISLAND, BRITISH COLUMBIA, CANADA | **BEST TIME OF YEAR** SUMMER (JULY AND AUGUST) | **IDEAL TIME COMMITMENT** FOUR DAYS | **ESSENTIAL TIP** DOUBLE-CHECK THE FERRY SCHEDULE FOR SEASONAL VARIATIONS | **PACK** BINOCULARS, PLUS APPROPRIATE CLOTHES AND SUN PROTECTION IF YOU PLAN ON CYCLING AND KAYAKING.

THE PIG WAR

On a midsummer day in 1859, the serenity of San Juan Island was interrupted by a gunshot. Thirteen years after the Oregon Treaty was signed, ambiguous borders between the US and Canada had created a tense environment on the islands. When Lyman Cutlar, a salty American homesteader, saw a black pig uprooting his potatoes, diplomacy was no option. He pulled the trigger and started the so-called Pig War. Aside from the swine, no lives were lost, and the land dispute was settled peacefully, but its legacy lives on in the pair of historic military camps – American Camp and English Camp – on the island.

■ THE PERFECT GETAWAY

Want an idyllic visit to San Juan Island? Book your trip in the late spring or early summer, when you'll miss the peak-season crowds but still enjoy clear skies and warm days. A large spectrum of accommodations can be booked in Friday Harbor, including a couple of very swish hotels and an affordable youth hostel, but the serenity and charm of a B&B further out on the island can't be beat. Many of them even have bikes to borrow if you want to get around by pedaling.

Over the next three days you'll be exploring the island, so start off with a cruise around the perimeter to get acquainted with your surroundings. History buffs will enjoy stopping at American Camp and English Camp, but the best park on the island is Lime Kiln Point State Park, where you can spend a few hours wandering the bluffs, scanning the skies for bald eagles and the ocean for orcas before unpacking a picnic overlooking the water. This is home to a lighthouse, and the rangers on hand will give you tips on spotting whales. Other day trips include a jaunt to the Krystal Acres Alpaca Farm and Country Store, or San Juan Vineyards for a taste of its award-winning siegerrebe. In the evening, head into town for the catch of the day at one of Friday Harbor's restaurants, then watch a flick at the little movie house or a performance by the island's local theater community.

If you extend your trip by a couple of days, the possibilities grow exponentially. Consider a side trip to one of the other islands: you can hike to the top of the modest Mt Constitution on Orcas Island for a fine view of the archipelago and distant snowcap of Mt Rainier, or you can circumnavigate Lopez Island by bike, a breezy trip that can be made in a leisurely afternoon.

ARMCHAIR

* ***Short Nights of the Shadow Catcher*** (Timothy Egan) A riveting biography about Edward Curtis, a photographer who worked to document and preserve local native customs during westward expansion.

* ***Snow Falling on Cedars*** (1999) A beautifully shot adaptation of David Guterson's award-winning tale of prejudice in a San Juan Island fishing community during the mid-20th century.

* ***Your Sister's Sister*** (2011) Shot on the islands in only 12 days on a shoestring budget, this indie film has a number of marquee stars.

* ***Free Willy*** (1993) This family drama about a young boy who befriends a captive orca was filmed in the area.

* ***Time Shadows and Tall Tales: San Juan Island in Earlier Years*** (Jack J Crawford) A colorful local history.

PLAN IT

The islands' small airport receives charter flights, but most visitors arrive via the Washington State Ferry from Anacortes, which accommodates cars. If you're flying into Seattle-Tacoma International Airport, it's a two-hour drive to the dock. The ferry weaves through the San Juan Archipelago before arriving at Friday Harbor; transfer to other islands via inter-island ferries. Island Bicycles in Friday Harbor rents a variety of bikes. For kayak rentals, try Sea Quest Expeditions.

DETOUR

Many lookouts from the islands offer views of the Olympic Mountains. For naturalists, they are an essential detour; no other place in North America can match the biodiversity in such a compact area. A two-day detour will follow the string of little towns around the edge of the Olympic Peninsula, and offers a chance to visit Olympic National Park. One of North America's great wilderness areas, most of the park remains relatively untouched by human habitation, with 1000-year-old cedar trees juxtaposed with pristine alpine meadows, moss-draped temperate rainforest, clear glacial lakes, and a largely roadless interior.

MONIKA WIELAND SHIELDS | SHUTTERSTOCK ©

OPENING SPREAD Boats moored at Roche Harbor on San Juan Island. **ABOVE** An orca breaches the surface, a common sight around the islands between April and October. **BELOW** Waves smash into the rocks under the gaze of Lime Kiln Lighthouse.

ORCAS AROUND THE ISLANDS

Three pods of orcas live around the San Juan Islands and are frequently sighted during the warmer months, usually between mid-April and October. The families are named J, K and L Pods and have a population that hovers around 80 whales. Each whale is individually identified by the unique patterns of black and white on their saddle patch, behind their large dorsal fin. Lime Kiln Point State Park is an excellent place to learn more about these magnificent creatures, as it has ranger-led programs and informative placards set up right on the water.

CLIMB THE NOSE OF EL CAPITAN

THE MOST FAMOUS ROCK CLIMB ON EARTH, THE NOSE ROUTE ON EL CAPITAN IS A SINGULAR EXPERIENCE MARKED BY DANGER, ENDURANCE AND DETERMINATION. IT IS A CLIMB STEEPED IN HISTORY, AND AN ADVENTURE SET IN STONE IN ONE OF THE WORLD'S MOST DRAMATIC NATURAL SETTINGS.

Climbing El Capitan was a seemingly impossible task. Its prow was too high, the technology too limited, the danger too great. That is, until adventurers like Warren Harding turned their sights skyward.

The first ascent of the Nose began on July 4, 1957, when Warren Harding and a crew of climbers set out to scale the face. Given the route's size, they opted to employ an expedition-style approach with fixed ropes and established camps. The siege of 'El Cap' lasted 47 days on the cliff, and spanned a period exceeding 18 months, marked by occasional broken ropes, tense relations with the National Park Service and a changing cast of characters that supported Harding's dream of making it to the top. But at last, on November 12, 1958, after an 11-day push on the wall – and a final 14-hour push by headlamp to the top – the team, then consisting of Harding, Rich Calderwood, George Whitmore and Wayne Merry, climbed their way into the history books, after the hardest, longest and most exposed rock climb ever undertaken.

To this day, an ascent of the Nose remains the Holy Grail of rock climbs. It takes anywhere from a few hours (for the most expert climbers) to four or five days for mere mortals. Most people choose to free climb most of the route, using only their hands and feet to move up the cliff, carrying a rope only for protection. They then step into aid-climbing equipment (as Harding did) to ascend the tougher sections (or pitches) of the route. A few, however, have managed to climb the Nose without any aid equipment at all. The first to do this was the rock-climbing dynamo Lynn Hill, who 'freed the Nose' in 1993.

This ascent is only for very experienced climbers – you need to be able to lead hard traditional climbs, aid climb efficiently and have the experience to keep yourself safe on the rock face for a five-day ordeal – but El Capitan is truly the stuff of legend.

ESSENTIAL EXPERIENCES

❋ **Gearing up for your climb in Camp 4 with your partner.**

❋ Taking your first step onto Yosemite granite as you step into the vertical.

❋ **Spending a night on the cliff with the wind all around you, a thousand feet up from the valley floor.**

❋ Chugging your way up perfect El Cap cracks.

❋ **Eating spaghetti from a can after a 12-hour day.**

❋ Arriving at the summit safely and catching the sunset on your four-hour hike down.

94

ELEVATION ABOUT 3000FT (914M) | **LOCATION** YOSEMITE NATIONAL PARK, CALIFORNIA, USA | **IDEAL TIME COMMITMENT** FOUR TO FIVE DAYS (AND FIVE YEARS' CLIMBING EXPERIENCE) | **BEST TIME OF YEAR** JUNE TO SEPTEMBER | **ESSENTIAL TIP** BRING MORE WATER THAN YOU THINK YOU'LL NEED.

DEFENDING CAMP 4

During its heyday in the 1960s and 1970s, people from across the globe came to Camp 4 to climb Yosemite's impossibly steep cliffs, swim naked in the Merced River, and drink far too many beers, and smoke far too many spliffs during all-night fireside bacchanals. Needless to say, the wild ways of Camp 4 were an issue for the National Parks Service, and at one point they tried to close the camp down to build a three-storey employee-housing unit. But climbers wouldn't have it. They united behind the Camp 4 cause and went to court to protect the camp. They won, and in 2003 Camp 4 was added to the National Register of Historic Places.

EXPLORE YOSEMITE'S WONDERS

Most visitors never leave the small area around
Yosemite Village, save for day hikes into the
wilderness. But beyond the Ansel Adams Gallery
and the tour buses, a vast wilderness awaits.
Within the 1189-sq-mile (3080-sq-km) World
Heritage Site, intrepid adventurers can backpack
for days on end past roaring waterfalls and giant
sequoia groves into a truly wild environment.
The park is home to deer and bears, and has the
tallest waterfall in California, Yosemite Falls. No
wonder John Muir, the Scottish-born naturalist and
activist instrumental to Yosemite's preservation,
considered it 'by far the grandest of all the special
temples of Nature I was ever permitted to enter.'

■ THE ADVENTURE UNFOLDS

One of the hardest elements of climbing the Nose is dealing with isolation and exposure. Imagine sleeping every night tied to the cliff. Picture yourself eating, drinking and dreaming in an environment that by its nature is hostile to life. The rewards are great, but difficult to fathom for those who have never explored the vertical world. Every day you awake to a bird's-eye view of Yosemite's waterfalls and meadows. Tourists below look like ants, the towering trees blend together to form a rough carpet over the valley, and the only noises you hear are the constant rush of the wind and the occasional hoot from another climber. Silence itself attracts adventurers to this inhospitable realm.

While there are harder, longer and more exposed climbs in the world today, the 31 vertical pitches of the Nose are simply classic. There are giant pendulums with names like the King Swing, and unique formations like the Texas Flake and the Great Roof. Every pitch takes you through a little piece of climbing history, passing challenges that pushed the limits of climbing legends such as John Long, Jim Bridwell, and Royal Robbins over the years.

Life on a 'big wall' is odd. Doing your morning business into a tube becomes second nature. That can of spaghetti becomes a point of contention between you and your climbing partner. You start to imagine you're near the summit, only to realize you are still two days away; you consider going down, then remember you're too high up for an effective retreat. Your only way out becomes up. And with every step, each gear placement, you slowly burn down, concentrating every ounce of muscle and mind to making it to the top.

■ MAKING IT HAPPEN

Before you head up the Nose, you should spend several days getting a feel for Yosemite's signature granite. Most climbers stay in the walk-in Camp 4 camping ground; if you don't have a climbing partner, you can easily find one here. The Yosemite Mountaineering School has been guiding in the valley since 1969 – but if you don't know what to pack, or have limited climbing experience, then you shouldn't attempt the Nose, even with a guide.

■ AN ALTERNATIVE CHALLENGE

There are tons of adventures to be had in Yosemite National Park, from day hikes to waterfalls to multiday backpack treks in a park the size of Rhode Island. Across the valley from El Capitan, Half Dome beckons hard-core climbers and fit hikers alike. One of the best hikes on this iconic cliff is the cable route up the back to the summit. This 14.9-mile (24km) round-trip hike normally takes 10 to 12 hours, and ascends around 4724ft (1440m). On the last 394ft (120m) or so of the climb, two cables assist you up to the summit.

97

OPENING SPREAD The fearsome El Capitan looms over Yosemite Valley. **ABOVE** Pine forest and dramatic Sierra Nevada peaks form the landscape of Yosemite National Park. **LEFT** A climbing team attempts the daunting ascent of The Nose, first scaled in 1958.

ARMCHAIR

❋ *Yosemite and the High Sierra* (Ansel Adams) This spectacular coffee-table book captures the best of Ansel Adams' photographic masterpieces.

❋ *Camp 4: Recollections of a Yosemite Rockclimber* (Steve Roper) Chronicles the author's 10-year stay in Camp 4.

❋ *My First Summer in the Sierra* (John Muir) Walden meets *On the Road* in this classic that combines transcendentalism with

youthful wonder, with Yosemite as its mighty backdrop.

❋ *To the Limit* (2007) This feature-length German movie with English subtitles follows climbing legends Thomas and Alexander Huber on their attempt to break the speed record on the Nose.

❋ *The National Parks: America's Best Idea* (2009) Six-part Ken Burns documentary series that takes you through Yosemite and the rest of America's national parks.

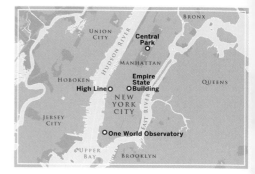

TAKE A FRESH LOOK AT THE BIG APPLE

NEW YORK: SO FAMILIAR FROM A MILLION MOVIES – YOU'VE SEEN IT ALL BEFORE, RIGHT? WRONG. PADDLE A KAYAK, CYCLE THE CITY'S BIKE PATHS, TAKE A HELICOPTER RIDE OR VIEW THE CITY FROM 100 STORIES UP FOR A DIFFERENT TAKE ON THIS ICONIC METROPOLIS.

The Big Apple looks really big. Towering. Gargantuan. Titanic, even. Of course, it always does: Lower Manhattan contains one of the densest concentrations of skyscrapers in the world; here, legion shards of shiny metal-and-glass rise like a supersized Giant's Causeway. But still, right now, it looks bigger than ever.

And that's because your own perspective has taken a dive. You are viewing this mighty metropolis not from the back of a yellow cab or on foot along the avenues, but from water level, from the seat of a kayak.

It's really quite surreal, gliding along the Hudson in this way, the splish of water on paddles mixing with the muted rumble of traffic and sirens. Being on the river feels serene: back to nature. Yet a glance to the side reveals not treetops but tower-blocks, the art deco masterpieces of the Empire State and Chrysler peeking out like roses between the thorns.

So, it's pretty special down here with the ducks, but doing battle with the Hudson is no walk in Central Park. The tidal river has quite a current; an out-and-back trip from one of the West Side piers – with a midway stop for a cold one – likely means rowing against the flow in one direction. There are also a frightening number of enormous ships to avoid, which make you feel very small indeed.

But this is something even novices can try, with a good guide and a little tuition. And the effort is worth it for the chance to get a view and a sensation few NYC visitors ever do. From your lowly, bobbing vantage, you can gaze over to Lady Liberty (rendered strangely small by perspective), float beneath the great gray hulk of the USS *Intrepid*, remind yourself that this glorious Gotham is an island – and earn that enormous, post-paddle slice of New York cheesecake to boot.

ESSENTIAL EXPERIENCES

* **Gazing up at the behemoth-like skyscrapers from a water-level perspective – and feeling really, really small.**

* Refueling after your exertions at a proper New York City deli – double pastrami on rye, anyone?

* **Rowing on the lake in Central Park – a little bit cheesy, a little bit brilliant.**

* Ascending 100 stories to One World Observatory for the ultimate 360° view of the city and beyond.

* **Taking Manhattan Kayak & SUP's after-dark tour and witnessing Midtown's lights from the water.**

* Exploring New York's green spaces – stroll along the elevated High Line and buy artisanal cakes from Union Square's farmers' market.

LOCATION NEW YORK, USA | **BEST TIME OF YEAR** MAY TO SEPTEMBER | **IDEAL TIME COMMITMENT** FOUR DAYS
ESSENTIAL TIP CHECK THE TIDES: BEGINNERS SHOULD SIGN UP FOR A TRIP THAT GOES WITH THE FLOW
PACK SUNSCREEN, SUN HAT, SWIMSUIT/SWIMMING TRUNKS.

The Hudson River flows for about 310 miles (500km) through New York State, from Lake Tear of the Clouds to the Atlantic Ocean, passing the Adirondacks, state capital Albany, and the Catskill Mountains. The Lenape called it Muhheakantuck (the 'river that flows two ways'); today it's named after British explorer Henry Hudson, who navigated it in 1609, trying to find the Pacific. The Hudson isn't the USA's longest waterway but it's one of its most important. Nearby, trade between Native Americans and settlers flourished, influential families (Roosevelts, Rockefellers) laid roots, America's first art movement began and writers such as Wharton and Irving set their tales.

CIRCUMNAVIGATE THE CITY

Manhattan Island has a perimeter of 28 miles (45km) – and there are several ways to make a circumnavigation. Experienced, fit kayakers should be able to paddle all the way around, from the Gotham-esque south to the trees and tidal pools of the north, in about eight hours; Manhattan Kayak & SUP runs guided trips. Too tough? Board the Circle Line's Best of NYC Cruise, which takes the effort out of waterbound sightseeing and only takes two and a half hours. Landlubbers might prefer the Great Saunter – every May the Shorewalkers preservation group organizes a mass hike around Manhattan.

■ THE PERFECT GETAWAY

New York, new schmork. More 'a perfect weekend in...' features have been written about the Big Apple than the city has yellow cabs. So this isn't another, but rather suggestions on how to see this old favorite in a new way. A kayak trip is a great start, best done in the warmer months, in light wind. For something a bit more Batman, paddle after dark. Your headlamp will pale next to all that city glitter; watch as the lights of the Empire State change color, dependent on occasion – red/pink for Valentine's Day, green for Earth Day. Of course, ascending this art deco icon remains one of the best ways to overlook the city. Not an original suggestion, maybe. But did you know it's open until 2am? Ride the elevator late at night to prove that, indeed, the city doesn't sleep; Thursdays to Saturdays, after 9pm, there's usually live music on the observation deck. For an even loftier perspective, take a Sky Pod lift up 100 stories of One World Trade Center – the tallest building in the western hemisphere – for a superlative view of the city from its observation deck. Or take a helicopter flight. Trips zip over the sights – the Statue of Liberty, the skyscrapers, the river you've just navigated.

Back on the ground, join the two-wheeled renaissance by cycling an entire loop of Manhattan on the 32-mile (51km) Manhattan Waterfront Greenway. Racks of Citi Bikes across the island mean you can jump on and off for food or museum stops on your way round. For a less strenuous perspective, take a stroll on the High Line. The 1.45-mile (2.33km) park is built on an old elevated freight rail line and offers a *Rear Window*-style perspective on the surrounding streets. It's especially romantic on a balmy night, when you can see the lit up city sparkling all around.

■ PLAN IT

New York City has two main international airports. JFK is in Queens; the AirTrain links it with the A-train subway line to Manhattan. Newark is in New Jersey; airport express buses to Manhattan take 45 to 60 minutes. Manhattan Kayak & SUP offers a range of kayak options. Guided trips start from one-hour sessions. Citi Bike passes are available for 24-hour and seven-day periods.

■ DETOUR

For alternative ways to go wild-ish in Manhattan, visit its green spaces. First, Central Park: hire a boat to row on the lake or try birdwatching – 230 species have been recorded here. Hudson River Park is a waterfront recreation area with bike trails, sports fields and, in summer, RiverFlicks – a series of free movie screenings. Bryant Park is an oasis off Times Square; not big but packed with facilities, from pétanque and ping pong to a free Reading Room. Union Square Park is home to the city's biggest Greenmarket, where family farmers, butchers and bakers sell their produce.

OPENING SPREAD Kayaking with a view of Manhattan's skyscrapers. **ABOVE (L)** Authentic NYC eats at Zucker's bagels.
ABOVE (R) Brooklyn Bridge viewed from the Dumbo Trail on the East River shore. **LEFT** E 42nd Street and the Chrysler Building.

ARMCHAIR

❋ *Canoeing and Kayaking New York* (Kevin Stiegelmaier) The top 50 paddles across the state.

❋ *Inside the Apple: A Streetwise History of New York City* (Michelle and James Nevius) A lively rundown of NYC's biggest moments.

❋ *The Bonfire of the Vanities* (Tom Wolfe) A novel of greed and corruption, set in 1980s New York.

❋ *Miracle on the Hudson: The Extraordinary Real-Life Story Behind Flight 1549* (Various authors) Perspectives from the survivors of the 2009 Hudson River plane crash.

❋ *The Age of Innocence* (Edith Wharton) This Pulitzer-winning novel skewers the East Coast high society of the 1870s.

❋ *Manhattan* (1979) Many films have been made here, but Woody Allen's classic is the biggest silver-screen love letter to NYC.

CRUISE THE MISSISSIPPI TO NEW ORLEANS

THE MISSISSIPPI: AMERICA'S MOST IMPORTANT RIVER. IT GAVE BIRTH TO THE BLUES, HUCKLEBERRY FINN, BUDWEISER, AND MUCH MORE. IT WITNESSED THE CIVIL WAR AND THE END OF SLAVERY. FOLLOW IT ALL THE WAY DOWN TO NEW ORLEANS AND BID IT FAREWELL AS IT LEAVES, SEEPING OUT INTO THE GULF OF MEXICO.

The USA is indeed a country renowned for classic road trips. Yet even among that plethora of riches, one of the most iconic is traveling down the Great River Road to follow the Mississippi down to New Orleans, LA.

Established in the late 1930s, the Great River Road is a 750-mile (1200km) journey from the Mississippi's headwaters in the northern lakes of Minnesota, floating downstream all the way to where the river empties into the Gulf of Mexico near New Orleans. You'll be awed by the sweeping scenery as you meander alongside North America's second-longest river, from the rolling plains of Iowa down past the cotton fields of the Mississippi Delta. And you'll never be more than 100 miles (160km) from a riverboat casino.

The Mississippi River defines New Orleans, not just geographically but emotionally, culturally, probably even metaphysically. New Orleans' location commands the entrance to the river, with the most important trade, conquest, and exploration of the continent tied to the Mississippi and her variegated moods. Through New Orleans, the river's depth averages around 200ft (60m). It runs some 2350 miles (3800km) from Minnesota to the Gulf of Mexico, with a drainage basin that extends from the Rockies to the Alleghenies, covering an astonishing 40% of continental USA. It drains more water than the Nile and only the Amazon and the Congo carry a greater volume of water out to the ocean.

Fittingly, the river's name is a corruption of the old Ojibwe word misi-ziibi, meaning 'great river'. It's a trip redolent with good ol' American history, glam and color, so make like the narrator in Gary US Bonds' famous 1960 tune, 'New Orleans': 'Well, come on ev'rybody / Take a trip with me / Well, down the Mississippi / Down to New Orleans / You know that ev'ry Southern Belle / Is a Mississippi Queen / Down the Mississippi / Down in New Orleans'.

ESSENTIAL EXPERIENCES

✳ **Visiting the Mark Twain Boyhood Home & Museum in Hannibal to bone up on your Huck Finn knowledge, and finding the places he transposed into his famous novel.**

✳ Exploring Memphis' Slave Haven Underground Railroad Museum to learn about the transportation of slaves up the river to freedom.

✳ **Making a pilgrimage to Elvis Presley's Graceland in Memphis, and getting a dose of the blues in Clarksdale.**

✳ Enjoying the French Market on the river banks in New Orleans.

✳ **Savoring river cuisine: slow-burning tamales and melt-off-the-bone ribs in Clarksdale; chili tamales and steaks in Greenville; and the full gamut of Cajun and Creole cuisine in New Orleans.**

102

DISTANCE APPROXIMATELY 770 MILES (1240KM) | **COUNTRIES COVERED** USA | **IDEAL TIME COMMITMENT** FOUR TO SIX DAYS
BEST TIME OF YEAR SEPTEMBER TO JUNE | **ESSENTIAL TIP** AVOID MARDI GRAS IF STAYING IN NEW ORLEANS.

Many words have been written about the Cajun and Creole cuisine of Southern Louisiana. You could spend weeks searching the alleys of New Orleans for the best samples, but even a few days will give you a taste for the marvelous cooking to be found. It's generally agreed that Cajun food is more rustic while Creole food is more refined, but the differences blur into one meta-cuisine more often than not. Try boiled crawfish (crayfish) in crawfish *étouffée*, a classic Cajun dish of seafood in a spicy reddish sauce served over rice.

MARK TWAIN

Mark Twain (1835–1910) grew up by the river in Hannibal, MO, during the time of slavery. Hannibal's characters, scenery, and politics would later inform Twain's fictional town of St Petersburg, home to the character Tom Sawyer and his best friend, the mischievous Huckleberry Finn. In addition to being a writer, Twain was a commercial steamboat pilot on the Mississippi, ensuring an intimate knowledge of the backdrop of towns, islands, nooks and crannies, and sandbars that made Huck's escape with Jim, the runaway slave, so realistic.

■ THE JOURNEY TODAY

You're on Hwy 61, the top is down, the wind is in your hair and you're following the Big Muddy. When you reach Gateway Arch in St Louis it blows your mind. At 630ft (192m) it is a massive statement against the clear blue sky. On a tour through the Anheuser-Busch Brewery's Victorian-era building, the guide tells you that beer was once made from Mississippi water and stored in barrels in dugouts on the riverbanks. Quaffing the two free Buds given away at the end, you're reminded of the old joke about how American beer is like making love in a canoe...

Now you're back in the car and on the trail of Elvis Presley. You pull out of St Louis, following the I-55S to Memphis, another classic Mississippi town. Graceland is there, of course, as is Sun Studio and Stax Records. It's Music City, man. You steep yourself in modern lore at the Smithsonian's Memphis Rock 'n' Soul Museum, which devotes itself to the history of blues music in the Mississippi Delta – the blues, of course, being the fuel that propelled Elvis's legendary Sun Studio sessions. Now it's time for a trip to the Mississippi River Museum, part of Mud Island River Park, itself linked to Memphis by monorail. Satiated with the rich history of the river, you slink back to the Peabody Hotel, where you're staying, to ponder the strange ritual there: every morning and afternoon at 11am and 5pm, a flock of ducks is marched from the penthouse to the marble lobby fountain. Weird, sure, but all part of the way they do things differently along the Mississippi River.

And if it was good enough for Elvis, who was known to be delighted by the Peabody ducks, then it's good enough for you.

■ SHORTCUT

Why not just stay in New Orleans? You'll never get bored and it's Mississippi Central. The best the city has to offer is contained within its neighborhoods. Unlike countless US metropolises, you can practically cover the entire city by residential roads without ever using the highway.

■ DETOUR

Clarksdale is the home of genuine Delta blues. Here you'll find the Crossroads, the intersection of Highway 61 and Highway 49, where Robert Johnson sold his soul to the devil, as immortalized in his tune 'Cross Road Blues.' Now all of the implied lonely fear and dark mysticism of the space is taken up by a tacky sculpture. Clarksdale's Delta Blues Museum has a small but well-presented collection of blues memorabilia including exhibits honoring Muddy Waters, BB King, John Lee Hooker, Big Mama Thornton, and WC Handy. As befitting such a town, Clarksdale has live music at least four nights a week. Red's is the best juke joint to see bluesmen howl.

105

OPENING SPREAD Steam paddle riverboat *Natchez* cruises the Mississippi River at New Orleans. **ABOVE** A lonely cypress tree awaits nightfall in Louisiana. **LEFT** The road hugs the Mississippi near Brainerd, Minnesota, not far from the great river's source, during fall.

ARMCHAIR

✳ ***As I Lay Dying*** (William Faulkner) The Mississippi is a feature of Faulkner's brilliant and slightly off-kilter novels about the South. This 1930 stream-of-consciousness novel is set in Yoknapatawpha County, Mississippi, a fictionalized version of his home county of Lafayette.

✳ ***The Adventures of Huckleberry Finn*** (Mark Twain) Synonymous with the river, Twain worked as a riverboat pilot, which informed this, the very first 'Great American Novel'.

✳ ***O Brother, Where Art Thou?*** (2000) The Coen Brothers are attracted to the river, and their version of Homer's *The Odyssey* uses the Mississippi to striking effect, notably in the scene where the trio of misfits are seduced by the mythical sirens.

✳ ***Mud*** (2012) Set amid Arkansas settlements on the banks of the Mississippi, this coming-of-age thriller is an atmospheric portrait of the river and those who make their lives on it.

HIKE ALASKA'S CHILKOOT TRAIL

THE KLONDIKE GOLD RUSH WAS 'THE LAST GRAND ADVENTURE,' WHEN
THOUSANDS FOLLOWED THE CHILKOOT TRAIL TO SEEK THEIR FORTUNE IN
THE YUKON. THESE DAYS IT'S HIKERS IN SEARCH OF ADVENTURE WHO ARE
RETRACING THE STAMPEDERS' STEPS ACROSS ALASKA'S FAMOUS TRAIL.

In 1896, Skookum Jim Mason, Dawson Charlie, and George Washington
Carmack found 'color' in a tributary of the Klondike River in Canada's Yukon
territory. A year later, when a steamship landed in Seattle with a couple of
tons of gold, the Klondike Gold Rush was on. Thousands of people quit their
jobs and sold their homes to finance a trip to the newly created boomtown of
Skagway in Southeast Alaska. In 1897–98 alone, almost 30,000 prospectors
tackled the steep Chilkoot Trail to Lake Bennett, where they built crude rafts
to float up the Yukon River to the goldfields. In all, it was a journey of around
600 miles (1000km), with gold-seekers often arriving in Dawson City only to
discover most of the streams were already staked.

At the height of this madness, Irish contractor Michael J Heney convinced
a group of English investors that he could build a railroad from Skagway
to Whitehorse over the White Pass. Construction began in 1898, with little
more than picks, shovels and blasting powder, and the narrow-gauge railroad
reached Whitehorse, today the Yukon's capital, in 1900. The construction of
the White Pass & Yukon Railroad was nothing short of a superhuman feat and
it sealed the fate of the Chilkoot Trail.

The actual Klondike Gold Rush lasted only to the early 1900s but its legacy
has endured, even blossomed, and is now the basis for Skagway's economy.
Today, most of downtown Skagway and the famous trail immortalized by
stampeders are part of the Klondike Gold Rush National Historical Park, and
a ride on the White Pass & Yukon Railroad is one of the most popular tours in
Southeast Alaska. Not only have Skagway's historic buildings been restored to
their boomtown appearance, but locals, dressed in turn-of-the-century garb,
still welcome the modern-day stampeders stepping off ferries and cruise ships.

106

ESSENTIAL EXPERIENCES

* **Riding the historic White Pass & Yukon Railroad as it climbs from Skagway to White Pass.**

* Bellying up to the bar at Skagway's Mascot Saloon, a museum dedicated to gambling, drinking, prostitution, and other vices during the Klondike Gold Rush.

* **Cruising to Skagway on the Alaska Marine Highway through glacier-studded Lynn Canal, North America's longest and deepest fjord.**

* Checking out the ton of supplies every miner had to carry over the Chilkoot Pass at Klondike Gold Rush National Historical Park Visitor Center.

* **Strolling Skagway's wooden sidewalks as if it's 1898.**

DISTANCE 33 MILES (53KM) | **ELEVATION** 3468FT (1057M) | **LOCATION** SKAGWAY, ALASKA, USA, TO LAKE BENNETT, BC, CANADA
IDEAL TIME COMMITMENT FOUR TO FIVE DAYS | **BEST TIME OF YEAR** MID-JUNE TO MID-SEPTEMBER | **ESSENTIAL TIP** PACK
YOUR PASSPORT – THE CHILKOOT TRAIL CROSSES AN INTERNATIONAL BORDER.

CLIMBING THE CHILKOOT PASS

Before the arrival of the railway, leg power was the only way to cross the Klondike. One amazing photo – one that's displayed even along the trail – is of a line of men carrying their loads up the Golden Stairs in the winter of 1897–98. Unless they could afford porters, stampeders carried roughly 49lb (22kg) on each trip up the pass, which included 1500 steps carved out of the snow and ice. Most could endure only one climb a day, which meant they made as many as 40 trips in 40 days before they could get the required 'year's worth of supplies' to the top.

■ THE ADVENTURE UNFOLDS

The Chilkoot Trail is as much a history lesson as it is a wilderness adventure. The well-developed trail is littered from one end to the other with artifacts from the era – everything from collapsed tramways and huge steam boilers to a rotting wagon wheel or a rusty coffee pot. The Chilkoot stretches 33 miles (53km) from Dyea, a ghost town that was once Skagway's rival, to Lake Bennett, just over the Canadian border. You can hike the trail in either direction but it's easier to begin in Dyea, following in the footsteps of the Klondike miners, which is what makes this adventure so appealing.

Located along the Chilkoot are nine camping grounds with wooden tent platforms and warming shelters. The 7.5-mile (12km) hike to the first two is relatively easy, because the trail follows the Taiya River. The climbing begins after the second camp site, Canyon City, but the most important camping ground by far is Sheep Camp, reached at mile 11.8. Just as in 1898, Sheep Camp still serves as the staging area for the climb to the summit. For most hikers, that's a 9-mile (14.5km), 10-hour trek to the next camping ground, in which they gain more than 2460ft (750m) in the first half. The final ascent to the 3468ft (1057m) Chilkoot Pass is via the famed Golden Stairs, a 45-degree rocky chute that is usually climbed by scrambling from one large boulder to the next on all fours.

At the top are snowfields, the USA–Canada border, and an emergency shelter. From there, the Chilkoot Trail is a gradual descent to Lake Bennett, where backpackers gather at the classic White Pass & Yukon Railroad depot for a scenic train ride back over the border to Skagway.

■ MAKING IT HAPPEN

Only 50 hikers per day are allowed on the trail. If you're intending to walk in the peak period from mid-July to mid-August, you will need to reserve your permits in advance through Parks Canada. For travel to Skagway, there's the Alaska Marine Highway. For other details about the hike, have a chat to the staff at the Chilkoot Trail Center. Contact the White Pass & Yukon Route Railroad for passage from Lake Bennett back to Skagway.

■ AN ALTERNATIVE CHALLENGE

Glacier Station, at mile 14 of the White Pass & Yukon Railroad, is little more than a sweeping curve in the tracks, a sign and a trail. But the trail leads 1.5 miles (2.5km) to a US Forest Service cabin and then to Laughton Glacier, which is a dramatic hanging glacier that spills over the 2953ft (900m) walls of the Sawtooth Range. Combining the train ride and a hike to a remote cabin makes this an easy alternative to the Chilkoot, while flagging down a train to return to Skagway is still a uniquely Alaskan experience.

MARK DAFFEY | GETTY IMAGES ©

MARK DAFFEY | GETTY IMAGES ©

OPENING SPREAD Following in the footsteps of the stampeders on the Chilkoot Trail. **ABOVE (L)** A reminder for walkers to exercise caution. **ABOVE (R)** Examining a Gold Rush-era boiler near Canyon City. **LEFT** Hikers make their way through a conifer forest along the trail.

ARMCHAIR

* ❋ *The Floor of Heaven* (Howard Blum) This novel of the Klondike Gold Rush has been made into a movie.

* ❋ *The Call of the Wild* (Jack London) An adventure classic, with a dog as chief protagonist and the Klondike as a backdrop.

* ❋ *Good Time Girls of the Alaska–Yukon Gold Rush* (Lael Morgan) Follow the women who followed the stampeders, including a prostitute who married the mayor of Fairbanks.

* ❋ *Klondike Trail: The Complete Hiking and Paddling Guide* (Jennifer Voss) From the Chilkoot Trail to paddling the Yukon River.

* ❋ *Songs of a Sourdough* (Robert W Service) The 'Bard of the Yukon' knew 'There are strange things done 'neath the midnight sun,' as recounted in the poem 'The Cremation of Sam McGee.'

* ❋ *Klondike Fever* (1980) Based on London's Yukon adventures, this Canadian film starred Rod Steiger and Angie Dickinson.

TAKE A BITE OF SAN FRANCISCO

IF YOU VISIT SAN FRANCISCO AND DO NOTHING BUT EAT, EVERYONE WILL STILL SIGH WITH ENVY. PICTURESQUE CABLE CARS AND THE GOLDEN GATE BRIDGE MIGHT SELL POSTCARDS, BUT YOUR VACATION SELFIES WITH FARMERS' MARKET FINDS, INVENTIVE CALIFORNIAN CUISINE AND EXPERTLY CRAFTED COCKTAILS WILL BE MORE BRAG-WORTHY.

Forget clichéd images of hippies and 'The Summer of Love.' This West Coast port has been transformed by Silicon Valley wealth into a trendsetting, high-rise metropolis. The city vibrates with new possibilities, just like during the mid-19th century Gold Rush when miners, sailors, ragamuffins and shady ladies strolled the Embarcadero. The only change is that now it's chefs, artisanal food makers and craft brewers showing up hoping to strike it rich.

The city's rich culinary history is one reason why residents obsess over food. In the 19th century, immigrants from China, Italy, Russia and beyond sailed through the Golden Gate and anchored themselves in neighborhoods such as Chinatown and North Beach. Of course, they brought their recipes with them. And don't forget that California was once Mexican territory, so the spices and sauces of Mexico have always been part of its culinary repertoire.

Today fearless experimentation and a cornucopia of ingredients – mostly grown or raised within 100 miles (and often far less) of the city – make San Francisco an essential foodie destination. Sustainable, local, seasonal and organic are still the hallmarks of Californian cuisine. Chefs here let the ingredients shine through, reflecting the philosophy of local food pioneer Alice Waters, who opened Chez Panisse across the Bay in Berkeley in 1971.

Unapologetic food snobbery is a way of life in SF. Eavesdrop and you'll quickly learn that everyone has an opinion about the best place to get a street taco or a bowl of ramen, which third-wave coffee roaster sells the tastiest single-origin beans, or which speakeasy-style bar has the coolest handmade bitters and elixirs. But it's not all about haute cuisine. San Franciscans are equal-opportunity eaters who love a good deal. Food truck picnics at the Presidio, a scoop of Bi-Rite Creamery ice-cream on a sunny day when the fog lifts, or a carne asada burrito from La Taqueria during a Mission bar crawl will cost you little, but the tastes will be remembered long after your trip.

110

ESSENTIAL EXPERIENCES

✳ **Grazing through the Ferry Building and snacking on free samples from the farmers' market.**

✳ Working up an appetite while cycling across the Golden Gate Bridge to Sausalito for fresh seafood.

✳ **Climbing the Filbert Street steps past colorful wild parrots to hilltop Coit Tower, then grabbing Italian food in North Beach.**

✳ Taking in the sights and smells of Chinatown's busy streets and narrow alleys – and finding the fortune cookie factory.

✳ **Slurping clam chowder in an edible sourdough-bread bowl at Fisherman's Wharf before boarding a ferry over to Alcatraz.**

✳ Admiring public murals in the Mission while munching on a gigantic burrito.

LOCATION SAN FRANCISCO, USA | **IDEAL TIME COMMITMENT** THREE DAYS | **BEST TIME OF YEAR** SEPTEMBER AND OCTOBER
ESSENTIAL TIP LATE SPRING AND EARLY SUMMER BRING GRAY, CLOUDY SKIES AND COOL TEMPERATURES, ESPECIALLY IN MAY AND JUNE.

MEET (OR BE) THE CHEF

Inside a former butcher shop in Noe Valley, beloved Omnivore Books (omnivorebooks.com) is where chefs go on their day off to buy vintage, rare and new cookbooks, and other food and drink titles, from the encyclopedic to the obscure. Check the bookshop's online calendar for upcoming in-store chef appearances and cookbook signings. If you want to actually be the chef instead of just shaking hands with one, several Bay Area cooking schools offer fun, casual and internationally flavored cooking classes, including the community nonprofit 18 Reasons, the Cheese School of San Francisco, and Berkeley's Kitchen on Fire.

CRAFT COCKTAILS & BEER

Ever since the Gold Rush, San Francisco has been making its own beer and pouring cocktails. Close to the former Barbary Coast red-light district, where many of the city's original barkeeps set up shop, Comstock Saloon serves throwback cocktails like Pisco Punch and the Martinez in an old-timey atmosphere. Other bars that give a nod to yesteryear speakeasies include Bourbon & Branch, Rickhouse, and Local Edition, all near Union Square. To taste the unusual style of steam beer that gold miners used to drink, reserve a tour and tasting at Anchor Brewing in Portrero Hill.

THE ADVENTURE UNFOLDS

Start your day with a coffee or a 'Gibraltar' (a double shot of espresso with a little steamed milk served in a glass tumbler) at an artisanal roaster such as Ritual, Sightglass or Four Barrel. Then wander to the Embarcadero, which sidles along the Bay, and into the restored Ferry Building. Inside this gourmet food hall, you can sample Californian olive oil and honey, Cowgirl Creamery cheeses from Marin County, and more. The farmers' market outside on Tuesdays, Thursdays and Saturdays is always thronged.

Ride a vintage streetcar west along the Embarcadero to North Beach, an Italian neighborhood, for Neapolitan pizzerias, old-school delis, and Liguria Bakery for tender focaccia. Afterward, zigzag uphill to Chinatown, where families fill dim sum halls and noodle shops. Or take the streetcar to Fisherman's Wharf to try sourdough bread from Boudin Bakery, and *cioppino*, a tomato-based seafood stew that features Dungeness crab.

The next day head to the Mission. Grab a breakfast taco or burrito before joining a guided cultural and historical tour of the area's famous murals with Precita Eyes, a nonprofit arts and education group. Spend a lazy afternoon in Golden Gate Park at the de Young art museum or the eco-conscious California Academy of Sciences. Stroll the Japanese Tea Garden, where allegedly the first fortune cookies were served in the US.

When your stomach starts growling, the avenues bordering the park are full of one-of-a-kind finds, such as cozy Outerlands cafe or Mourad, serving Moroccan-Californian fusion cuisine. Foodies chasing Michelin stars need to book months in advance for dinner at the likes of Benu or State Bird Provisions. Otherwise backtrack east to the Hayes Valley district, whose chic shopping streets hold the city's densest concentration of eateries.

MAKING IT HAPPEN

San Francisco International Airport is about a 25-minute taxi ride south of the city (rush-hour traffic permitting). The airport is linked by BART trains to the Mission and downtown San Francisco. City hotels are expensive, with most options around Union Square, Nob Hill, SoMa, the Marina, and Fisherman's Wharf. Alcatraz boat tours are popular, so book well ahead.

A DETOUR

Just over an hour's drive from the city is the Napa Valley wine-growing region. It's also a destination for cutting-edge chefs and their fans. You'll find the most restaurants per capita in the hamlet of Yountville, made famous by chef Thomas Keller's French Laundry. For cooking classes and wine tastings, the Culinary Institute of America has two campuses: historical Greystone Cellars in St Helena and downtown Napa near Oxbow Market, packed with shops, restaurants and bars.

ANDREW MONTGOMERY | LONELY PLANET ©

KRIS DAVIDSON | LONELY PLANET ©

OPENING SPREAD San Francisco's great signifier, the Golden Gate Bridge. **ABOVE (L)** Betty Carr has been baking at Mom's Apple Pie since 1983. **ABOVE (R)** The Haight Ashbury 'hood is synonymous with the summer of love. **LEFT** A streetcar makes its way up the city's steep streets.

ARMCHAIR

* *The San Francisco Ferry Plaza Farmers' Market Cookbook* (Peggy Knickerbocker and Christopher Hirsheimer) Flavorful recipes for every season to make at home.

* *The Zuni Cafe Cookbook* (Judy Rodgers and Gerald Asher) Advice on wine and cooking from the San Francisco restaurant whose roast chicken can't be beat.

* *Tartine* (Elisabeth M Prueitt and Chad Robertson) The first in a series of cookbooks from the influential Mission bakery.

* *The Omnivore's Dilemma: A Natural History of Four Meals* (Michael Pollan) Because Bay Area foodies always want to know exactly where their food comes from.

* *Drinking the Devil's Acre: A Love Letter to San Francisco and Her Cocktails* (Duggan McDonnell) For every aspiring Barbary Coast bartender. Cheers!

TRACE THE LIFE OF AMELIA EARHART

AMELIA EARHART: AUTHOR, WOMEN'S-RIGHTS ADVOCATE, CELEBRITY, FASHION ICON, AVIATION PIONEER. ON HER FINAL JOURNEY, SHE ONLY HAD TO CROSS THE PACIFIC TO COMPLETE A QUEST TO BE THE FIRST WOMAN TO FLY AROUND THE GLOBE – ONLY TO DISAPPEAR WITHOUT TRACE.

In 1932, Amelia Earhart, aged 34, became the first woman to fly solo nonstop across the Atlantic. Five years later, she set out to be the first woman to fly around the world, this time along with a navigator, Fred Noonan. On May 21, 1937, she took off from Oakland, California on the first leg of a journey that would take her from the US to New Guinea via South America, Africa, India and Southeast Asia, and across the Pacific.

Simply listing her stops on this monumental 22,000-mile (35,000km) journey is enough to impart its scope and achievement: Burbank, California; Tucson, Arizona; New Orleans, Louisiana; Miami, Florida; San Juan, Puerto Rico; Cumana, Venezuela; Paramaribo, Suriname; Fortaleza, Brazil; Natal, Brazil; St Louis, Senegal; Dakar, Senegal; Gao, Mali; N'Djamena, Chad; Al-Fashir, Sudan; Khartoum, Sudan; Massawa, Ethiopia; Assab, Ethiopia; Karachi, Pakistan; Calcutta, India; Sittwe, Burma; Rangoon, Burma; Bangkok, Thailand; Singapore; Bandung, Indonesia; Surabaya, Indonesia; Hupang, Indonesia; Darwin, Australia; and Lae, New Guinea.

On July 2, 1937, she left Lae bound for Howland Island, the last leg of her journey. She never made it, the plane vanishing completely without trace. This disappearing act has spawned many theories as to what happened. Was she shot down from the sky by the Japanese, held prisoner on Saipan and executed as a spy? Was Noonan a raging alcoholic who fatally compromised the mission with his erratic behaviour? Of course, there's the obligatory UFO theory, de rigueur for disappeared pilots. So this one goes: Earhart was in the employ of US intelligence. This led her to make contact with an alien ship, which either malfunctioned on contact or deliberately blew her out of the sky, depending upon which conspiracy theorist you believe.

ESSENTIAL EXPERIENCES

✳ **Making a pilgrimage to the Amelia Earhart Birthplace Museum in Atchison, Kansas.**

✳ Photographing the Amelia statue at Burbank Airport, where she took off to begin her journey.

✳ **Photographing Amelia's original home in Toluca Lake, California, which has been carefully preserved and maintained by the current owners (Amelia planned her fatal trip in the courtyard here).**

✳ Visiting Trepassey in Newfoundland, Canada, the launching place of Amelia's first-woman-across-the-Atlantic flight in 1928.

✳ **Traveling to Lae, the launching place for the beginning of the end.**

DISTANCE 22,000 MILES (35,000KM) | **COUNTRIES COVERED** USA, PUERTO RICO, VENEZUELA, SURINAME, BRAZIL, SENEGAL, MALI, CHAD, SUDAN, ETHIOPIA, PAKISTAN, INDIA, BURMA, THAILAND, SINGAPORE, INDONESIA, AUSTRALIA, NEW GUINEA | **IDEAL TIME COMMITMENT** THREE MONTHS | **BEST TIME OF YEAR** ANY TIME YOU FEEL HEROIC | **ESSENTIAL TIP** DON'T CRASH.

'AMELIA – IS THAT YOU?' PART 1

It was first thought that the mystery of Earhart and Noonan had been solved in 1941, when British soldiers discovered two sets of bones and shoes on remote Nikumaroro Island in the Pacific. However, a British doctor declared that the bones were of two European men and the matter was put to rest. Then in 1998 the doctor's notes were re-examined by modern specialists, who concluded that he must have got it wrong. According to them, one set of bones belonged clearly to a Caucasian female, 170cm (5ft 7in) tall – which just happened to be Earhart's vital statistics. Typically, the bones have long since vanished, allowing the mystery to remain.

'AMELIA – IS THAT YOU?' PART 2

In 2010, it was announced that more bone fragments had been found, on another deserted Pacific island located along the course of Earhart's final flight. Found nearby was old make-up, glass bottles and shells that had been prised apart. Scientists at the University of Oklahoma tried to extract DNA from the bones to test the theory that Earhart and Noonan died as castaways. The results proved inconclusive, and the bones may very well be a turtle's, as a turtle shell was also found nearby. Yet, even that fact opens up a can of worms, because the shell was hollowed out. Did our castaways perhaps use it to collect rainwater?

■ THE JOURNEY TODAY

As you settle into the padded leather seat of your Lockheed Electra 10E, you watch the sun rise beneath you, a truly wondrous sight. The Electra has custom-fitted gas tanks, larger than normal capacity, so you feel safe and secure as you slice through the air, knowing you have enough fuel to make the 2556-mile (4113km) journey to Howland Island. You caught a bit of dysentery in Bandung, but it appears to have eased now – hopefully, you think, for your navigator's sake sitting behind you.

You quickly leaf through your log, noting all the stages of the journey and how happy and elated you have felt. But you know you can't take too many things for granted, because the journey from Lae to Howland is the longest stretch you've done across water. At that point, your navigator tells you how utterly thankful he is that you had the foresight to strip all nonessential items from the plane so that more fuel could be taken on. You understand that Howland is but a tiny speck in the Pacific, very easy to miss, and so you are further reassured by the US Coast Guard, which sent ships to the island with instructions to burn all their lights at once for you to use as landing beacons.

After a while, you see something ominous: storms ahead. 'I thought they said the forecast was favourable!' cries your navigator, and you bite your lower lip with worry. 'We've come this far,' you reply. 'Nothing to fear.'

Inside, though, you are scared because although you're near Howland you can't see the ships. You radio to the lead ship: 'Where are you? We must be near but we can't see you.' You check the fuel: it's low. 'Please reply,' you continue. 'We're at 1000ft.' And then the sky cracks.

■ SHORTCUT

For the potted history, visit one or more of the various Earhart landmarks scattered across the US, detailed in Essential Experiences on the previous spread. But there is no easy or 'short way' into the mystery of everyone's favorite aviator: over 80 years later, people still can't agree on how she disappeared or even what her true purpose was.

■ DETOUR

Fans should visit Amelia's hometown of Atchison, Kansas. On a hillside near Warnick Lake, an artist has created a huge earthworks portrait of the aviator, complete with goggles and scarf. The main attraction, however, is the Amelia Earhart Birthplace Museum housed in the building where she was born. The rooms and interiors are as they were during her childhood, and feature family portraits, the furniture that she owned, replicas of the Lockheed Electra 10E that flew her to her death, as well as photographs, interactive displays, maps, and numerous curios. What it doesn't have is the answer to the mystery.

OPENING SPREAD & ABOVE (R) Amelia Earhart with a sports plane she bought in 1928. **ABOVE (L)** A memorial in Harbour Grace, Newfoundland, from where Earhart flew across the Atlantic. **ABOVE (R)** Her birthplace in Atchison, Kansas. **LEFT** New Guinea, where Earhart was last sighted.

STUART FORSTER | ALAMY ©

SHARON DAY | SHUTTERSTOCK ©

ARMCHAIR

* ***The Search for Amelia Earhart*** (Fred Goener) This 1966 book worked on the assumption that the Japanese had captured her.

* ***Flight For Freedom*** (1943) This film popularized the theory that Earhart was working for US intelligence.

* ***'The 37s'*** (1995) This episode of *Star Trek Voyager* played up the UFO angle, suggesting Earhart and Noonan had been abducted.

* ***Amelia*** (2009) The obligatory glossy Hollywood biopic starring Hilary Swank as the titular aviatrix.

* ***Close Encounters of the Third Kind*** (1977) In Steven Spielberg's film, Earhart can be seen walking out of the alien mother ship along with other abductees.

WINDSURF THE COLUMBIA RIVER GORGE

HOIST YOUR SAIL FOR A MAGIC CARPET RIDE ON STEROIDS. DANCE OVER THE CHOP AS YOU BLAZE A TRAIL PAST A PARADISE OF PRISTINE FORESTS AND MOUNTAIN VISTAS, FIZZING SO FAST YOU'LL NEED A DE-ADRENALINE SHOT TO BRING YOU BACK DOWN.

Launching a windsurf or kiteboard in your own private wind tunnel is a secret fantasy of sailboarders worldwide. Fortunately, turning this dream into reality is as simple as making your way to the Columbia River Gorge in the Pacific Northwest. Extending more than 80 miles (130km), this enormous canyon is the only navigable route through the mountain range known locally as the Cascades. And therein lies its attraction, because differences in wind pressure at opposite ends of the Cascades, coupled with the mountainous terrain, have combined to create a jet stream that effectively blasts its way through the gorge. The result is the ultimate wind-ride for experienced boarders who come from every part of the planet to savor the rush.

With dozens of designated launch sites, the gorge provides epic conditions at any time of year. But when the westerlies kick in, 37mph (60km/h) wind gusts are not uncommon, which is why it is regarded as a true windsurf and kiteboarding mecca, not to mention a preferred contest location for the pros.

In the warmer summer months, winds average a moderate 12–15mph (20–25km/h), with the added bonus of sheltered spots for anyone looking to learn. Take advantage of this before heading out into the more treacherous zones, and whatever you do, don't attempt to cross the river unless you're a seasoned veteran. Not only is the gorge still a busy shipping route, as it has been for 200 years, there's also plenty of flotsam, not to mention extremely strong currents.

But the Columbia River has more to offer than just wind-borne recreation pursuits. It's also one of the few places where you can snowboard in the morning and pull in for a kite session in the afternoon.

Oh, and did we mention it's also a pristine wilderness boasting a bewildering concentration of waterfalls, including the 623ft (190m) Multnomah Falls, the tallest falls in Oregon?

118

ESSENTIAL EXPERIENCES

❋ **Looking back up at the misty heights of the Cascades as you set off on dawn patrol.**

❋ Having your sail punched by the fist of Thor.

❋ **Feeling your arms ripping from your shoulders as you do everything you can to keep your ride under control.**

❋ Getting lifted higher, further, longer than you've ever been before.

❋ **Chilling post-session with your homies, ready to do it all again tomorrow.**

LENGTH 81 MILES (130KM) | **LOCATION** HOOD RIVER, OREGON, USA | **IDEAL TIME COMMITMENT** HALF A DAY | **BEST TIME OF YEAR** JUNE TO SEPTEMBER | **ESSENTIAL TIP** PACK YOUR SMALLEST KITE/SAIL TO HANDLE THE 30MPH+ (50KM/H+) WINDS.

KEEP CLEAR

Oregon isn't quite *Deliverance* territory but it still pays to observe the local laws while you're riding the river. Sailboarders can pay hefty fines for obstructing shipping laneways, and if you spot a sheriff's boat, steer clear as you're not allowed within 1640ft (500m). The tankers are particularly hazardous, as their size causes large 'wind shadows' – if you do get too close, you might find there is literally no power to blow you out of harm's way. It's the kind of situation that could have you squealin' like a pig...

UNDERGROUND THREAT

The fate of the Columbia River lies in the success or failure of one of the most extensive environmental cleanup operations in the world. Until their decommission at the end of the Cold War, nine nuclear reactors along the banks of the river discharged plutonium into the water course. The real danger today is that a million gallons of radioactive waste has leached into underground aquifers and is slowly moving towards the river. Experts predict that the cleanup, which began in 1989, may take up to 50 years and, if it stalls or fails, the poisoned water from the aquifers could easily pollute the river.

■ THE ADVENTURE UNFOLDS

Cruising the historic Columbia River Highway (Hwy 100) is the perfect precursor to riding the Columbia River Gorge. Completed in the 1920s, Hwy 100 was purposefully designed to showcase the mountains, canyons, cliffs and spectacular waterfalls for which the gorge is renowned. It also means you can check out the lay of the land and river before you set sail.

The real action starts at your launch site on the banks of the Columbia River. You've picked your spot after consulting the weather charts and knowledgeable locals back in Fort Hood, knowing that along the gorge even a few miles can mean drastically different water and atmospheric conditions. You pull on your wetsuit, rig up your smallest kite and prepare for launch. The water is freezing, like the locals said it would be. Above the far shore, clouds skitter above a sheet of conifers that cloak the hills, a small gust catches your kite and you're off, skidding across the water like a new-age Messiah.

Lurching forward, you notice the changing hues of the river, signifying shifts in the current. Like an enormous mass of living liquid, it's constantly on the move. Ahead, an overladen barge slugs its way along the well-plied shipping lane. You angle your arms and shift your weight as another gust approaches, and like a hand from the heavens it plucks you from the water and throws you up toward the mountains.

Shredding your aerial maneuver, you land majestically as another gust shunts you forward, as if your kite is caught in the doors of a freight train. Then you either hang on for the ride of your life, or get dragged into a world of pain.

■ MAKING IT HAPPEN

Head to Hood River, the nearest town, about 37 miles (60km) from the gorge. Be warned that this place fills up fast whenever races are on or the wind is nuking. An easier and cheaper accommodation option is to camp at sites within the Columbia River Gorge National Scenic Area, which spans the entire length of the gorge. Renting a car will give you the flexibility to choose your launch site depending on the wind, the atmospheric conditions and the river's strong currents.

■ AN ALTERNATIVE CHALLENGE

Still working on your pro credentials? No worries, try the Sandspit at Hood River where you'll find moderate, consistent conditions along with some of the planet's most experienced sailboarders and kitesurfers to help hone your skills before you take on the gorge. Alternatively, you can always hike the nearby hills and get a bird's-eye view of the action. Even on a calm day you can watch and learn from dozens of shredders. Wear proper boots, though – the area is notorious for rattlesnakes.

ZACK FRANK | SHUTTERSTOCK ©

OPENING SPREAD Windsurfers make use of Columbia River Gorge's unique atmospheric conditions. **ABOVE** The gorge has been designated a National Scenic Area. **LEFT** The footbridge affords a closeup view of the spectacular Multnomah Falls.

ARMCHAIR

✳ **Pokin' Round the Gorge** (Scott Cook) A lover's guide to the Columbia River region, featuring saucy images and secret spots ideal for intimacy!

✳ **The World Kite and Windsurfing Guide** (Udo Hoelker) Once you've shredded Columbia River, plan your next trip with this formidable resource showcasing more than 1200 of the best windsurf locations worldwide.

✳ **Wild Beauty: Photography of the Columbia River Gorge, 1867–1957** (Terry Toedtemeier & John Laursen) A coffee-table book revealing the magnificence of this area and how it changed following dam construction that began in the late 19th century.

✳ **The Windsurfing Movie** (2007) Directed by Johnny DeCesare, this film shot at locations around the world is considered the definitive movie about windsurfing.

RIDE THE CALIFORNIA ZEPHYR

THE CALIFORNIA ZEPHYR SHOWS HOW THE WEST WAS WON: RIDE THIS ROUTE, WHICH STRADDLES NORTH AMERICA'S MIGHTIEST MOUNTAIN RANGES, TO APPRECIATE ENGINEERING MASTERY, NATURAL SPLENDOR, THE COMPANY OF NEW FRIENDS, AND THE ADVENTUROUS SPIRIT OF PIONEERS PAST.

Zephyrus was the ancient Greek god of the west wind, blower of the gentlest spring breezes. Trains on his namesake rail route, which puff across America in the same direction, from Chicago to the Pacific coast, are rather less demure.

The California Zephyr doesn't do gentle. The scenery outside the windows of the 'Silver Lady' is massive and majestic, domineering and elemental. For sections, the mountains, soaring up to over 13,000ft (4000m), are tipped with snow, year round; gorges are gouged by white water; hostile desert extends seemingly forever; tunnels and switchbacks battle with the Continental Divide. This is wild country, which man has, just about, sneaked through.

It was in 1869 that Abraham Lincoln's dream was realized: railroaders hammered in the final spike at Promontory, Utah, and the Atlantic and Pacific sides of the United States were finally connected by train. This paved the way for convoys of cowboys, gold prospectors, oilmen and outlaws to expand into the western frontier. A journey that would previously have taken months to complete on horse and foot could now be done, for a few dollars, in just a week.

Today that original line, the Overland Route, transports freight only (unless snowfall forces Zephyr trains to divert onto its historic tracks). But the California Zephyr, which has run under various guises since 1949, follows some of the same line, and showcases similarly impressive feats of engineering along the way: the 6.2-mile (10km) Moffat Tunnel, which burrows through the Continental Divide to save a 162-mile (260km) detour around it; and the stretch of track atop 7060ft (2160m) Donner Pass, which allowed the first rail passage over the Sierra Nevada, and just happens to be one of the country's most scenic stretches of track.

Like the breeze, travel west. Starting from Chicago you should still pass the mountains in daylight, even if the train departs late. You'll also be channeling the spirit of those original pioneers and traveling into dazzling desert sunsets.

ESSENTIAL EXPERIENCES

* **Hitting the Obama trail on a tour of Chicago's rejuvenated South Side.**

* Disembarking at Winter Park for high-altitude pistes and miles of cross-country ski trails.

* **Rafting, mountain-biking and hiking around Glenwood Springs, or simply enjoying the views of the Glenwood Canyon.**

* Winning big at the casinos of fluoro-kitsch Reno.

* **Finding a prime Sightseer Lounge Car seat to take in the peaks, canyons and cascades of the Sierra Nevada.**

* Complementing your train travel with a visit to the California State Railroad Museum in Sacramento.

* **Raising your binoculars at Suisun Marsh, a vast brackish wetland teeming with birds.**

* Sailing out to Alcatraz Island, the notorious prison stranded in San Francisco Bay.

DISTANCE 2400 MILES (3900KM) | **COUNTRIES COVERED** USA | **IDEAL TIME COMMITMENT** 10 DAYS
BEST TIME OF YEAR YEAR ROUND | **ESSENTIAL TIP** TRAVEL EAST–WEST FOR THE BEST SUNSETS.

THROUGH THE ROCKIES

In 1870, America's railway-building pioneers plowed south from Denver, their goal being to reach El Paso, Texas. The Denver & Río Grande Western Railroad (D&RGW) aimed to conquer the Rockies, cutting through the ranges rather than detouring around them. The tracks never made it to Texas, terminating instead at Santa Fe, New Mexico. But the D&RGW was still impressive. Its 10,400ft (3120m) Tennessee Pass was the highest mainline track in the USA. The Durango & Silverton Narrow Gauge section, which serviced gold mines in the San Juan Mountains, is now a 45-mile (72km) heritage track plied by steam locos, and one of the best rides in the country.

■ THE JOURNEY TODAY

You've swapped blackjack tips with a croupier from Reno, and discussed politics with a student bound for Sacramento. Meanwhile, when you look out of the window, the most remarkable mountain scenes are streaming by – white-whip tops and river-rumbled gorges. And you haven't even had to move a single muscle.

The Sightseer Lounge Car is the place to be. In these panoramic carriages, walls have been swapped for windows, offering uninterrupted views of whatever you're passing: the marshy Mississippi, the bright lights of Denver, the drama of the Rocky Mountains. This is also the place to chat, to meet the Americans who've swapped airplanes and automobiles in favor of the train.

They're a growing breed, from a low base. In 1970, after battling decades of competition against the airplane and motorcar, usage was so low that the Zephyr ceased operation until 1983. But in 2016 it carried more than 417,000 passengers, an 11% increase on 2015. Air travel is increasingly laden with security rigmarole and cramped seating, and fuel prices are once again on the rise. Put simply, US trains make sense.

In a frantic world, this is travel at its most civilized. Seats are comfy, even in Coach class. A reasonably priced dining car offers sit-down meals – though if you want to bring your own supplies that's fine. You'll even get commentary, with experts from the California State Railroad Museum pointing out the sights between Sacramento and Reno. Still, it's nice to get off now and then. This iconic journey is steeped in cultural history and landscapes as old as the hills. But with so many stops with so much potential, it's a journey you can mold into your own glimpse of railside USA.

ARMCHAIR

✳ ***Stranger on a Train*** (Jenny Diski) The British author travels America by rail, documenting the fleeting landscapes and quirky characters she meets, quite reluctantly, en route.

✳ ***Nothing Like it in the World: The Men Who Built the Railway That United America*** (Stephen E Ambrose) The story of the hardy souls who constructed the transcontinental railroad.

✳ ***Riding the Rails in the USA*** (Martin W Sandler) From opening up the Wild West to shifting modern-day commuters, a look at the impact of trains in American life.

✳ ***California Zephyr*** (Hank Williams) Classic country-music crooner's paean to the eponymous train.

✳ ***Denver & Río Grande*** (1952) High-drama Hollywood version of the construction of the railroad over the Rocky Mountains, filmed on location near Durango, southern Colorado.

SHORTCUT

Ridden nonstop, trains on the Zephyr route take 51 hours and 20 minutes to connect Chicago with San Francisco. While getting off en route is more fun, you can still get a taste of America during your two and a half days on board: the panoramic viewing lounges offer tantalizing views of the plains and mountains, and the bar and dining cars allow long chats with the locals.

DETOUR

Take a different route from Chicago to the Pacific Ocean. Plowing a more southerly trail than the Zephyr, Amtrak's Southwest Chief (40 hours) heads from Chicago to LA via the red-rock badlands of the American West; stop off at Albuquerque for Pueblo culture, great hiking and mountain-biking trails and forays into New Mexico, and Flagstaff, for a historic downtown crammed with eclectic vernacular architecture and vintage neon, and access to the Grand Canyon. Alternatively, trains on the Empire Builder route head north from Chicago, meeting the West Coast in the Pacific Northwest (Seattle or Portland), having trundled for 46 hours via the sweeping plains of North Dakota and Montana's big-sky country.

JOE RAEDLE | GETTY IMAGES ©

OPENING SPREAD The Zephyr pulls up to the platform in California. **ABOVE** The view from the rear of the train at Green River, Utah, one of the seven states it passes through. **BELOW** More scenic wonders reveal themselves from your window seat.

TRAIN DRIVER FOR THE DAY

The Western Pacific Railroad Museum occupies the former train servicing depot in Portola, California, a small town nestled in the upper reaches of the Feather River Canyon. Amid its vast collection of locos and cabooses, which you're encouraged to climb on and over, are an engine car and four passenger cars from the original California Zephyr train. Better still, from mid-April to mid-November any train buff can play train driver – the museum's Run A Locomotive program allows you to rent one of a selection of its vintage diesel engines and operate it under the supervision of a private instructor.

LEAVE THE LAS VEGAS STRIP

THERE'S PLENTY TO DO IN SIN CITY AWAY FROM THE FAMOUS CASINO STRIP, FROM PLAYING AROUND WITH HEAVY MACHINERY TO WINERY VISITS, GO-KART RACES AND TRAMPOLINE DODGEBALL.

You know you want to. Anyone who had a sandbox as a kid would want to; anyone who's driven past a building site and peered inside would want to. And now here you are perched up in the cabin of a proper bulldozer, about to push some dirt around. Serious dirt, too – tons of it. Press a few buttons, pull a few levers. The big engine revs, the caterpillar tracks start moving, the shovel digs into the earth...

They say you can do just about anything in Las Vegas, although when they say that they're probably thinking more along the lines of gambling and strippers than building a big mound of dirt and then driving over it. But it takes all kinds in this place, and it's only once you get away from that famous neon-lit Strip that you realize just how much there is to do in Vegas. Forget the gambling and postpone the Elton John show. There's work to be done.

The bulldozer is part of Dig This, which has to be about the most bizarrely great attraction in Vegas. The idea is simple: drive a real bulldozer or excavator, and do all the work those big machines normally do. Dig trenches, move huge tyres around, and drive over large mounds of dirt. It's brilliant in its simplicity, and the perfect salt-of-the-earth antidote to the glitzy fakery of the Strip.

It's also just the beginning. Once you're done playing in your giant sandbox there's plenty of amusement awaiting in Vegas that doesn't involve cards and chips. Take a helicopter ride over the Grand Canyon and combine it with dinner and wine-tasting at a vineyard. Play dodgeball on trampolines. Take off in a jetpack. Race go-karts. Eat at Michelin-starred restaurants. Fly an aerobatic plane. Party in a pool. Drink at a dive bar.

And don't gamble a cent.

ESSENTIAL EXPERIENCES

❋ **Visiting the Neon Museum's Boneyard and witnessing old neon cowboys brought back to life.**

❋ Knocking back a few drinks with the locals at Double Down Saloon, Vegas' dingiest and best dive bar.

❋ **Jumping behind the controls of a bulldozer at Dig This and living your childhood sandbox dreams in full size.**

❋ Taking a helicopter joy flight over the Grand Canyon – or just getting dropped off at a winery.

❋ **Enjoying the sun, the water, the DJs, the cocktails and the cabanas at one of Las Vegas' famous pool parties.**

❋ Indulging your inner child with a game of ultimate dodgeball at Sky Zone Indoor Trampoline Park.

LOCATION LAS VEGAS, NEVADA, USA | **BEST TIME OF YEAR** THERE'S NO BAD TIME TO VISIT; POOL-PARTY SEASON RUNS FROM MARCH TO SEPTEMBER | **IDEAL TIME COMMITMENT** FOUR DAYS | **ESSENTIAL TIP** MAKE USE OF YOUR CONCIERGE **PACK** CLOTHES TO GO OUT IN, AND CLOTHES TO GET DIRTY IN.

BIGGER IS BETTER

The first casino on the Las Vegas Strip was a Spanish-style place called El Rancho Vegas, which had 110 rooms and a gambling floor consisting of two blackjack tables, one roulette wheel, and a craps table. That was back in 1941 – how things have changed. The biggest building on the Strip now, by size, is the Palazzo, which has 3068 rooms and 105,000 sq ft (9800 sq m) of gambling floor – it topples the Pentagon as being the largest non-industrial building in the USA. For pure punting, however, the biggest is the MGM Grand, which has 139 gaming tables and more than 2500 slot machines spread out over 171,500 sq ft (16,000 sq m) of casino space.

MR LAS VEGAS

Elvis has been there. Elton John has done plenty of shows there. Celine Dion never seems to leave. But none of them can claim the title of Las Vegas' most frequent performer – that would be Wayne Newton, or 'Mr Las Vegas,' who has done more than 30,000 shows in Sin City. Newton, a singer and entertainer most famous for the single 'Danke Schoen', has done cameos in his fair share of Vegas-based films as well, including *The Hangover, Ocean's Eleven* and *Smokin' Aces*. The road to the airport is even named after him: Wayne Newton Boulevard.

THE PERFECT GETAWAY

Away from the Strip, away from the lure of all those neon lights and singing slot machines, there's plenty to keep visitors to Las Vegas occupied. Dig This, the earthmoving theme park, is one of the more inventive attractions, but the fun doesn't stop there. Sky Zone Indoor Trampoline Park is another place popular with overgrown children, where you can bounce around doing somersaults and trying to avoid being hit with squishy balls. Makes a change from blackjack.

Meanwhile, those who've hit the jackpot should get high with a helicopter joy flight – some tours soar over the Grand Canyon, others take in the Hoover Dam, and still others go further afield, taking guests out to Pahrump Valley Winery, near the California state line. Have a meal, some wine, and then fly back to Vegas.

Take in a little of the town's history at the Boneyard. The Las Vegas Neon Museum's huge yard is strewn with over 200 old neon signs and billboards dating back as far as the 1930s, a monument to a city that outgrew itself several times over. Several have been restored to their former, functioning glory.

Another Vegas institution and a must-visit for anyone jaded by all the glitz is Double Down Saloon, a dive bar that's proud to call itself such. The bar is dark and dingy, it's patronized by Vegas' more interesting characters, and the live music borders on 'experimental', but the drinks are cheap.

Want to slow down? Pay a visit to the Mob Museum to learn about Vegas' past. Want to speed things up? Leap into a go-kart at Pole Position Raceway; strap on a jet-pack at Lake Las Vegas Water Sports; or take to the skies in an aerobatic plane with Sky Combat Ace. Finally, don't miss Vegas' famous pool parties. Be it Wet Republic, Encore or Rehab, the formula is basically the same: get thousands of party-goers in the pool, add a DJ, some drinks, and see what happens. You've probably got a fair idea of the results.

PLAN IT

Summer is when Vegas is busiest, but attractions are open year-round. Access is by plane from almost anywhere in the US and some Canadian centers; alternatively, hire a car in Los Angeles and take a drive made by many before you. Accommodations in Las Vegas are relatively cheap; the casinos know they'll recoup those losses. How much you decide to give back is up to you.

129

DETOUR

There's no way you'll stay out of Vegas' gambling dens forever. So where to go, and what to do? Top of the list has to be watching the fountains at the Bellagio, which is spectacular, crowded, and doesn't cost a cent. Next up, wander the canals of Venice – or, at least, the canals of the Venetian Casino. Then step back a little further into fake Italian history with a stroll through the Roman-themed Caesars Palace. It's all tropical island dreaming under the rainforest atrium over at the Mirage, while the Wynn is just pure luxury. Finish up with drinks at New York New York, the casino that never sleeps (actually, that goes for all of them).

KRIS DAVIDSON | LONELY PLANET ©

OPENING SPREAD Retired Vegas signage lights up The Neon Museum. **ABOVE** The Strip in its illuminated glory. **LEFT** Command your very own bulldozer at Dig This.

ARMCHAIR

✳ **Fear and Loathing in Las Vegas** (Hunter S Thompson) Hunter S Thompson goes on his now-famous drug-spiked rampage through Sin City, changing journalism in the process.

✳ **Leaving Las Vegas** (John O'Brien) Man leaves wife and job, goes to Vegas to drink himself into oblivion and... well, that would spoil it.

✳ **The Hangover** (2009) Four guys, one bachelor party, one baby, one tiger, and one former heavyweight champion of the world. It will seem unlikely until you experience Vegas for yourself.

✳ **Ocean's Eleven** (2001) Attempting to steal from a Las Vegas casino is a really, really bad idea. Unless, of course, you've got George Clooney, Brad Pitt and Matt Damon on board.

✳ **Casino** (1995) Wait, there's a dark side to Las Vegas? Involving the Mob? Robert De Niro and Joe Pesci portray it perfectly.

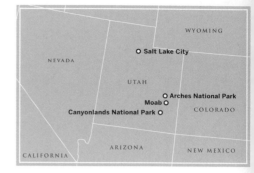

MOUNTAIN BIKE MOAB'S SLICKROCK TRAIL

DISCOVER THE ICONIC SLICKROCK THAT HAS MADE THE UTAH TOWN OF MOAB A WORLD-FAMOUS DESTINATION FOR FAT TIRE FANS. PEDAL THROUGH THE DESERT ON A BIKE, EXPLORING ROCKY OUTCROPS AND TESTING YOUR METTLE ON STICKY DROP-OFFS IN THIS WILD WILE E COYOTE COUNTRY.

Most people associate Utah with deserts and Mormons, but to mountain bikers the western town of Moab could be an acronym for Mother of all Biking towns.

Originally a ford on the Colorado River, Moab was first settled (and swiftly abandoned) as a Mormon outpost in 1855. It boomed with the discovery of uranium in the region in the 1950s. Thirty years later, the Cold War ended, and so did Moab's largest industry. In its place came mountain bikes, refashioning Moab as one of the States' premier outdoors destinations. How many other towns have generic-brand hotels that advertise on-site bike workshops?

Pinched between Arches and Canyonlands national parks, Moab's surrounds are a mat of sand and red rock – the so-called 'slickrock' that makes mountain biking here so magnificent. Named because its surface was so slick for horses, the ancient Navajo sandstone is more like stickrock for mountain bikes, allowing riders to almost defy gravity as their wheels grip the steeply sloped rock.

The trail that attracts the vast bulk of mountain bikers is the Slickrock Trail, arguably the most famous mountain bike route in the world. Originally designed for trail bikes, the 12-mile (20km) loop rolls across Swiss Cheese Ridge and the Lion's Back, a rock ridge looming above Moab. Its orange rock is like a set of cycling moguls, with ledges that drop into pits of sand followed by stiff climbs back out.

But there's no need to get fixated on the Slickrock Trail: Moab has myriad bike experiences and great natural beauty to help dilute the adrenaline rushes. Novices can admire the swirling patterns in the rock as they curl around Bartlett Wash, or pass dinosaur footprints on the Klondike Bluffs Trail. Experienced riders will want to add Porcupine Rim and Poison Spider Mesa to their resumé – these trails are almost as famous as Slickrock – while multiday desert rides beckon the most adventurous on the White Rim and Kokopelli trails.

ESSENTIAL EXPERIENCES

* **Earning your mountain bike stripes on the mighty Slickrock Trail.**

* Touring through canyon country as you ride a ledge above the Colorado and Green Rivers on the White Rim Trail.

* **Braving the exposure of the Portal on Poison Spider Mesa.**

* Dodging dinosaur footprints on the ride to Klondike Bluffs.

* **Soaking in the view along Porcupine Rim, while still remembering to keep an eye on the ledges.**

DISTANCE 12 MILES (20KM) | **LOCATION** MOAB, UTAH, USA | **IDEAL TIME COMMITMENT** THREE TO FOUR HOURS **BEST TIME OF YEAR** APRIL TO MAY, SEPTEMBER TO OCTOBER | **ESSENTIAL TIP** IF CYCLING IN SUMMER, RIDE ONLY IN THE COOL OF THE EARLY MORNING OR EVENING.

CRYPTOBIOTIC CRUSTS

One of the most fascinating features of the desert around Moab are cryptobiotic crusts. These living crusts cover and protect desert soils, literally gluing sand particles together so they don't blow away. Cyanobacteria, which are among the world's oldest living forms, start the process by extending mucus-covered filaments that wind through the dry soil. Over time, these filaments and the sand particles that stick to them form a thin crust that's colonized by microscopic algae, lichens, fungi, and mosses. Unfortunately, this thin crust is instantly fragmented under the heavy impact of bicycle wheels. Once broken, the crust takes 50 to 250 years to repair itself, so it's imperative to stick to trails when you ride.

DESERT SOLITAIRE

The landscapes you ride through around Moab can have a haunting, almost apocalyptic beauty that's captivated many, including one of America's great writers, Edward Abbey (1927–89). Abbey worked as a seasonal ranger at Arches National Monument (now Arches National Park, about 3 miles (5km) from Moab) in the 1950s. He wrote of his time here in *Desert Solitaire: A Season in the Wilderness*, describing the simple beauty and subtle power of the vast landscape. Read it – and its polemic against cars and the paving of the wilderness – and you may see this desert and its mountain-biking potential in a new light.

■ THE ADVENTURE UNFOLDS

They call it the Slickrock practice loop, but really it's the procrastination loop as you delay the moment you must confront the trail more famous than Moab itself: the Slickrock. Even this short loop has moments that have you closing your eyes in hope, including a jump into sand that throws you over the bars.

On the Slickrock Trail, your guiding lines are the painted white dashes that stretch like rollercoaster tracks across the rock. Few people can ride this trail without stopping to push, and you've covered less than two miles before you're taking your bike for a walk, pulling it up and out of Wooly Gully. One more walk and you've emerged at the top of Swiss Cheese Ridge, the highest point of the trail, where you can pretend you're soaking in the view over Moab to the Portal and not simply trying to suck in more oxygen.

Past Portal Viewpoint, the descent begins. The Colorado River is below, carving its way toward the Grand Canyon, but your attention is on your braking hands. As you turn from the river, you round Shrimp Rock, wondering how this table of rock – it looks nothing like a shrimp – received such a name. Later someone reveals it's because of the shrimps that live in the pool of water at its base.

You're tiring as the trail continues over rock and through sand (is this really just 12 miles?) until eventually you're back at Abyss Viewpoint, staring into the box canyon below. There's just a mile to ride, following your outward trail back to the practice loop, though practice sure didn't make perfect on Slickrock, and you have the blood and scabs – the bacon, as mountain bikers call them – to prove it. But so does everyone else here.

■ MAKING IT HAPPEN

Boutique Air flies to Moab from Denver and Salt Lake City, while Greyhound has buses to Green River, around 50 miles (80km) away, with shuttle connections to Moab. In town, a number of companies offer bicycle shuttles to trailheads. Bike stores abound, but book ahead for bike hire. The Slickrock Trail is in Sand Flats Recreation Area.

■ AN ALTERNATIVE CHALLENGE

Moab's reputation for adventure may be founded on mountain bikes, but dig deeper and there's a lot more here than knobblies and slickrock. Rafting the Colorado River has become Moab's adventure understudy, with a menu that ranges from flat-water trips to the Confluence right up to turbulent week-long journeys into the legendary class V rapids of Cataract Canyon. Other Moab adventures of renown include four-wheel driving (Hells Revenge trail is right beside Slickrock, while the Moab Jeep Safari is held every Easter) and canyoneering – there's a reason the national park is called Canyonlands.

133

OPENING SPREAD Mountain-biking the singletrack trails of Moab. **ABOVE (L)** An adult and a juvenile prairie dog; the rodents build burrows in the soil. **ABOVE (R)** Riding the dramatic terrain of the Slickrock Trail. **LEFT** Arches National Park is just a few miles to the north.

ARMCHAIR

❋ **Mountain Biking Moab Pocket Guide** (David Crowell) Excellent guide to 42 of the best mountain bike trails around Moab.

❋ **Rider Mel's Mountain Bike Guide to Moab** (Rider Mel) Irreverent guide to 39 Moab rides, spiral-bound for ease of use.

❋ **In the Land of Moab** (Tom Till) Ogle the Moab landscapes in this photographic ode to red-rock country.

❋ **Between a Rock and a Hard Place** (Aron Ralston) Epic real-life survival tale in which the author amputates an arm after being trapped in a Canyonlands canyon; the story hit the big screen as *127 Hours*.

❋ **Wagon Master** (1950) A John Ford western filmed around Moab.

❋ **The Collective** (2004) Visually stunning 16mm film about mountain biking with several scenes shot in Utah.

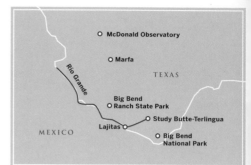

ROAD TRIP THE RIVER ROAD (RÍO GRANDE)

HUGGING THE RÍO GRANDE THROUGH SOME OF THE MOST SPECTACULAR AND REMOTE SCENERY IN THE COUNTRY, THE RIVER ROAD TAKES YOU UP, DOWN, AND THROUGH A RUGGED TEXAS LANDSCAPE OF LOW DESERT ARROYOS, SWEEPING VISTAS AND STONY MOUNTAINS.

For almost 125 miles (200km), the River Road (Camino del Río) snakes north along the great Texas river, the Río Grande, beginning near the Big Bend National Park. It's a wonderfully dramatic route and one you'll never forget, with vast desert and mountain landscapes, hot springs, hiking and horseback riding to enjoy. It's pretty rugged – at one point there's a 15% grade, the maximum allowable. The start point of the road is the Terlingua-Study Butte region. Here, 3 miles (5km) east of the park, two dusty little towns – Study Butte and Terlingua – run together at the junction of the River Road and Hwy 118. Leaving Terlingua to the west, the river road passes through the desert and through Lajitas, which looks like a town but is actually a resort – a shock to the system after Terlingua's desert appeal.

Past Lajitas, the road continues to the Big Bend Ranch State Park. It's much less explored than its big brother, but it has easily accessible turnouts for hiking or picnicking along the river road. These shouldn't be ignored. Make the easy 0.8-mile (1.2km) trek into narrow, dramatic Closed Canyon, where the cliffs rise above you to block out the sun. The road through this region is equally spectacular. Around 45 miles (70km) further is the tiny town of Ruidosa, between the Río Grande and the stunning mountains. Blink and you'll miss it, although that would be too bad because if you keep going past Presidio and around 30 miles (50km) west, just past Ruidosa, you'll come to the turn-off for Chinati Hot Springs, where locals adore the isolation of the outdoor tubs, camping grounds, and cabins. Turn north at Presidio for the famous UFO-spotting town of Marfa, 60 miles (96km) up US 67. If you plan to go back along the River Road, travel as least as far as Colorado Canyon (20 miles (32km) from Lajitas) for the best scenery.

134

ESSENTIAL EXPERIENCES

* **Hiking the Big Bend National Park, one of the most remote spots in North America.**

* Visiting the evocative ghost towns west of Big Bend.

* **Chasing the Marfa lights for as long as it takes, or at least until a local tells you to give up.**

* Eating as much chili as you can stand, while watching competitors in the Terlingua chili championships burn tongues, mouths and minds.

* **Looking for Willie Nelson everywhere you go.**

* Bird-watching in the Río Grande Valley.

* **Rafting and canoeing along the Río Grande, one of North America's best river trips.**

DISTANCE 125 MILES (200KM) | **COUNTRIES COVERED** USA | **IDEAL TIME COMMITMENT** ONE WEEK
BEST TIME OF YEAR APRIL TO EARLY JUNE AND SEPTEMBER TO NOVEMBER | **ESSENTIAL TIP** TAKE NECESSARY SAFETY PRECAUTIONS IN THE NATIONAL PARK. DRINK WATER AND TAKE PLENTY WHEN HIKING.

CHILI CHALLENGE

Every November, Terlingua is invaded by chili freaks who are after the very best in homemade chili. But it's no small-town festival they seek – the Terlingua Chili Cookoff is so big, there are actually two events to accommodate the hundreds of entrants. There's the International Chili Championship, organised by the Chili Appreciation Society International – you need to qualify to enter it. And then there's the Original Terlingua International Frank X Tolbert-Wick Fowler Championship Chili Cookoff, a name that's almost as much of a mouthful as the chili. It's less competitive and more like a big party.

THE JOURNEY TODAY

It's been a great road trip, one of the best. You pulled off the highway and scrambled to the top of a huge butte. Exhilarated, you squint your eyes until you can actually see a waterline: the ghost of an ancient ocean that has deposited years' worth of corals, skeletons, shells and sediment. You have been overloaded with new experiences, driving through this blistering and beautiful landscape, but to be here in West Texas is the quintessential Texan experience, with miniature towns, even ghost towns, and lots of dust and heat transforming the landscape into a shimmering haze.

The highlight of your River Road experience has been the Big Bend National Park, vast enough for a lifetime of discovery. It's a white-water rafting, mountain-biking, and hiking paradise, and also one of the country's least visited national parks. You found out for yourself why that is so: it's hotter than hell! But you put up with it because it's so wonderful, with so much to do. The area around the park is also enticing, and home to many artist retreats, historic hotels and quaint mountain villages. The park's diverse geography means an amazing variety of wildlife, while the 110 miles (177km) of paved road and 150 miles (241km) of dirt road make scenic driving even more exciting.

West of Big Bend, you pull into Terlingua, which happens to be a favorite haunt of none other than Mr Willie Nelson himself, and you can see why: its relaxed vibe never fails to attract travelers and artistic souls. Then you're on your way to stay at the Hotel Paisano in Marfa, where you're hopeful of spotting a 'Marfa light' or two. From there, you travel to Marathon, an artsy hamlet with art galleries, great eateries and the best hotel in the region: the Gage Hotel, with rooms straight out of the Wild West: wide wooden blinds, saddles as

ARMCHAIR

❋ **El Mariachi** (1992) Made by Robert Rodriguez for $7000, this film became an inspiration to film-school students everywhere. It's about an unlucky traveling mariachi and is shot on the Texas–Mexican border.

❋ **No Country for Old Men** (2007) The Coen Brothers' harrowing adaptation of Cormac McCarthy's novel is about a west Texas welder who finds drug money and decides to keep it.

❋ **Lone Star** (1996) A compelling drama set against the unsettled racial atmosphere of a Texan border town.

❋ **Traffic** (2000) Filmed in part on the El Paso-Juarez borderlands, this multilayered thriller explores the US government's 'war on drugs'.

furniture, and cowhides on the bed. Yep, that's doin' it easy, River Road style.

◼ SHORTCUT

If scenic driving is your thing, concentrate on the Big Bend National Park roads for a mini-experience of West Texas landscapes. Maverick Dr (22 miles (35km)) is notable for its scenery and wildlife. Ross Maxwell Scenic Dr (30 miles (48km)) takes you past the grand panorama of the Chisos Mountains, and a view of Santa Elena Canyon's 1500ft (457m) sheer rock walls. Río Grande Village Dr (20 miles (32km)) is best at sunset, when the mountains glow brilliantly with different red and orange hues.

◼ DETOUR

The middle of West Texas has some of North America's clearest and darkest skies, a legacy of being so far away from city life and its attendant light pollution. That's why the University of Texas McDonald Observatory is here. With some of the biggest telescopes in the world, it's perched on top of 6790ft (2069m) Mt Locke, 18 miles (30km) northwest of Fort Davis on Hwy 118. The observatory offers guided tours and 'Star Parties', when professional astronomers give tours of the night sky.

ALL CANADA PHOTOS | ALAMY ©

OPENING SPREAD Road through Big Bend National Park. **ABOVE** The great kiskadee flycatcher can be found in the Lower Río Grande Valley. **BELOW** The Río Grande.

MARFA LIGHTS

What are the fabled Marfa lights? Strange atmospheric conditions? Certainly, they are 'UFOs' in the literal sense – unidentified flying objects – and they've been sighted by numerous people over the years, appearing, disappearing, moving around the sky, and often changing color. Accounts go back to 1883, when a cowboy first reported them, believing they were Apache signal fires. Today, reports keep streaming in although a large proportion turn out to be car headlights. Aside from these, there is a genuine phenomenon here and it still hasn't been fully understood, a mystery making the Marfa lights one of West Texas's top attractions.

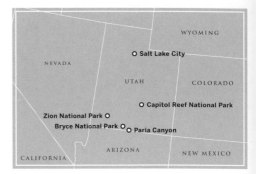

CANYONEER UTAH'S PARIA CANYON

A HIKE DOWN PARIA CANYON IS LIKE NOTHING YOU KNOW. WITH ITS NATURAL AMPHITHEATERS, ANCIENT PETROGLYPHS, MINIATURE RATTLESNAKES, AND THE CONSTANT THREAT OF FLASH FLOODS, NEGOTIATING THE WORLD'S LONGEST SLOT CANYON IS AN EXERCISE IN AMAZEMENT.

Before Europeans 'discovered' it, Paria Canyon was part of a route used by the indigenous Paiute people to move between what is now southern Utah and northern Arizona. Archaeological evidence indicates that their ancestors inhabited the region for more than 10,000 years. Paria is actually Paiute for 'muddy water,' which is something you'll get used to as the canyon narrows, forcing you to wade through the chocolate-colored river.

As the last ice age came to an end, water runoff from ancient glaciers slowly cut deeper into the soft sandstone, bestowing Paria Canyon with a succession of bizarre and intriguing geological formations. This is Mother Nature at her most sublime and poetic, from the swirling patterns of the Wave at Coyote Buttes to the equally mesmerizing red rock of the Paria amphitheater. As the water wore through the sandstone, the wind stripped the rock back to reveal changes in hue that have astonished visitors for millennia. The sun adds its final touch by glazing the shapes as if a potter on peyote had shaped the whole canyon. Thus, when you canyoneer through Paria, you are bearing witness to 85 million years of outrageous geology.

Typically, canyoneering is a hybrid of mountaineering that requires an acute route-finding sensibility plus the rope skills to descend and ascend any obstacles in your way. The awesomeness of Paria is that anyone with a good level of fitness is capable of negotiating any or all of the 37-mile (60km) route. That said, this is not a place you can take for granted: it's prone to flash floods, which means a happy hike can turn to disaster in an instant.

If you intend to tackle it yourself, make like a cub scout and 'be prepared.' Paria Canyon may be popular but it's still extremely remote, contains little drinking water and is largely inaccessible – getting rescued from here is not simply a matter of dialing emergency on your cell phone.

138

ESSENTIAL EXPERIENCES

✳ **Marveling at a brilliant ray of sun blasting through the Narrows onto the rock, illuminating it like pure gold.**

✳ Walking the Wave at Coyote Buttes.

✳ **Stargazing through the 'roof' of the canyon, and remembering the spirits of those who passed here long before.**

✳ Catching a glimpse of a bald eagle or peregrine falcon.

✳ **Giggling at the 'miniature' rattlesnakes common in the canyon, then remembering they can kill you with one bite.**

DISTANCE 37 MILES (60KM) | **LOCATION** PARIA CANYON-VERMILION CLIFFS WILDERNESS, UTAH, USA | **IDEAL TIME COMMITMENT** FOUR TO SIX DAYS | **BEST TIME OF YEAR** SPRING AND FALL | **ESSENTIAL TIP** BRING A WATERPROOF SACK FOR YOUR SLEEPING BAG.

TSUNAMI IN A SLOT CANYON

In a region famous for its thunderstorms, a slot canyon is the last place you want to be when the rain comes down. Paria Canyon has an enormous catchment area, making a flash flood here more like a tsunami. With an average of eight flash floods a year that can reach speeds of up to 50mph (80km/h) and approximately 33ft (10m) in height, bringing with them rolling rocks and all manner of debris, this is one mother of a wave nobody wants to catch. The deaths of seven experienced hikers in a Utah slot canyon in 2015 was a tragic reminder that the dangers of flash flooding cannot be overestimated.

KEEP CALM AND CARRY ON

If you're hiking the Paria River Canyon, the end of the line is technically where it meets the 'other' longest known slot canyon, Buckskin Gulch. Even more prone to flash floods than Paria, the gulch is ill advised for the inexperienced but a must-do for canyoneers who know their ropes. For 13 miles (21km) of its 37-mile (60km) length, Buckskin Gulch forms a corridor that is barely narrow enough to slip through and so steep you lose sight of the sky. A bewildering array of deep and shallow pools, fettered with perilous quicksand and rock jams, the gulch is the icing on Paria's cake.

THE ADVENTURE UNFOLDS

Paria Canyon's extraordinary length means it's packed with twists and turns that constantly leave you wide-eyed while testing your physical dexterity. When you first enter the canyon, it's little more than an unassuming desert streambed. Within a few hundred paces, you're moving through the Navajo sandstone. It's only after about 4 miles (6km), when you enter the Narrows and are most at risk of getting caught in a flash flood, that suddenly you are moving between sheer walls of brightly colored wind-streaked rock that stretch nearly 500ft (or 150m) straight up towards the deep blue sky. And so it begins.

A hike through Paria is all about the journey. Sure, you can't wait to arrive at star attractions such as the confluence with Buckskin Gulch or the wide arms of Wrather Arch, but it's the spaces, the moments in between, that carve themselves indelibly into your memory.

In parts you'll be scrambling up and along steep, smooth sections of limestone, so bring 'sticky' footwear, such as rubber-soled hiking shoes. Also carry your own drinking water. Hooking up with an experienced local or hiking with a guide is also strongly recommended, as this is the only way you'll discover many of the hidden gems that are all too easy to miss.

At all times only 20 people each day are allowed to start the hike, 10 by prior booking and 10 by lottery chosen 24 hours earlier. During the peak season there are literally thousands of adventurers hoping and praying for one of the few hundred golden tickets available. If you really want to experience Paria in the sandstone flesh, you need to apply four months before you actually want to hike.

MAKING IT HAPPEN

There are several campgrounds at the Whitehouse trailhead, just off Rte 89, from where you can begin your adventure. Permits are required to hike Paria Canyon; get the latest information from the Bureau of Land Management. You must adhere to the 'leave no trace' policy, which means picking up any evidence you were there, including your poo, bagging it and carrying it out with you.

AN ALTERNATIVE CHALLENGE

You don't have to be in it to experience the beauty of Paria Canyon. Take a ride in a hot-air balloon and absorb the scenery as you float above this alien landscape. Or make your way to one of the many lookouts, such as Paria View, where you might spot a majestic peregrine falcon. The surrounding meadows are home to mule deer and elk. If you're here just before the start of summer, you might get lucky and spy pronghorn antelopes heading to the forest, where they'll give birth to the next generation of mythical-looking creatures that inhabit this untamed region.

WHIT RICHARDSON | GETTY IMAGES ©

OPENING SPREAD The incredible patterns of the Wave at Coyote Buttes. **ABOVE** Sunset over the Paria River. **LEFT** A hiker drinks in the view of the red stone pyramids and buttes of Paria Canyon on the border of Utah and Arizona.

ARMCHAIR

❋ *Southern Paiute: A Portrait* (William Logan Hebner) Records the many trials and tribulations of the Paiute people since Europeans arrived, as told to Hebner by living members of the Paiute tribe. Accompanied by evocative photographs by Michael Pyler.

❋ *Hiking and Exploring the Paria River* (Michael R Kelsey) The guidebook covers the region's short and day walks, as well as the epic hike along the southern length of the Paria River gorge.

❋ *Between a Rock and a Hard Place* (Aron Ralston) Ralston had to hack off his own arm after he got stuck in the Blue John Canyon. His autobiographical account offers a tantalising glimpse into what drives an outdoor adventurer.

❋ *127 Hours* (2010) The six-time Oscar-nominated film tells Aron Ralston's story.

TAKE A SPIN DOWN ROUTE 66

THIS IS IT: THE GRANPAPPY OF ALL ROAD TRIPS. NOTHING BEATS THE 'MOTHER ROAD', AS NOVELIST JOHN STEINBECK DUBBED IT IN THE GRAPES OF WRATH. IT'S LIKE A TIME-TUNNEL INTO RETRO AMERICA: THINK DINERS, SODA FOUNTAINS, AND MOTOR COURTS.

Route 66 snakes across the very heart of America. It first connected Chicago with Los Angeles in 1926, and in-between gave rise to a flurry of small towns that provided all the comforts of home to those perpetually on the move: drive-ins, motor courts – the whole transient, garish bit. Everything around here has to have a nickname, and the Oklahoma entrepreneur Cyrus Avery was no exception. Known as the 'Father of Route 66,' he came up with the idea for a new national highway linking the Great Lakes with the greater Pacific Ocean and formed an association to promote and build it. The new highway, itself earning the handle the 'Main Street of America,' was to connect existing roads, many of them through rural areas. It proved immensely valuable during the Depression, allowing countless migrants to escape the Dust Bowl for more salubrious climes such as California. Conversely, the jubilant postwar boom saw newly cashed-up Americans taking their newfound optimism out for a spin on the wide, open road, which ran through Illinois, Missouri, Kansas, Oklahoma, Texas, New Mexico, Arizona and California. This is where the well-worn cliché 'get your kicks on Route 66' kicked in.

However, an ambitious new interstate system spelt the end, paving over much of Route 66 while bypassing the rest of it and its collection of kinky roadside artifacts. Entire towns began to disappear and Route 66 was officially decommissioned in 1984, although preservation associations began to spring into action. Today, what remains of the gravel frontage roads and blue-line highways connects you to places where the 1950s never ended – and that's the journey's enduring appeal. But even if retro Americana doesn't start your motor, it's still an awesome trip, with big horizons and superb natural beauty: the Grand Canyon, the Mississippi River, Arizona's Painted Desert and Petrified Forest National Park, and the Pacific beaches of Santa Monica.

ESSENTIAL EXPERIENCES

* **Enjoying that essential Route 66 small-town flavor in McLean, Tucumcari, Santa Rosa, and Needles.**

* Counting off the unique parade of Mother Road icons including the Gemini Giant; Black Madonna Shrine; Meramec Caverns; Red Oak II; Arcadia Round Barn; Cadillac Ranch; Big Texan Steak Ranch; Rainbow Rock Shop; WigWam Motel; Jack Rabbit Trading Post; Elmer's Place; and Bob's Big Boy.

* **Stopping to enjoy some of America's best national parks, natural monuments, and outdoor recreation areas, all close to the road, including the Chain of Rocks Bridge; Wilson's Creek; Sandia Tramway; Sky City; El Morro and El Malpais; Petrified Forest and Painted Desert; Grand Canyon; Wupatki Monument; the Mojave Desert and Santa Monica State Beach.**

142

DISTANCE 2400 MILES (3862KM) | **COUNTRIES COVERED** USA | **IDEAL TIME COMMITMENT** TWO WEEKS
BEST TIME OF YEAR BETWEEN MAY AND SEPTEMBER TO AVOID WINTER SNOW | **ESSENTIAL TIP** GO WITH THE FLOW.

LAS VEGAS

It would be a crime to drive all that way without seeing wild and wonderful Las Vegas. Really, if Route 66 is tacky (and we mean that in a good way, of course), then it's got absolutely nothing on Vegas. Casino gambling, hot nightlife and plastic glamour – all of that and more can be yours on 'The Strip' (otherwise known as Las Vegas Blvd). If that doesn't appeal, why not get spontaneously hitched by one of the multitude of Elvis impersonators at Vegas' drive-thru wedding chapels. Starting west of Needles, Vegas is almost 160 miles (257km) north on US95.

ROADSIDE WEIRD

If you're a lover of kitsch, Route 66 is most definitely your kind of trip. Some of its best loved sights include Illinois's Gemini Giant, a fiberglass astronaut with a rocket in his hand, and the Black Madonna Shrine in Eureka, built by a Polish émigré Franciscan monk. It features a series of folk-art grottoes hand-decorated with shells, glass and statuary surrounding an open-air chapel. Inside hangs a copy of the 'Black Madonna' painting, associated with miracles in the Old World. Other oddities include Holbrook's WigWam Motel in Arizona, where you can stay in concrete tepees filled with cosy 1950s furniture.

THE JOURNEY TODAY

The car top's down, 'Route 66' is pumping on the radio, and your mind is free, easy and wild. You've only been on the road a short while but already 'The Main Street of America' has delivered the goods. Let's see, now: join an automobile club – check; make sure the car has a spare tire and tool kit – check; GPS installed on the dashboard – check; tank full of gas – check; jettison preconceptions of small-town American life – check!

Route 66 has been an eye-opener. You've drunk Jack Daniel's with country-and-western stars in Missouri. Old-timers in Oklahoma have assailed your ears with tall tales of cowboys and Indians. You've visited Native American tribal nations and contemporary pueblos across the Southwest. You've followed the trails of miners and desperados deep into the Old West. And you've been to Cadillac Ranch, the subject of many a rock song, a surreal art installation where old-school Caddys are buried nose-down in the dirt.

It hasn't all been plain sailing though, and despite your GPS you've gone and got yourself lost trying to find one more roadside curio town. You have suffered through realignments of the route, dead-ends in farm fields and tumbleweed-filled desert patches, and rough driving conditions.

However, getting lost is what makes this trip all the more interesting. And besides, ending up in an unplanned stop at a small town is really what it's all about: the taste of the Mother Road is often at its most piquant in such places, where the vintage neon signs flicker after sunset and there's only one bar in which to mix it with the locals. And then the next morning, you can cure your hangover with a greasy, full breakfast at one of those old-time diners you've seen so often on TV. What's not to love?

SHORTCUTS

If you're in a hurry, take the interstate through most of southern Illinois, Missouri and Texas, and concentrate on New Mexico and Arizona. As long as the weather holds, the shoulder months (April, May, and September) can be good, especially for avoiding crowds, but most events happen in summer. Also, some attractions are closed (or at least keep shorter hours) during the off-season.

DETOUR

The Grand Canyon is arguably the USA's most famous natural attraction. An incredible spectacle of colored rock strata and the many buttes and peaks within the canyon itself, the meandering South Rim gives you access to amazing views. It can be visited as a day trip from Flagstaff or Williams. The foremost attraction is the canyon rim, paralleled by a scenic drive east, and a 9-mile (15km) hiking trail west to Hermit's Rest.

145

ANDREY BAYDA | SHUTTERSTOCK ©

LITTLENY | GETTYIMAGES ©

OPENING SPREAD Out on the highway, looking for adventure, on Route 66. ABOVE (L) Old road signs in Arizona. ABOVE (R) Delgadillo's Snow Cap Drive-In restaurant in Seligman, Arizona, a Route 66 icon since 1953. LEFT The famous Cadillac Ranch, near Amarillo, Texas.

ARMCHAIR

❋ *The Grapes of Wrath* (John Steinbeck) This is the classic Route 66 novel, set during the Dust Bowl years. It was made into a film in 1940 by John Ford, who won an Oscar (Best Director), as did Jane Darwell (Best Supporting Actress) in the role of Ma Joad.

❋ *Bound for Glory* (Woody Guthrie) A road-trip autobiography about life during the Depression.

❋ *On the Road* (Jack Kerouac) A beatnik hymn to the open road, as is Walt Whitman's *Song of Myself*.

❋ *Easy Rider* (1969) The classic countercultural road trip starring Dennis Hopper, Peter Fonda and Jack Nicholson follows much of the old Route 66.

❋ *Thelma & Louise* (1991) Another era-defining movie shot on the route, as things unravel for Geena Davis and Susan Sarandon.

MOUNTAIN BIKE THE GREAT DIVIDE

MOUNTAIN BIKE THE WORLD'S LONGEST OFF-ROAD CYCLING ROUTE, PEDALING FROM BANFF IN CANADA TO ANTELOPE WELLS ON THE UNITED STATES-MEXICO BORDER, CROSSING THE CONTINENTAL DIVIDE 30 TIMES ON THE WAY. THIS IS A TRUE CYCLING EPIC TO DIGEST IN BITE-SIZE PIECES.

Hikers have long had options to walk the length of the United States, following the Pacific Crest, Continental Divide, or Appalachian trails. Now mountain bikers have their own dedicated trail: the Great Divide Mountain Bike Route (GDMBR to its friends).

Conceived as an idea by the Adventure Cycling Association in the early 1990s, it became a reality in 1998, running from Antelope Wells to Roosville on the Canadian border; it was extended to Banff in 2003. Though the route is long and committing, it's not overly technical. Following mostly unsealed roads and trails, it's a touring-style trail rather than a single-track attack.

The trail statistics alone border on exhausting. Covering around 2730 miles (4400km), the GDMBR travels through two Canadian provinces and five US states. Crossing the Divide 30 times – the highest point is Indiana Pass in Colorado, at 12,000ft (3630m) – its climbs total around 200,000ft (60,000m), or the equivalent of cycling to the summit of Mt Everest from sea level almost seven times.

For most riders, the route begins in Canada at the Banff Springs Hotel, pedaling south towards the USA through a chain of national and provincial parks. By Great Divide standards, it's a low-elevation ride, rising only to 6430ft (1960m) at Elk Pass.

After the curiosity of a border crossing at Roosville, the route enters Montana and the most technically tricky sections of the ride. Through the mountains of Idaho, Wyoming and Colorado, the GDMBR ends across rough, corrugated tracks in New Mexico, hitting the Mexican border in the barren Chihuahuan Desert...an awfully long way, both in distance and terrain, from Banff.

If you want to do it the fast way, the entire route was once cycled in just under 23 days – an average of about 118 miles (190km) a day – though it's probably more realistic to aim for about 37 miles (60km) a day.

146

ESSENTIAL EXPERIENCES

✳ **Detouring to Fernie, for a day or two on some of Canada's finest mountain bike trails.**

✳ Handing over your passport at the border at Roosville.

✳ **Watching for bears as you ride through tough mountain country near Glacier National Park, with one of the highest concentrations of grizzlies in North America.**

✳ Rolling through forests of aspen in the fall.

✳ **Coasting to a stop beside the lonely border-control building outside Antelope Wells at ride's end.**

ROCKY MOUNTAINS

Even if you're riding alone, you'll have one fairly constant companion as you cycle the Great Divide Mountain Bike Route, and that's the Rocky Mountains. Stretching for around 3100 miles (5000km) from the Cassiar Mountains near Canada's border with Alaska, to the Sangre de Cristo Mountains of northern New Mexico, the Rockies have rightly been called the 'backbone of North America.' The Continental Divide – the ridge line that sheds water either east to the Atlantic Ocean or west to the Pacific Ocean – meanders erratically through the Rockies, often far from the highest summits and ranges...to the inevitable relief of GDMBR mountain bikers.

■ THE ADVENTURE UNFOLDS

Packing your panniers at the Warm River Campground, you're excited at the thought of riding into another state today. The tough and forested climbs of Montana are behind you, and soon Idaho will be as well. Two states down, three to go. Wyoming sits somewhere toward that mountain horizon ahead.

Crossing the border you enter natural royalty of sorts, with the road pinched beautifully between Yellowstone National Park to the north and Grand Teton National Park to the south, the latter's peaks rising with stunning abruptness. You're back in bear country, but it's the mosquitoes that force you to quicken your pace even as the ascent does its very best to slow you down.

The next few days will be ones of incredible contrast. Through the Wind River Range, you rise into a stunning alpine area, but there's desert not far ahead. Atlantic City has none of the bells and whistles its name suggests – this Atlantic City is a tumbleweed kind of place, making it an appropriate gateway into the Great Basin, North America's largest desert. Soon, the earth is just that: bare earth. You climb through heat, the land scuffed brown, with the Divide rising off in the distance. Wild horses roam far from the trail. Was it just a few days ago you were surrounded by water and mountains around Jackson Lake?

Still, the desert has its own beauty, and for a short time the trail even gives you the chance to ride along the Divide, rather than zigzagging across it, which has been the pattern much of the way. Into Rawlins, and another state is almost done. The Colorado Rockies, the highest points of your journey, loom to the south. But first you have one more tough climb out of Rawlins and this desert.

ARMCHAIR

❊ **Cycling the Great Divide: From Canada to Mexico on America's Premier Long Distance Mountain Bike Route** (Michael McCoy) Guide to cycling the trail from one of its creators.

❊ **National Audubon Society Field Guide to the Rocky Mountain States** (Peter Alden and John Grassy) All-in-one natural history guide to the Divide, covering geology, flora, fauna, and even all-important weather patterns.

❊ **Journal of a Trapper** (Osborne Russell) For those days when it all seems too tough; a classic account of a young fur trapper's adventures in the Rockies and Grand Tetons in the mid-19th century.

❊ **Ride the Divide** (2010) Award-winning feature film starring mountain biker Mike Dion following riders in the annual race along the length of the Great Divide Mountain Bike Route.

■ MAKING IT HAPPEN

Riders on the GDMBR must be totally self-supported and self-sufficient. You will need to camp much of the way, and distances between food and water sources can be lengthy and tough. Come well researched. Most towns along the route are small, so also come well provisioned with spare parts.

■ AN ALTERNATIVE CHALLENGE

Just as the GDMBR parallels the Continental Divide walking trail, the newer Sierra Cascades Bicycle Route follows the hikers' Pacific Crest Trail. Also created by the Adventure Cycling Association, this route begins in Sumas (Washington), on the Canadian border, and ends 2392 miles (3850km) later in Tecate (California), on the Mexican border, following the Cascade Range and Sierra Nevada. Along the way, it passes through the likes of Mt Rainier, Crater Lake, Yosemite, and Kings Canyon National Park, while crossing 20 mountain passes and bisecting the Pacific Crest Trail around 25 times. Most of the route traverses National Parks and recreation areas so services are generally easy to find. Plan ahead for overnight stays in Yosemite, Kings Canyon and Sequoia National Parks.

GIBSONPICTURES | GETTY IMAGES ©

OPENING SPREAD Following the mountain bike trail through old-growth forest. **ABOVE** A quite literal interpretation of mountain biking in Canada. **BELOW** Wild horses cross the Great Basin desert in the southern United States.

DON'T JUST RIDE IT, RACE IT

The creation of the Great Divide Mountain Bike Route has, in turn, spawned a pair of mountain bike races along the route. In the Tour Divide, self-supported cyclists leave Banff in the second week of June and must follow the exact course of the GDMBR until they arrive in Antelope Wells, usually about four weeks later. The Great Divide Race also begins in June, but leaves from Roosville, cycling only the US section of the GDMBR. Rules in both are straightforward – follow the GDMBR to its end, with no prearranged outside assistance allowed.

CARIBBEAN

①　HIKE THE RAINFORESTS OF ST LUCIA　②　DANCE SALSA IN SANTIAGO DE CUBA

③　LIVE LIKE JAMES BOND IN JAMAICA　④　EXPLORE THE PRISTINE REEFS OF BONAIRE

⑤　MAKE LIKE A PIRATE IN NASSAU

EXPLORE THE AMERICAS

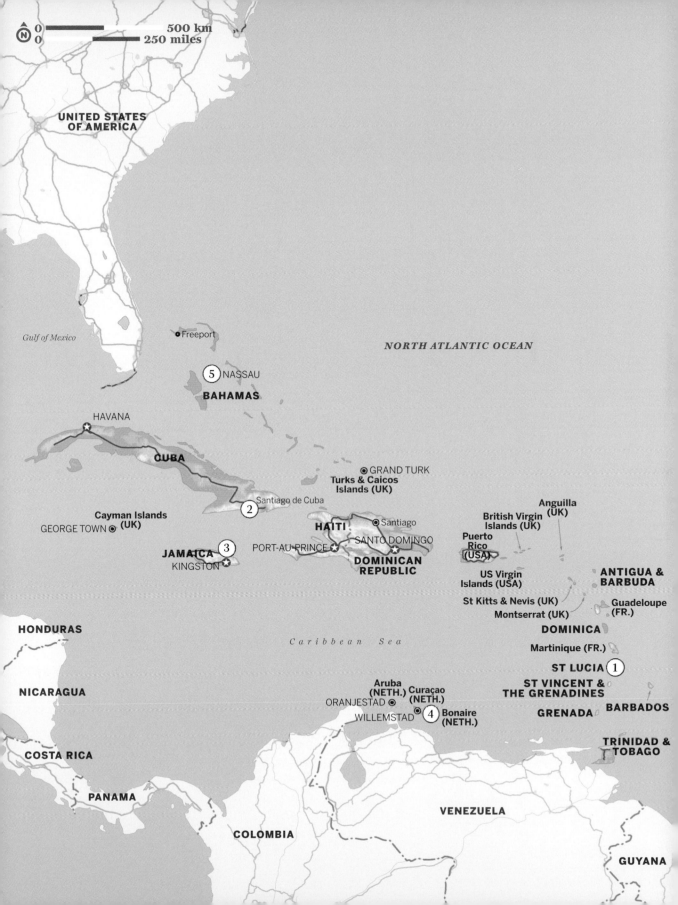

0 500 km
0 250 miles

UNITED STATES
OF AMERICA

Gulf of Mexico

NORTH ATLANTIC OCEAN

Freeport

⑤ NASSAU
BAHAMAS

HAVANA

CUBA

Santiago de Cuba
②

GRAND TURK
Turks & Caicos
Islands (UK)

Anguilla
(UK)

British Virgin
Islands (UK)

Cayman Islands
GEORGE TOWN ◉ (UK)

JAMAICA ③
KINGSTON

Santiago
HAITI
PORT-AU-PRINCE SANTO DOMINGO
DOMINICAN
REPUBLIC

Puerto
Rico
(USA)

US Virgin
Islands (USA)

St Kitts & Nevis (UK)
Montserrat (UK)

ANTIGUA &
BARBUDA

Guadeloupe
(FR.)

DOMINICA

Martinique (FR.)

ST LUCIA ①

ST VINCENT &
THE GRENADINES

HONDURAS

Caribbean Sea

Aruba
(NETH.) Curaçao
ORANJESTAD ◉ (NETH.)
④ Bonaire
WILLEMSTAD ◉ (NETH.)

GRENADA

BARBADOS

NICARAGUA

TRINIDAD &
TOBAGO

COSTA RICA

PANAMA

COLOMBIA

VENEZUELA

GUYANA

HIKE THE RAINFORESTS OF ST LUCIA

HIKE THE VINE-CHOKED TRAILS OF THE WILD ST LUCIAN RAINFOREST, WATCHING OUT FOR RARE, ONLY-IN-ST-LUCIA PARROTS AND EXPLORING TUMBLEDOWN 18TH-CENTURY FRENCH FORTS. WHEN YOU'RE TIRED OF WALKING, WHOOSH THROUGH THE CANOPY ON A ZIPLINE OR AERIAL TRAM TOUR.

You're deep in the tropical forest, rays of sunlight barely piercing the canopy of the chataignier trees towering nearly 70ft (21m) overhead, their enormous trunks wreathed by strangler figs. Your path is lined with giant ferns, and strewn with exotic flowers – bitter ginger, spiky orange heliconia, ghostly wild orchids. What's that rustling in the bushes? A feral pig? An enormous iguana? A rare, red-rumped agouti?

Typical Caribbean vacation? Not in St Lucia.

Don't get us wrong – St Lucia's silvery beaches, their reefs brimming with colorful fish, are some of the world's finest. But for the active traveler, this eastern Caribbean nation is a paradise of a different sort. Its jagged volcanic terrain and diverse ecosystems offer days of exploration. Hike through the rare elfin woodlands on the slopes of Mt Gimie, climb the knife-like summits of the Pitons, or bike among the colonial plantations, their trees dripping with guavas, mangoes, breadfruits and cacao pods. Or if that's not adventurous enough, you could fly through the rainforest on a zipline.

St Lucia is sometimes called the 'Helen of the West Indies' because, like Helen of Troy, it's so beautiful and so often fought-over. Originally inhabited by Carib Indians, the island was wrestled back and forth between the French and the British 14 times between the mid-1600s and 1814, when the British finally took control as part of the Treaty of Paris that ended the Napoleonic Wars.

Independent since 1967, the island has been an open secret among in-the-know travelers for years. Less trafficked than many nearby countries, it's the perfect spot for those whose ideal vacation is about more than lounging on a beach with a piña colada in hand. You can do that too, of course, and it will be all the sweeter after a long morning of trekking through the flower-perfumed cloud forest or scaling the stony sides of an ancient volcano.

152

ESSENTIAL EXPERIENCES

✳ **Spotting the psychedelically colored St Lucia Amazon parrot, only found on the island, flitting through the forest canopy.**

✳ Goggling at enormous, prehistoric-looking ferns and wild tropical flowers along one of the rainforest trails.

✳ **Tackling one of the iconic peaks – Gros or Petit Piton, or Mt Gimie – for views across the turquoise Caribbean.**

✳ Slathering yourself in volcanic mud at Sulphur Springs, perfect for post-hike muscle relaxation.

✳ **Cooling down with a dip at one of the southwestern beaches, followed by a cocktail while lounging in the pearly gray sand.**

✳ Dining on local classics such as saltfish and green fig, or a spicy bowl of pumpkin soup.

HIGHEST ELEVATION 3120FT (950M) | **LOCATION** ST LUCIA | **IDEAL TIME COMMITMENT** THREE DAYS TO A WEEK | **BEST TIME OF YEAR** DECEMBER TO MAY | **ESSENTIAL TIP** AVOID CASTRIES WHEN THE CRUISE SHIPS ARE IN TOWN – CROWDED!

ZIPLINING

In keeping with St Lucia's reputation as an adventure island, ziplining is one of the more popular activities, with several companies offering tours. Strap on a harness to fly through the trees, Tarzan-style, taking in the sights and smells of the canopy as you go. If that's not your speed, there's also an aerial tram tour, which allows you to tour the forest from above in a slightly more sedate manner. In addition to the famous St Lucia Amazon parrot, keep your eyes peeled for yellow and blue St Lucian warblers and tiny purple-throated Carib hummingbirds.

■ THE ADVENTURE UNFOLDS

A St Lucia getaway is all about mixing sporty adventure and relaxation. Think of the island as being divided in two – the busier, modern north around the capital, Castries, and the slower, lusher, more intimate south. We recommend the latter. Base yourself in the hills around the town of Soufrière, with its views of the Pitons, the two volcanic towers jutting into the horizon. There are many quirky, family-run hotels in the area, some with only a few rooms. Breakfast on local fare such as hot bakes (a fluffy, doughnut-like fried bread) and cocoa tea (a milky, cinnamon-spiked hot chocolate) to fuel you up, then head out to explore the wilderness.

If it's hiking you're after, you've got an embarrassment of riches. For a more relaxed amble, there's the 2.5-mile (4km) Des Cartiers Rainforest trail, ideal for spotting the emerald green St Lucia Amazon parrot, recognizable by its bright blue face, ruby throat and yellow-tipped tail. Nearby, the Edmund Forest Reserve has a 7-mile (11.2km) trail traversing the valley rim, piercing through a tunnel of vines, ferns and bromeliads. Occasionally the forest opens up, giving you glimpses of the sea and of Mt Gimie, the island's tallest peak. The fit might consider taking a side trail up to the summit. If you're game for that, you could try the Pitons as well.

Gros Piton is a better choice for the average hiker, with volcanic stone 'stairs' leading up to dizzying views across the Caribbean all the way to St Vincent. Or leave your hiking boots behind and hop on a mountain bike, bouncing along a series of trails hacked out of the jungle. You could also skip the sweating in favor of a different adrenaline rush, strapping in to a zipline what whizzes through the dense rainforest canopy. After, cool off with a dip in the crystalline waters at Anse Chastanet beach, followed by a splurge-y dinner at one of the resorts on the southwest coast.

■ MAKING IT HAPPEN

Fly directly to St Lucia from a handful of US and European cities, including London, New York, Miami and Toronto. Most flights arrive at Hewanorra International Airport in Vieux Fort. Hotels and resorts can arrange your transfer. Book early, especially if you're traveling in high season. May brings crowds for the St Lucia Jazz & Arts Festival, while June is Carnival. Most hikes require a day pass; some require guides.

■ A DETOUR

Connected by a causeway to the north of St Lucia, Pigeon Island was once a pirate hideout, manned by the 16th-century French privateer Jambe de Bois (Wooden Leg). Today, the 44-acre (18-hectare) island is home to the ruins of old French and English forts, as well as to two golden beaches. Poke around the ruins, climb the lookout point for views across the ocean, then settle in with a local Piton beer.

JUSTIN FOULKES | LONELY PLANET ©

JUSTIN FOULKES | LONELY PLANET ©

OPENING SPREAD St Lucia's imposing Pitons rise above the jungle canopy. **ABOVE (L)** Some welcome assistance for your Grand Piton hike. **ABOVE (R)** With the Pitons ever present, the island offers idyllic beaches aplenty. **LEFT** Exploring the Grand Piton trail.

ARMCHAIR

✳ *Omeros* (Derek Walcott) An epic poem telling the story of natives, African slaves, British colonialists, and their descendants on St Lucia, by the island's Nobel-winning native son.

✳ *The Struggle for Survival: An Historical, Political, and Socioeconomic Perspective of St Lucia* (Anderson Reynolds) By a St Lucian economist, this book offers background on the island's politics, economics and culture.

✳ *The St Lucia Island Club* (Brent Monahan) A historical murder mystery set among the plantations of 1910 St Lucia.

✳ *Saint Lucia: Portrait of an Island* (Jenny Palmer) Lush photographs of the island along with quotes from Derek Walcott.

✳ *Coconut. Ginger. Shrimp. Rum: Caribbean Cooking for Every Season* (Brigid Washington) A mouthwatering Caribbean cookbook with a forward from St Lucian chef Nina Compton.

DANCE SALSA IN SANTIAGO DE CUBA

GET YOUR HIPS MOVING ON A CUBAN DANCE FLOOR IF YOU REALLY WANT TO FIND OUT WHAT MAKES THIS ASTONISHING ISLAND TICK. LEARN TO DANCE AND YOU'RE GUARANTEED TO DISCOVER MORE ABOUT THE UNIQUE CULTURAL MIX THAT UNDERPINS LIFE IN THE COOLEST COMMUNIST OUTPOST.

You can sense Cuba's musical undercurrent from the moment your plane touches down. Baggage handlers throw suitcases around with a rhythmic flourish and customs officials shimmy in their booths to the tinny splutterings of a wall-mounted loudspeaker. Music is everywhere, and even when it's not playing, most Cuban hips seem to be twitching to a built-in rhythm.

To understand the island's people and rich mix of cultures, you really need to step onto a Cuban dance floor. Under the disheveled colonial arches of a dance school in Santiago de Cuba, you'll take your first steps into the world of salsa, guided by a trained dancer. With one-to-one tuition, moves are built up slowly over the course of a week until you're performing increasingly complex steps, learning to spin with your partner in beguiling grace. There's a dance-school work ethic as once again you 'take it from the top' to perfect each section, but the pay-off comes quickly. Within a few days, early nerves start to give way to a noticeably Latin swagger in the hips and a seductive shimmy in the shoulders. And then comes the cry of 'Salsa libre!' from the instructor, the signal that it's time to improvise your moves for the next couple of bars. For some that means a creative and fluid interlude, for others a mess of limbs and helpless laughter.

Broad smiles and tired feet spill out onto the street at the end of a day's class, but your musical adventure continues. Wander the streets and live music is all around you, from the city's world-famous venue, Casa de la Trova, to a host of smaller local bars, giving you plenty of opportunity to finesse your moves. By the final night, while you certainly won't be the hottest dancer in town, you will be able to hold your own on a Cuban dance floor. You'll have a feel for the blend of Spanish canción and African rhythms that underpin Cuban son music, and you'll have had an experience that has taken you to the very heart of Cuban life.

ESSENTIAL EXPERIENCES

✳ **Discovering the rhythms and instruments that go into making son, one of Latin America's most influential forms of music.**

✳ Sitting in on a band's practice session or discovering musicians honing their skills in bars around town.

✳ **Learning to dance to traditional Cuban son and testing your skills for real on the dance floors of Santiago de Cuba.**

✳ Photographing classic American cars with Santiago de Cuba – Cuba's 'most Caribbean city' so they say – as your backdrop.

✳ **Learning Spanish in formal language lessons, then using your new language skills in dance lessons.**

✳ Sampling Cuba's famous rum cocktails and getting the low-down on the history of the hard stuff at the Museo del Ron.

LOCATION SANTIAGO DE CUBA, CUBA | **BEST TIME OF YEAR** SUMMER (JUNE TO AUGUST) IS FESTIVAL SEASON; COOLER WEATHER IN SPRING OR AUTUMN IS BETTER FOR DANCE CLASSES | **IDEAL TIME COMMITMENT** ONE TO TWO WEEKS | **ESSENTIAL TIP** LEARN SOME SPANISH TO GET THE MOST FROM YOUR TRIP | **PACK** DANCING SHOES.

THE CUBAN BEAT

Cuban son originated in the eastern part of Cuba and is a happy combination of forceful African rhythms and poetic Spanish melody. The ethnomusicologist Fernando Ortiz called it 'a love affair between African drum and Spanish guitar.' The traditional set-up includes six musicians playing guitar, *tres* (a Cuban guitar with three sets of double strings), bass, bongos, claves and maracas. In the 1920s many bands added trumpet to the mix. Cuban son is probably the forerunner of salsa and one of the most influential forms of music in Latin America. You'll find a Casa de la Trova in most large towns — it's the best place to hear it being played live.

SANTERÍA RELIGIOUS BELIEFS

A mixture of African, Catholic and Native American traditions, Santería is a syncretic religion that focuses on building relationships between humans and powerful mortal spirits called *orishas*. Followers believe that if they carry out the right ritual, these spirits will help them fulfill their destiny. But these powerful spirits also rely on their followers. They need to be worshipped and rely on offerings of food and even animal sacrifice if they are to continue to exist. Many *orishas* are associated with Catholic saints, such as St Barbara, known as Changó, and St Lazarus, known as Babalú-Ayé. There is no holy text or equivalent of the Bible – the beliefs are instead passed on by word of mouth.

■ THE PERFECT GETAWAY

Learning to dance in Cuba isn't just about perfecting salsa moves or discovering the more subtle world of Cuban son. This is an escape for those who want to connect with the real Cuba, and experience as much of the island as possible. And there's no better way to do that than by staying with a Cuban family.

You'll instantly see the stark contrasts between the classic American cars and colonial architecture outside and the communist propaganda that forms prime-time TV. You'll see the gulf between younger Cubans, excited about the future and the country's tentative rapprochement with the United States, and an older generation who loved Fidel Castro and blame the US trade sanctions for all of Cuba's problems. You'll be introduced to a vibrant and sociable extended family who wander in and out of each other's homes, but you'll also develop an awareness of how the winds of change are affecting everyday life in Cuba.

Politics aside, Cubans love to have fun and want you to see that side of their country. Make a few friends and you'll find yourself being taken into bars to meet musicians or into houses to see bands practice. You'll discover the *tres* (a guitar with three sets of double strings), an instrument that gives Cuban music a distinctive sound, and you may be handed a pair of claves (wooden percussion) and invited to join in. Hang around for a glass of rum and you'll notice the African influence that delivers a more rhythmic, vibrant form of music in Santiago de Cuba than other parts of the island. It's also the source of Santería, the local religion that was brought to the island by African slaves and merged with Catholic and Native American traditions.

■ PLAN IT

Antonio Maceo Airport is 4 miles (7km) south of Santiago de Cuba; international flights arrive here from Miami, Montréal, Paris, Rome, Toronto and a handful of Caribbean airports. There are direct flights from the Cuban capital, Havana, every day. Local families rent rooms – look for the distinctive blue insignia on the door marked 'Arrendador Divisa.' A number of Cuban dance and language specialists, such as Caledonia Languages, can organize rooms and dance lessons.

■ DETOUR

Santiago de Cuba province is home to Cuba's highest mountain, the 6476ft (1974m) Pico Turquino. It sits at the heart of the Sierra Maestra and was the stronghold of Fidel Castro and Che Guevara's rebel forces pre-1959. Its cloud forest teems with wildlife, including the world's smallest toad and some astonishing birds. The hike up Pico Turquino starts from Las Cuevas, 80 miles (130km) west of Santiago de Cuba. At the summit is a bust of José Martí, hero of the second independence war.

159

ROBERTO MACHADO NOA | GETTY IMAGES ©

JAN SOCHOR | GETTY IMAGES ©

OPENING SPREAD Santiago de Cuba street musicians in full cry. **ABOVE (L)** Serving rum, Cuba's national drink. **ABOVE (R)** Religion in the region blends African, Catholic and Native American influences. **LEFT** Women practice their moves at the city's School of Rumba.

ARMCHAIR

❋ *Our Man in Havana* (Graham Greene) The tale of a British vacuum-cleaner salesman who enlists in the British secret service and sends in bogus reports that mysteriously start to come true.

❋ *Ay, Cuba!* (Andrei Codrescu) The Romanian writer visits Cuba to compare the island with his homeland in 1989.

❋ *The Reader's Companion to Cuba* (edited by Alan Ryan) Collected works of writing on Cuba.

❋ *Trading with the Enemy: A Yankee Travels Through Castro's Cuba* (Tom Miller) Cuban lore gleaned from an eight-month tour of the island.

❋ *Buena Vista Social Club* (1999) Documents a group of aging musicians who take traditional Cuban music to the world.

❋ *Dance with Me* (1998) Contrasts Cuban dancing styles in the tale of a Cuban émigré who opens another world for a ballroom dancer.

LIVE LIKE JAMES BOND IN JAMAICA

THE OLD-TIME GLAMOUR OF JAMAICA COMES ALIVE AT GOLDENEYE – A RESORT ON ORACABESSA BAY, WHERE BOND CREATOR IAN FLEMING USED TO WRITE HIS SPY NOVELS LOOKING OUT TO A JADE-GREEN SEA. ITS SPIRIT LIVES ON IN THE HANDS OF CHRIS BLACKWELL, FOUNDER OF ISLAND RECORDS.

It is early evening and the Caribbean waters are turning a blush pink with the falling light. The pale, glass-green water of GoldenEye's still lagoon is transformed into a jewel-like emerald now that the sun is no longer high in the sky. This is when the sun sends its shafts deep into the pool of water to light the lagoon as if from within, creating a place that's hard to beat even on Jamaica. A few stilted, candy-colored villas have their shutters open so their occupants can better hear the surf and birdsong. Concealed by thick, glossy vegetation, the crickets provide exotic percussion to the sound of reggae emanating from the curl of white beach nearby. This is where a group of guests gather, chicly attired in Etro and flip-flops, sipping on beer and the local rum punch.

They are drinking at the bar at GoldenEye, a resort occupying 52 acres (21 hectares) of prime real estate on the north coast of Jamaica. The salty air carries not just their voices, but the unmistakable scents of Jamaica: tangy curry and chargrilled sweetcorn cooked on the barbecue. Whether the aroma emanates from the resort's restaurant or the nearby village of Oracabessa, it is hard to tell.

There is music too. But then GoldenEye's owner, Chris Blackwell, was the man who founded Island Records, launching Bob Marley and exporting reggae to the world. He also knew author Ian Fleming who, along with Noël Coward and screen legend Errol Flynn, lived on the island in its silver-screen heyday – when everyone from Liz Taylor to Sophia Loren showed up to party. GoldenEye was Fleming's former home, which Blackwell has owned since 1976. By turning it into one of the most exclusive resorts in the Caribbean, Blackwell has opened up the island's glamour to outsiders, without turning the place into a luxury cliché.

160

ESSENTIAL EXPERIENCES

* **Rafting Rio Grande, one of Jamaica's largest rivers, at a gentle pace.**

* Swimming in YS Falls, a seven-tiered cascading waterfall on the island's south coast. Closer to GoldenEye (30 minutes by car) is a thrilling river-tubing ride, led by experienced guides, down the White River.

* **Climbing Blue Mountain Peak (the island's highest mountain at 7336ft (2236m)), combining your trek with a stay at another of Blackwell's hotels, Strawberry Hill, in these mist-wrapped, coffee-growing hills.**

* Taking a jet-ski safari from GoldenEye to Robins Bay. The sport is a favorite hobby of Blackwell's.

LOCATION ORACABESSA BAY ON JAMAICA'S NORTH COAST | **BEST TIME OF YEAR** FEBRUARY IS THE COOLEST MONTH, JULY AND AUGUST THE WARMEST, AND CHRISTMAS AND NEW YEAR THE MOST FUN | **IDEAL TIME COMMITMENT** ONE WEEK
ESSENTIAL TIP HEAD OUT OF THE RESORT TO EAT LOCALLY AND DANCE ON A FRIDAY OR SATURDAY NIGHT
PACK NO TIES, JACKETS OR LOUBOUTIN HEELS – IT'S ALL ABOUT GOING BAREFOOT.

JAMMING IN JAMAICA

For the past half century, Chris Blackwell has helped tell Jamaica's story through music, from the founding of Island Records in 1959 to the export of Bob Marley's 'One World, One Love' message to every corner of the earth. His passion for Jamaica is also reflected in his Island Outpost group of hotels, which includes GoldenEye, Strawberry Hill in the Blue Mountains, The Caves, and Geejam, which has its own recording studio. Thus his two worlds come together, with Blackwell's musical roots never far from his present. His love of a good rhythm is reflected in the inspired playlists available in every room at GoldenEye – created by Bruno Guez, who founded Quango Records.

■ THE PERFECT GETAWAY

Oracabessa Bay used to be a port for Jamaica's banana trade. It was also the spot that inspired Ian Fleming, who from 1949 spent three months of every year in Jamaica, writing his famous spy novels at a rate of 2000 words a day. He wrote 14 novels while living at GoldenEye, which Fleming first discovered for himself after British Intelligence sent him to report on U-boat activities in the Caribbean during World War II. He was easily seduced by Oracabessa's soporific pace. This led him to build his villa on the rocks, which still forms the heart of the resort that carries the GoldenEye name.

To stay in this villa, sketched by the author on his desk blotter, is expensive, starting at US$6000 a night for use of the three-bedroom main house plus two satellite villas, Sweet Spot and Pool House, all of which come with their own staff. But it is also authentic, with the villa's original footprint still overlooking a white beach, reached by a flight of stairs. The lawn is still cut just so, and the flowers grow in tropical abundance, concealing the villa and its inhabitants from prying eyes.

Near this landmark, clapboard and cedar villas with shingle-roofs have been added, forming a private enclave of suites and cottages that are neither too flashy nor too basic to sit with the glamour of Fleming's beloved home. Explore just a little further out into GoldenEye's gardens, and one discovers trees planted by the likes of Kate Moss and Michael Caine. Venture further still, up into the hills behind the resort, and there is Noël Coward's House, Firefly, where guests can enjoy the picnic hour under the welcome shade of trees. Take a boat out for the afternoon and it is easy to see what the inspirations were behind Fleming's fiction. And at the end of each day, pull out the backgammon board, best enjoyed with a martini in hand, and listen once again to the surf and the chatter of crickets.

■ PLAN IT

GoldenEye is a magnet for celebrities who want to escape the cameras and sink into a relaxed world of like-minded souls. The resort is at its most glam over Christmas and New Year when the big names arrive from London, New York and LA. The usual way to get here is via the international airport at Montego Bay, a 90-minute drive from the resort. You can transfer to a helicopter; the 25-minute flight takes in Jamaica's dramatic coastline.

■ DETOUR

Firefly was the hilltop home of English playwright Noël Coward, who made Jamaica his home for 20 years. The villa's views of Jamaica's north coast were not lost on the pirate-turned-governor, Sir Henry Morgan, who used this eyrie as his lookout prior to Coward taking up residence in 1948. Cut to the present day and Firefly's spirit remains, as if the great wit has only just walked out the door to take in the still evening air from his garden bench. Inside the house, there is an elegant salon dominated by a grand piano featuring photos of Coward's former guests, including Marlene Dietrich. By prior arrangement through GoldenEye, resort guests can enjoy a picnic in Firefly's gardens, a sunset cocktail, or even arrange a private wedding ceremony.

163

OPENING SPREAD Another glorious day in GoldenEye's lagoon. **ABOVE** Local fishing boats set off to the Caribbean Sea. **LEFT** The island's Blue Mountains.

ARMCHAIR

❋ **Dr No** (Ian Fleming) Of all the 007 books largely or partly set in Jamaica, *Dr No* is the one to read while staying at GoldenEye.

❋ **The Long Song** (Andrea Levy) A gripping novel set in Falmouth on the island's north coast, it investigates unsettling truths about slavery on Jamaica.

❋ **My Wicked, Wicked Ways** (Errol Flynn) Errol Flynn helped define the island's glamorous history after his yacht washed up here in 1942 following a storm. This is his autobiography.

❋ **The Italian Job** (1969) Noël Coward, who lived on Jamaica, here plays the role of Mr Bridger, a prison-bound criminal who bankrolls a robbery.

❋ **The Harder They Come** (1972) This Jamaican crime film, based on a 1940s real-life villain, stars singer Jimmy Cliff. Its soundtrack was the catalyst for reggae breaking into the USA.

EXPLORE THE PRISTINE REEFS OF BONAIRE

THIS DUTCH CARIBBEAN ISLAND HAS SOME OF THE WORLD'S MOST UNSPOILED REEFS THANKS TO DECADES OF ENVIRONMENTAL PROTECTION. WHETHER NEWBIE OR DIVE PRO, THE JEWEL-LIKE CORALS AND 350 FISH SPECIES FOUND HERE ARE CERTAIN TO STUN.

Bonaire may be in the Caribbean, but you don't come here for the beaches. While some of them are quite pretty, they're narrow and composed more of sharp coral than sand. No, this flat, arid island is famous for something else: diving. It is unique for its abundance of shore dives, where you can stride out into the ocean to explore shallow fringing reefs.

And oh, what extraordinary reefs they are! We're talking about spots worthy of bucket lists and bragging rights, places you'll tell your grandchildren about. Haul your gear down the famous 1000 Steps (don't worry, there are actually fewer than 70) to the beach and wade into the gently lapping waters. Here, bulbous brain corals, gardens of waving sea fans, and neon-hued sponges make for a psychedelic scene. Rainbow parrotfish and giant groupers hover, while tiny tangs flit about. The clarity of the water here makes it a favorite spot of underwater photographers, who capture barracudas, tarpon and eels. Near town, the *Hilma Hooker*, a 240ft (73m) cargo ship impounded in the early 1980s with 25,000lb (11,340kg) of marijuana in a false bulkhead, lies sunken between two reefs. Dive down to investigate her rusty hull and massive bronze propeller. Or traverse the double reef at Angel City, floating amid schools of angel fish and looking out for stingrays in the sandy channel between reefs.

The reason Bonaire's reefs are so spectacular is an intentional policy of conservation. At a time when few countries were thinking about human impacts on the environment, Bonaire took steps to protect its marine life. Spearfishing has been banned since the early 1970s, coral collecting was prohibited a few years later, and, in 1979, the Bonaire National Marine Park was established to oversee some 10 sq miles (26 sq km) of reef and wetlands. Once you take your first dive in Bonaire's glittering waters, you'll thank the island's leaders for their foresight.

ESSENTIAL EXPERIENCES

* **Dragging your gear down the 1000 Steps to watch rainbow parrotfish and hawksbill turtles swim over grand formations of star coral.**

* Exploring the coral-encrusted wreck of the *Hilma Hooker*, a drug-smuggling ship that sank in 1984.

* **Delighting in the whimsical sight of flocks of flamingoes loafing around the salt flats.**

* Hiking the desert hills of Washington-Slagbaai National Park in search of iguanas and blue lizards.

* **Sailing to the islet of Klein Bonaire to see the old slave shelters and snorkel the shallow reef.**

* Snapping underwater photos of trunkfish, barracuda, eels and multicolored sponges in the gin-clear waters of Salt Pier.

LOCATION BONAIRE | **IDEAL TIME COMMITMENT** FOUR TO SEVEN DAYS | **BEST TIME OF YEAR** BONAIRE HAS PLEASANT, DRY WEATHER MOST OF THE YEAR; WINTER IS MORE CROWDED THAN OTHER SEASONS | **ESSENTIAL TIP** THE WATERS OF THE LEEWARD (WEST) COAST ARE ALMOST ALWAYS CALM. THE WINDWARD (EAST) COAST IS TOO ROUGH FOR SAFE SWIMMING.

SLAVERY IN BONAIRE

After the Dutch claimed Bonaire, along with Curaçao and Aruba, in 1633, the island became a possession of the Dutch West Indies Company. Enslaved Africans were brought here to grow crops and harvest salt alongside native and convict laborers. Salt harvesting was a particularly brutal task, done by hand under a broiling sun. Bonaire also served as a market for enslaved people bound for Curaçao. Today you can visit the old slave huts, their ceilings too low to allow a person to stand up fully. Slavery was abolished in the Netherlands and its holdings in 1863, and many Bonaire residents today are descended from the enslaved salt harvesters.

FLAMINGOES

The salt flats of Bonaire are one of the few nesting places for the American Flamingo, making the island home to several thousand of the enormous pink birds at any given time. During breeding periods, the flamingoes retreat to Pekelmeer Flamingo Sanctuary near the island's solar salt works, where visitors can watch them with binoculars from the road. The rest of the year they can be found in Washington-Slagbaai National Park and other salty, marshy areas around the island, where they forage for the carotenoid-rich brine shrimp that give them their vivid color.

■ THE ADVENTURE UNFOLDS

Bonaire is roughly boomerang shaped, with most of the dive sites, hotels and restaurants lining the protected inner angle of the west coast. There are more than 60 dive spots on Bonaire itself, and another 26 on Klein Bonaire, an uninhabited islet just west of Kralendijk. Take a boat here to explore sites adjacent to the open water, which means swimming alongside sea turtles and barracudas in swift currents. Or just snorkel – Klein Bonaire has some of the top spots for non-divers.

And what about when you're done diving? On the southeast coast, Lac Bay has calm surf and a beach bar, making it an ideal spot for hoisting a piña colada while watching the windsurfers skip across the water. Or, hey, you could try windsurfing yourself – there's a school right here.

If you'd rather be on the water than in it, join a kayaking tour of the mangroves around Lac Bay, some of the best preserved in the Caribbean. The mangroves and sea grass here are a nursery for baby sea animals, including queen conch, rays and seahorses. Skim across the shallows, then hop out for a spot of snorkeling amid the forest of knobby roots.

And yes, there are plenty of things to do that don't involve the water. Hike among the cacti at Washington-Slagbaai National Park, go flamingo-spotting, check out the salt works, and visit the handful of historic sites, including a lighthouse, a fort, old slave huts and colonial churches. For Instagram-worthy uniqueness, the Donkey Sanctuary is a don't-miss. Donkeys have lived on Bonaire since the Spanish brought them in the 1600s. The sanctuary is home to some 600, many of whom were found dehydrated or hit by cars. Come meet some fuzzy friends and feed them a carrot or two.

■ MAKING IT HAPPEN

Visitors to Bonaire fly into Flamingo International Airport in the capital of Kralendijk. If you stay in Kralendijk you can get around by foot. To explore the rest of the island, rent a car (reserve ahead) or call a taxi. Hotels and resorts are scattered along the west coast. There are numerous dive shops; all marine park visitors must pay an entrance fee – US$25 for divers; US$10 for non-divers.

■ DETOUR

Bonaire's northern tip – about a fifth of the island's total territory – is a national park composed of two former plantations. These plantations once produced salt, charcoal and aloe, and raised goats. Today you can explore landscapes of cacti and spiky shrubs, looking out for iguanas and some of the 200-plus bird species, as well as the odd feral donkey. Bring a picnic lunch, plenty of water and a 4WD, and drive the park's rugged loop tracks, stopping to swim at hidden beaches, hike into the volcanic hills and say 'hi' to the flamingoes that gather in the salt flats.

WESTEND61 | GETTY IMAGES ©

WALTER NIEDERBAUER | 500PX ©

OPENING SPREAD Make friends with sea turtles and vibrant tube sponges in the waters off Bonaire. **ABOVE (L)** A local iguana surveys his terrain. **ABOVE (R)** Flamingoes feed in the briny shallows. **LEFT** Thin strips of white sand characterize the coastline of the island.

ARMCHAIR

* ***Bonaire: Point to Point*** (Federico Cabello) Lush underwater photography of Bonaire's best dive sites, to whet your appetite.

* ***Birds of Aruba, Bonaire, and Curaçao: A Site and Field Guide*** (Jeffrey V Wells, Allison Childs Wells and Robert Dean) A comprehensive guide to the hundreds of bird species you can see on Bonaire and its sister islands, with details on the geography and geology of the islands.

* ***Under the Black Flag: The Romance and the Reality of Life Among the Pirates*** (David Cordingly) A historian's entertaining look at the real-life pirates of the Caribbean who once terrorized these waters.

* ***Ocean Parks: Bonaire National Marine Park*** (2016) This Smithsonian nature documentary takes you underwater to explore the reef and its conservation.

MAKE LIKE A PIRATE IN NASSAU

ONCE A RUM-SOAKED BOLT-HOLE FOR BUCCANEERS, NASSAU IS NOW A GETAWAY FOR LOVERS, WHERE COUPLES GET ROMANTIC IN THE FRAGRANT BACK GARDENS AND LABYRINTHINE WINE CELLARS OF AN 18TH-CENTURY PIRATE'S MANSION, NOW KNOWN AS THE GRAYCLIFF HOTEL.

A warm wind is blowing off the Caribbean Sea, the hibiscus is in bloom, and you and your beloved are sitting with your feet kicked up on your private balcony high in the hills overlooking the cobblestoned Old Town of Nassau. Add a glass of golden rum in hand and you've got a pretty good idea of what it was like to be a gentleman pirate surveying his bounty in the mid-1700s.

This is the Graycliff Hotel, built in 1740 by the fearsome pirate Captain John Howard Graysmith, who plundered Spanish galleons throughout the Caribbean with his schooner, *Graywolf*. Graysmith built the Georgian-style mansion atop a hill looking down over the gin-clear water so he could spot any incoming ships. Later, the house became a garrison for the US Navy, Nassau's first inn, and a playpen for Jazz Age Americans looking to party during the years of Prohibition.

Today, you're free to roam about the hushed hotel, whose creaky antiques and mismatched Oriental rugs suggest an era of long-ago – and possibly ill-begotten – opulence. Swim in the Spanish-tiled pool, crack open a musty tome in the leather-lined library or puff a Cohiba straight from the hotel's own cigar factory. The hotel restaurant is famous for its French-Caribbean cuisine, and the wine cellar, with more than 250,000 bottles from 400 vintners, including such precious rarities as an 1865 Château Lafite and a 1727 Rüdesheimer Apostelwein (one of the most expensive bottles in the world), is world-renowned. In-between naps, swims, and wine-soaked feasts, you and your love can stroll down the hill into Nassau town for all manner of 21st-century amusements. Continue the pirate theme at the interactive Pirates of Nassau museum, climb the hand-hewn limestone steps to 18th-century Fort Fincastle, or snorkel the technicolor reef surrounding the island. Perhaps you'll even find a chest of lost pirate treasure!

ESSENTIAL EXPERIENCES

* **Puffing a hand-rolled Cuban cigar made on-site at the Graycliff's Cuban-staffed cigar factory.**

* Sipping a mellow, vanilla-inflected cognac from the hotel's Cognateque, alongside some 9000 bottles of cognac and port.

* **Gawking at psychedelically colored fish along the reefs of New Providence.**

* Shopping for duty-free gemstones, batik fabric tablecloths, sticky rum cakes, and local straw baskets along downtown Nassau's West Bay St.

* **Shaking your booty to local goombay music at Arawak Cay, downtown Nassau's beloved outdoor food center – a must-try for its conch fritters.**

LOCATION NASSAU, NEW PROVIDENCE, THE BAHAMAS | **BEST TIME OF YEAR** MID-DECEMBER TO MID-APRIL | **IDEAL TIME COMMITMENT** THREE TO FOUR DAYS | **ESSENTIAL TIP** AVOID THE CROWDS BY HEADING SLIGHTLY WEST OF CABLE BEACH: THE SANDS ARE JUST AS BEAUTIFUL BUT MUCH QUIETER | **PACK** FORMAL DINNER ATTIRE, SUNSCREEN AND AN EXTRA SUITCASE FOR BRINGING BACK LOCAL RUM.

PARADISE ISLAND

You can't spend any time in Nassau without noticing what looks like a pink Disney castle across the harbor. This is the Atlantis resort at Paradise Island, a jaw-droppingly huge resort-meets-amusement park with a Disney-esque Lost City of Atlantis theme. You don't have to be a resort guest to gawk at the lobby's indoor shark tanks, brave the twisting slides at the 140-acre on-site waterpark, or try your luck at the blackjack tables in the massive Atlantis casino. The complex is home to some of the area's best see-and-be-seen restaurants, including an outpost of the Nobu sushi empire and establishments owned by celebrity chefs Todd English and Jean-Georges Vongerichten.

SHAKE IT AT JUNKANOO

Masked dancers whirl, cowbells clang, drums beat a ceaseless tattoo. This is Junkanoo, the Bahamas' national festival and the equivalent of New Orleans' Mardi Gras or Brazil's Carnaval, which starts every year in the early morning hours of Boxing Day (December 26). With origins in West African secret societies, Junkanoo grew as a tradition among slaves on the British plantations, who hid their faces with masks to obscure their identities. Today, the festival is an integral part of Bahamian identity, with dancers and teams competing for the most elaborate costumes and dances. If you're not around then, head over to Nassau's Arawak Cay to watch dancers practice on weekend evenings.

■ THE PERFECT GETAWAY

A long weekend is an ideal amount of time for a romantic Nassau getaway. Plan on spending your first day hitting the beaches. Cable Beach is the island's main sandbox. Paddle in the turquoise surf, rent a boogie board, or just lie on a lounge chair and relax under the white-hot Caribbean sun. Afterwards, chow down on cracked conch (fried conch, a type of sea snail) and Bahamian-style mac 'n' cheese at Arawak Cay, aka 'the fish fry,' a collection of crayon-colored shacks just west of downtown Nassau. Wash everything down with a glass of 'sky juice', a high-octane blend of gin and coconut water, the local specialty.

On your second day, take advantage of the Graycliff's grounds and swimming pool. Stroll among the hibiscus and bougainvillea in the walled garden, float in the tiled pool, visit the on-site cigar factory, and chat (en español, of course) with the Cuban cigar rollers who work here. In the afternoon, hit up West Bay St, Nassau's main shopping district. Duty-free gems are a major draw, but if you don't fancy an emerald the size of your fist, there are plenty of fun souvenirs to choose from – look for local woodcarvings (bonefish are popular subjects). In the evening, dine at the Graycliff Restaurant, where French-style dishes have a Caribbean influence – think crispy duck with Bahamian citrus sauce.

On your third day, follow a pirate-themed itinerary through Nassau's historic sites – Fort Fincastle, the Pirates of Nassau museum, Blackbeard's Tower – before catching your flight home. If you've got extra time, hop a fast ferry to the pink-sand shores of Eleuthera. Either way, don't forget your souvenir bottle of local firewater Ron Ricardo.

■ PLAN IT

Fly into Nassau's Lynden Pindling International Airport and catch a taxi to the Graycliff Hotel, about 20 minutes away. Book well in advance at the Graycliff, especially during the winter high season. If you're planning on scuba diving or taking a snorkeling excursion, arrange this in advance. The Bahamas Ministry of Tourism website has helpful information about transportation and tour operators.

■ DETOUR

With more than a few days, hop the two-hour fast ferry to Eleuthera, the skinny island east of New Providence. Eleuthera's 'mainland' is a quiet place of pineapple plantations, empty pink-sand beaches and crumbling lighthouses. Rent a car and drive to Lighthouse Beach, a stretch of coral-colored sand at the southern tip. Off the northeast coast, Harbour Island, known locally as 'Briland', is a car-free village of pastel cottages, boutiques and the kind of bistros where you can eat a US$50 lobster in your bare feet. It's popular with celebrities; if you see Mick Jagger, just nod and smile.

STEPHEN FRINK | GETTY IMAGES ©

BRET CHARLTON | GETTY IMAGES ©

OPENING SPREAD Waves break against the sand on a beautiful Nassau beach. **ABOVE (L)** Snorkeling in clear Bahamian waters. **ABOVE (R)** Chose your vessel on which to explore the island's coastline. **LEFT** All dressed up and ready for Junkanoo, on New Year's Day.

ARMCHAIR

* *Under the Black Flag: The Romance and the Reality of Life Among the Pirates* (David Cordingly) The former head of exhibitions at England's National Maritime Museum explores the golden age of piracy in the Caribbean.

* *Islands in the Stream* (Ernest Hemingway) This posthumously published Hemingway novel was partially set on the nearby islands of Bimini.

* *Bahamian Anthology* (College of the Bahamas) This collection features stories, plays, and poetry by Bahamian writers.

* *Never Say Never Again* (1983) Underwater scenes from this James Bond flick were filmed around New Providence.

* *Pirates of the Caribbean* The Graycliff's builder John Howard Graysmith may not have been as glamorous as Johnny Depp, but these fun Disney films will get you in the *aarghh* spirit.

MEXICO & CENTRAL AMERICA

1 DIVE THE YUCATÁN'S CENOTES 2 CLIMB VOLCANOES IN NICARAGUA

3 PLUNGE INTO THE CAVES OF BELIZE 4 LET THE KIDS GO WILD IN COSTA RICA

5 CELEBRATE LOST SOULS IN OAXACA 6 TRAVEL ALONG THE RUTA MAYA

7 RIDE THE COPPER CANYON RAILWAY

EXPLORE THE AMERICAS

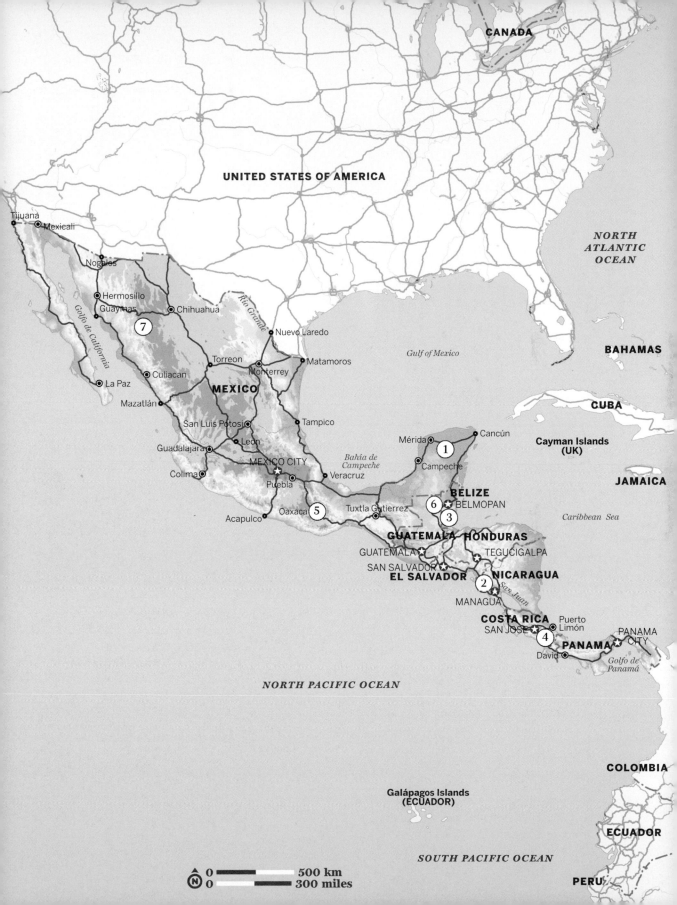

DIVE THE YUCATÁN'S CENOTES

THE MAYA REVERED THESE OTHERWORLDLY POOLS, WITH SHAFTS OF
SUNLIGHT TANGIBLE ENOUGH TO CLIMB, CLUSTERS OF THIGH-THICK VINES,
AND VISIBILITY MEASURED IN HUNDREDS OF FEET. DIVERS WILL DISCOVER
MANY SECRETS BELOW THE SURFACE OF THESE UNIQUE MEXICAN WONDERS.

Cenotes played a key role in prehistoric Maya civilization, and they remain
a central part of the natural heritage of the Yucatán. Formed by the erosion of
calcium-laden rock in the shallow shelf that makes up the peninsula, cenotes
are sink holes. What makes them unique is that these columnar caves reach
far down into the freshwater aquifer, providing water in an area that, while
lush and humid, often experiences droughts. Only a handful of rivers cut
through the area, leaving much of this plateau and its plants, animals and
humans dependent on rainwater. Scientists are realizing that many of what
were once thought to be independent caves are actually connected; indeed, the
Yucatán's cenotes may be part of the largest underground system in the world.

Even more interesting, thanks to centuries of cenotes being used as
anything from ceremonial burial grounds to waste baskets, the silt at the
bottom of these unique freshwater caves is often rich with information about
the plants, animals and populations of prehistoric times. Many of the artifacts
on display in museums in Mexico and at famous sites such as Chichén Itzá
were dredged up from the depths. Traveling into these caverns is like diving
into a museum.

Cenote diving is both interesting and dangerous: this is not an open-water
dive. You may encounter all sorts of interesting challenges that separate this
experience from the run of the mill. Layers of silt are easily stirred up and,
without currents to wash it away, can turn crystal-clear visibility into zero
visibility in seconds. Extreme pressures at certain depths trap toxic gases,
which remain suspended or dissolved in the water but which are poisonous
and can even eat away at diving equipment if precautions aren't taken. Some
cenotes have forests of dead trees at the bottom, which can tangle or ensnare
the careless. So it's vital to dive with someone experienced not just in diving,
but in all the various surprises each cenote may have in store.

ESSENTIAL EXPERIENCES

* **Gazing up in awestruck wonder at a cavern ceiling pierced by shafts of sunlight that seem tangible as steel.**

* Gliding past ethereal rock formations in inky dark caves that are larger than a football stadium.

* **Observing close up the bottom of these time capsules: prehistoric artifacts, indigenous peoples' skulls, even the occasional mastodon.**

* Plunging into the crystalline water hundreds of miles inland, knowing that if you could follow it indefinitely you'd find it leads all the way to the sea.

* **Taking in the wonders of the Maya ruin Chichén Itzá, where the Well of Sacrifice was used for sacrificing humans to the gods.**

174

LOCATION YUCATÁN, QUINTANA ROO, MEXICO | **IDEAL TIME COMMITMENT** ONE DAY PER DIVE | **BEST TIME OF YEAR** NOVEMBER TO MARCH | **ESSENTIAL TIP** RESERVE TWO-THIRDS OF YOUR TANK FOR THE RETURN.

THE CHICXULUB CRATER

A vast number of the Yucatán's cenotes, especially those near Mérida in the state of Yucatán, trace the outer border of the Chicxulub crater, a massive meteor impact that dates back to prehistoric times. The event occurred right at the K–T boundary, which was the time the dinosaurs vanished, and the crater's size (over 112 miles (180km) across) proves it had to have been an earth-changing catastrophe. It may be that the Chicxulub impact not only paved the way for mammals to thrive, but created the area's most interesting natural attractions as well.

HENEQUIN

In the late 19th century, the Yucatán was Mexico's richest and most prosperous *estado*, thanks to the use of local henequin fibers in ropemaking. Like tequila, the fibers come from agave. The industry took off after the invention of the henequin fiber press (an intricate Rube Goldberg–looking machine), and soon henequin plantations stretched for thousands of square miles, ruled by barons who exploited the indigenous populations and made fortunes off cheap land and labor. Only when the era of the clipper ships ended did the need for rope subside, and today most plantations remain as atmospheric ruins, if they remain at all.

■ THE ADVENTURE UNFOLDS

Cenote diving often begins with a hazard: just getting the gear down to the water can be tricky, requiring careful placement of feet on slippery rocks, climbing down ladders or even leaping in from above. But the care at the start pays off in spades when you're underwater, gliding through vast chambers or narrow tunnels in water so clear you almost forget it's not air.

Take your time to absorb the above-ground portion of the cave: the sunlight filtering through the canopy and the tangle of vegetation, vines and moss on the cavern sides. Some cenotes have stalactites that almost kiss the surface. Others have shallows where you can see rocks and blind fish swimming.

Descending, you'll find that visibility is limited only by your torch, or by the sunlight that filters in from above. Use your fins sparingly, to avoid churning up dust. You may need to hold onto a guide rope to avoid getting lost. Make sure emergency procedures have been discussed before you dive, and always reserve two-thirds of the tank for your return trip.

As you dive deeper, the chambers take on the aura of cathedrals and it seems as if you're flying, weightless, through Earth's natural apses. If your location is close to the sea, you may notice the blurry halocline, where the heavier saltwater mixes with the fresh rainwater in the aquifer above.

Only those experienced in deepwater scuba-diving should go all the way to the bottom of some cenotes. Many have 'Peligro – No Pase!' signs that must be heeded carefully. Layers of dissolved acid or treacherous passageways are just a few of the possible dangers, but the rewards of a cenote dive are long-lasting.

■ MAKING IT HAPPEN

Cancún, Mérida, and Playa del Carmen hotels have cenote tours and there are cenote-experienced dive shops nearby. Trips start at around US$100 per person, and may be much more depending on the type of dive and location. Keep safety at the top of the priority list – two-thirds of your tank must remain for the return half of the dive. Lesser-known cenotes may require private permission and/or off-road driving to reach.

■ AN ALTERNATIVE CHALLENGE

For those visitors who are not yet PADI-certified or who are uncomfortable assuming the risks inherent in a non-open-water dive, cenote snorkeling may be the perfect alternative. Most of the popular tours, such as Dos Ojos and Río Secreto, offer snorkel-only options; often the group is a mix of snorkelers and divers. Snorkelers should not apply any kind of sunscreen before entering the water, because the oils will rub off into the water and leave a sheen that – in these current-free holes – has nowhere to go.

177

OPENING SPREAD A diver explores a cavernous cenote. ABOVE Cenote Zací is located in the middle of the small Yucatán city of Valladolid. LEFT The Kukulkan pyramid in the Unesco-listed ancient Maya complex of Chichén Itzá.

ARMCHAIR

* **Cancún, Cozumel & the Yucatán** (Lonely Planet) A great guide to the area, with lots of insider tips and practical advice about lodging, food, dives and more.

* **Exploring Maya Ritual Caves: Dark Secrets from the Maya Underworld** (Stanislav Chládek) A unique look into many cenotes and caves around the peninsula, with excellent photography.

* **Mayan Folktales** (Susan C Thompson, Keith S Thompson & L López) Explains some of the cultural history behind the cenotes and what they meant to the Maya who revered them.

* **Fifty Places to Dive Before You Die** (Chris Santella) Includes cenotes in the list, along with many other fascinating dives.

CLIMB VOLCANOES IN NICARAGUA

SUMMIT THE GRAY SLOPES OF CERRO NEGRO THEN SURF DOWN ITS ASHY SIDE ON A WOODEN BOARD. CLIMB THE JUNGLE-SHROUDED CONCEPCIÓN AND MADERAS VOLCANOES ON OMETEPE ISLAND IN THE MIDDLE OF LAKE NICARAGUA. OR CIRCLE THE STEAMY CRATER OF MASAYA, WATCHING THE SUNSET THROUGH THE VAPOR.

From the top, it feels as if you're standing on the world's largest dune – nearly 2400ft (731m) of gray-black sand rising in the midst of the emerald Maribios mountain range. But this is no sand dune. This is Cerro Negro, a live volcano whose ashy sides are the result of constant volcanic activity. Peering down the steep slope, you wait for the signal. Then – *uno, dos, tres* – you're off! Perched atop a modified snowboard, you're tearing down the side of the volcano like a surfer on a monster wave. This is adventure, Nicaragua-style.

Nicaragua, the wedge-shaped country in the center of Central America, is sometimes referred to as 'the land of lakes and volcanoes.' Its landscape is dotted with nearly two dozen volcanoes running in a diagonal line from northwest to south, cutting through the country's two enormous lakes. These volcanoes create an extraordinary opportunity for adventures. You can swashbuckle up the vine-choked sides of remote forest volcanoes, traverse the rim of sulfur-steaming craters, ride horses up slopes of volcanic stones and swim in lagoons created by long-ago eruptions.

While surfing down Cerro Negro (Black Hill) is a must for adrenaline-heads, some of our favorite volcano trips are more classic hikes. On Ometepe, a figure-eight-shaped island in the middle of vast Lake Nicaragua, you can climb two giants – Concepción and Maderas – ascending through coffee, cacao and banana plantations. On Maderas, the rainforest gives way to an ancient crater turned lagoon, where you can swim in the water listening to the cries of howler monkeys. In the northwest, camp near the summit of the active volcano Telica, where the dark of night makes it possible to see hints of bubbling orange magma deep in the crater. In Volcán Masaya National Park, climb the two peaks for grand views – check ahead, though, since the park sometimes closes due to dangerous rumblings. This is good advice for any of the country's volcanoes – some are dormant, others are very much alive.

ESSENTIAL EXPERIENCES

* **Screaming with glee as you surf down the ashy slope of Cerro Negro on a volcano board.**

* Surveying the choppy waters of Lake Nicaragua after a sweaty trek to the peak of Concepción.

* **Cooking dinner on an open fire near the crater of Telica, then tiptoeing over to peer in at the magma more than 300ft (90m) below.**

* Relaxing with a bottle of local Flor de Caña rum at one of Granada's many al fresco cafes after a long day's hike.

* **Wandering the coffee groves at one of the farmstays on the slopes of Ometepe's Maderas volcano.**

178

ELEVATION OF SAN CRISTÓBAL, NICARAGUA'S TALLEST VOLCANO: 5725FT (1745M) | **LOCATION** THE WESTERN SIDE OF NICARAGUA | **IDEAL TIME COMMITMENT** 10 DAYS | **BEST TIME OF YEAR** NOVEMBER TO APRIL | **ESSENTIAL TIP** CHECK WITH INETER, THE INSTITUTE THAT MONITORS SEISMIC ACTIVITY, BEFORE ANY SOLO TREKKING NEAR ACTIVE VOLCANOES.

REVOLUTION AND WAR

Though it may no longer be obvious to the casual traveler, Nicaragua is still very much marked by the bloody conflicts of the 20th century. From 1937 to 1979, the country was ruled by the corrupt Somoza family dictatorship, which was backed by the US. In the 1970s, the Sandinistas, a leftist political group, launched a guerilla war, eventually overthrowing the Somozas. The Reagan administration then backed the Contras, a right-wing militant group, to fight the Sandinistas. A bloody war ensued, with kidnappings, rapes, torture and widespread use of landmines. Almost no one over the age of 30 doesn't live with memories of the conflict.

OLD AND NEW LEÓN

The original city of León was founded in 1524 by the Spanish conquistador, Francisco Hernández de Córdoba, who named it after the city in Spain. But León was built on a hotbed of seismic activity, and suffered major earthquakes in 1594 and 1610. Eventually the Spanish colonists decided to relocate to its present location, about 20 miles 32km) away. Over the years, the buildings of Old León were buried under ash erupting from the nearby volcano Momotombo. The ruins were discovered in the late 1960s, and excavations have been ongoing. Today you can visit the ghostly city, and contemplate life in the volcano's shadow.

■ THE ADVENTURE UNFOLDS

Nicaragua's volcanoes – and most of the country's cities and people – are fairly close to the Pacific Coast. Two cities in particular make excellent bases for volcano exploring. In the northwest is León, Nicaragua's second-oldest city, with a vibrant university community, excellent museums and crumbling, centuries-old cathedrals. León offers quick access to Cerro Negro, Telica, and San Cristóbal, Nicaragua's tallest volcano. Granada, halfway down the coast on the north shores of Lake Nicaragua, is postcard Central America: cobblestone streets, colonial houses in poppy-bright colors, plazas with spouting fountains and vendors selling sliced mangos from pushcarts. From here it's a 45-minute drive to the Volcán Masaya National Park, or a quick bus and ferry ride across the lake to Ometepe. Ometepe's main ferry port, Moyogalpa, is in the northern half of the island, at the foot of Concepción, and has the bulk of the accommodations. The southern half of the island, around Maderas volcano, is much more rural, with unpaved roads and tiny farming and fishing hamlets.

For the intrepid volcano-hound, we suggest a three-part trip. Start your adventure in León, an easy bus ride from the country's main airport in Managua. Surf down Cerro Negro, camp by the crater of Telica, and hoof it up to the summit of San Cristóbal. Then spend your evenings enjoying street food like *nacatamales* (Nicaraguan-style tamales, stuffed with meat or vegetables) and *quesillo* (local cheese and pickled onions rolled up in a warm quesadilla) at the outdoor markets, and drinking red wine at student bars. After a few days in León, bus it to Granada to explore the Volcán Masaya National Park and the city's colonial splendor. Visit the churches, relax your volcano-sore muscles on a bench in the old-world central plaza, and dine at modern Nicaraguan restaurants in candle-lit old mansions. Then catch a ferry to Moyogalpa on Ometepe to climb Concepción, then stay at a rural farm in the island's south while tackling Maderas. Don't forget to enjoy the local bounty: lake fish, volcano-grown coffee, fresh papaya, and local chocolate.

■ MAKING IT HAPPEN

Most visitors to Nicaragua fly into the country's main airport in the capital city of Managua. From here, it's a two-hour bus or taxi trip north to León, or an hour south to Granada. November through April is Nicaragua's dry season, which makes for especially pleasant hiking. Both León and Granada offer a wide range of accommodations, from backpacker hostels to luxury boutique hotels. Most guided hikes can be booked just a day or two in advance.

■ A DETOUR

A quick daytrip from Granada, the turquoise waters of the Laguna de Apoyo fill an ancient volcano crater. Nearly 650ft (approx. 200m) deep, the lake is ringed by green mountains, making it a spectacular place to kayak, tube or just float on your back, staring at the sky. It's also a favorite spot for scuba divers. At sunset, climb into the hills for panoramic views over the water. The surrounding jungle is home to capuchin monkeys, anteaters, wild cats known as jaguarundis, and hundreds of types of butterfly. If you'd like to stay overnight, several ecolodges offer rustic-chic bungalows.

OPENING SPREAD Concepción as viewed from its sister volcano, Maderas. **ABOVE** Surfing down the slopes of Cerro Negro. **LEFT** The city of León.

181

ARMCHAIR

❋ *The Country Under My Skin: A Memoir of Love and War* (Gioconda Belli) Belli's enthralling memoir of going from a silver spoon Managua childhood to joining the Sandinista revolution.

❋ *Blood of Brothers: Life and War in Nicaragua* (Stephen Kinzer) A history of Nicaragua's turbulent 20th century.

❋ *Azul* (Rubén Darío) The landmark 1888 book of poems from the León-bred 'Father of Modernism'.

❋ *Nicaraguan Cooking: My Grandmother's Recipes* (Trudy Espinoza-Abrams) Try Nicaraguan classics like *gallo pinto* (rice and beans) at home.

❋ *The Jaguar Smile* (Salman Rushdie) The novelist's nonfiction account of visiting Nicaragua in the late 1980s, at the invitation of a Sandinista cultural organization.

PLUNGE INTO THE CAVES OF BELIZE

PSYCH YOURSELF FOR A JOURNEY INTO THE MAYAN UNDERWORLD – DELVE INTO THE VERY ROCK ON WHICH BELIZE IS FOUNDED TO DISCOVER A DARK REALM OF GUSHING RIVERS, ANCIENT ARTIFACTS AND THE SKELETAL REMAINS OF SACRIFICIAL VICTIMS DISPATCHED A MILLENNIUM AGO.

To the ancient Maya, the caverns, sinkholes, lakes and underground rivers in Belize – which now offer such great opportunities for tubing, kayaking, swimming and abseiling – were not adventure playgrounds but gateways to Xibalbá, 'Place of Fear': the Mayan underworld, ruled by death gods.

The geology, of course, is more prosaic. Many of the physical features that make Belize so beguiling – its picturesque karst outcrops, the barrier reef that skirts its shoreline, and the caves pocking the northern interior – are manifestations of its porous limestone bedrock, repeatedly exposed then re-covered by rising and falling seas. Rain erosion created the fissures, potholes and pinnacles that now decorate the land and offshore reefs.

Most characteristic of these features are cenotes: sinkholes formed by the collapse of the roofs of caves carved out by underground rivers. To the Maya, these were sacred; the source of water and gateways to the underworld, they were places to bury the dead, perform religious ceremonies and make sacrifices. Intrepid travelers are reminded of past rituals by handprints, petroglyphs and pictographs etched or painted on rock walls, and by the bones and skulls that still litter some caves, possibly the remains of human sacrificial victims.

Only in the past 20 years have Belize's subterranean marvels been opened up for exploration. Now those with a head for heights (and depths) can abseil nearly 300ft (91m) into the jungle-filled Black Hole, or canoe or tube through Barton Creek Cave. Two Blue Holes offer contrasting aquatic experiences: take a cooling dip in the cerulean waters flowing through a vast inland cenote, or don snorkel or scuba equipment to explore the offshore sinkhole at Lighthouse Reef. And the hike, wade, swim, and scramble to and through Actun Tunichil Muknal at the edge of Tapir Mountain Nature Reserve reveals a poignant sight: the skeleton of a young girl, sacrificed a millennium ago and now sparkling with calcite crystals.

ESSENTIAL EXPERIENCES

✳ **Trekking through steaming jungle and wading through waist-deep rivers to reach the sacrificial Crystal Maiden in Actun Tunichil Muknal.**

✳ Spotting tapirs, anteaters, monkeys, a dizzying array of birds and – if you're really lucky – a jaguar at Cockscomb Basin Wildlife Sanctuary.

✳ **Meeting the modern-day Maya in their villages in the southern Toledo district.**

✳ Chilling out on the Northern Cayes and snorkeling or diving the Western Hemisphere's longest barrier reef.

✳ **Taking the rough road to remote Caracol, the vast, jungle-clad Mayan city founded at least two millennia ago.**

✳ Abseiling nearly 300ft (90m) down into the rainforest-lined Black Hole.

LOCATION CENTRAL BELIZE | IDEAL TIME COMMITMENT THREE DAYS TO ONE WEEK | BEST TIME OF YEAR NOVEMBER TO MAY
ESSENTIAL TIP TAKE A LIGHTWEIGHT DRY BAG FOR CARRYING YOUR CAMERA AND ANYTHING ELSE YOU DON'T WANT TO GET WET.

THE LIVING MAYA

As you gaze slack-jawed at crystal-encrusted skeletons or explore ancient, tumbledown temples, don't forget that, though the heyday of Classical Mayan civilization ended some 11 centuries ago, Maya peoples still inhabit Belize today. In fact, over 10% of the country's population is Maya, divided into three linguistically distinct groups. The Yucatecs of the north originated over what's now the Mexican border, while the Kekchi migrated from Guatemala. The Mopan also arrived from Guatemala, though their roots were in Belize. An eye-opening stay in one of the Maya villages of the south can be arranged through the Toledo Ecotourism Association (TEA).

ANIMAL MAGIC

Belize boasts more than its fair share of natural treasures; over 40% of the country's area is protected by national or private organizations, affording rich wildlife watching. Though named a jaguar reserve, you'd be fortunate to spot Latin America's biggest cat at Cockscomb Basin Wildlife Sanctuary, but you could see howler monkeys, Baird's tapirs, coatis, some of its 300 bird species, and perhaps even a selection of Belize's other cats: ocelots, margays, pumas and jaguarundis. Elsewhere, the lagoons of Crooked Tree Wildlife Sanctuary attract profuse birdlife, while cats including jaguars stalk the forests of Blue Hole National Park.

THE ADVENTURE UNFOLDS

Dawn's pink kiss is still fading from the sky as you set off through the jungle. Mist lingers in woolly tufts on the forest canopy ahead: moisture condensing in cold air, telltale signs of caves and streams, your guide tells you. A flash of movement sends your heart leaping up to your mouth. That it's merely a coatimundi scampering down a tree brings both relief and disappointment – is a close encounter with a jaguar to be longed for or dreaded?

An hour's trek through dense forest is punctuated by waist-deep river crossings. You stop briefly at Actun Uayazba Kab – 'Handprint Cave' – to admire the eponymous stencils, and to boost the adrenaline with a short abseil past cliff niches holding pottery artifacts. But the real adventure begins at the hourglass entrance to the Underworld: Actun Tunichil Muknal, the 'Cave of the Stone Sepulchre.' The shiver as you slip into the shimmering turquoise pool can't be explained by the cool of the water alone. The ancient Maya believed this to be a gateway to Xibalbá, where the dead return and the jaguar retreats at night.

You flick on your headlamp and swim into the cave, scrambling upstream, chest-deep in chilly water. Eventually you clamber onto rocks coated with crystal flows; here you leave your shoes and pad on in stockinged feet through successive caverns, past wide pottery *ollas* (jars) and stelae carved to represent blood-letting tools, finally ascending into the Cathedral.

Although the soaring ceiling justifies the name, it could be called the Catacomb. Skulls sparkle with calcite and ahead lies the object of your mission: the Crystal Maiden, a young girl, resting where she was killed over a thousand years ago.

MAKING IT HAPPEN

Belize's caves dot the center and west of the country; most are accessible only on organized tours. A couple of outfits are currently licensed to take visitors into Actun Tunichil Muknal; these tours, along with other caving adventures in the west of Belize, are best booked through your accommodation or the lodges in San Ignacio. The Black Hole abseil is run by Caves Branch Adventure Company, just off the Hummingbird Highway.

DETOUR

The world's second-longest barrier reef – a 186-mile (300km) limestone shelf topped with choice coral – skirts Belize's coast, in some spots within spitting distance of the shore, which makes for fine snorkeling. The country's Northern Cayes host scuba-divers, with dozens of fine dive sites easily accessible. The headline act is the Blue Hole, a vividly hued sinkhole on Lighthouse Reef, 1000ft (305m) across and 400ft (122m) deep. Other sites offer opportunities for spotting whale sharks, manta rays, sea turtles, manatees and countless smaller species.

HENRY GEORGI | GETTY IMAGES ©

OPENING SPREAD Looking out from the mouth of Belize's Río Frio cave. **ABOVE** Adventurers tackle Caves Branch River by inflatable raft. **LEFT** A puma stalks the Belize savanna forest – the species is the country's second-largest cat after the jaguar.

ARMCHAIR

* *The Maya* (Michael D Coe) An accessible, intelligent introduction to the dominant culture of ancient Belize.

* *Diving & Snorkeling Belize* (Tim Rock) A colorful guide providing detailed information on dive sites and species to spot.

* *Time Among the Maya: Travels in Belize, Guatemala and Mexico* (Ronald Wright) This perceptive travelogue describes enlightening encounters with modern-day Maya.

* *Belize & Northern Guatemala: Travellers' Wildlife Guide* (Les Beletsky) Detailed introduction to the species to spot and where to see them.

* *The Mosquito Coast* (1986) Harrison Ford plays a fanatical inventor bent on creating a utopia in Central America. Paul Theroux's book was set in Honduras, but the steaming jungle in Peter Weir's film is Belize.

LET THE KIDS GO WILD IN COSTA RICA

EXPLORE YOUR FAMILY'S WILD SIDE ON A COSTA RICAN ADVENTURE, WHERE IT'S POSSIBLE TO SEE A VOLCANO, HEAR HOWLER MONKEYS SCREECHING IN THE CLOUD FOREST, AND SURF WARM BLUE WATERS, ALL IN THE SAME DAY.

186

The sound of cicadas fills the forest like a screeching jet engine. You step over a dark trail of leafcutter ants carrying triangles of leaves over a snake-like tree root that's invaded the path. One of the many tall trees above your head rustles and you look up to see a troop of white-faced monkeys eating fruit. A monkey catches your gaze, then turns quickly to run up the branch, a baby clinging to her back. Your kid points at her, with an expression of pure awe.

Welcome to Costa Rica, arguably the easiest place to see wildlife in the Americas. But the nature-in-all-its-glory adventure doesn't end here. The same day you explore that forest you may have also visited a live volcano, and the Pacific coast with its sandy beaches and surfable waves could be steps away. As one of the safest and more developed countries in the region, Costa Rica is easy to get around; if you plan it right, you won't have any car trips longer than three hours. There are thrills for every age: soft beaches for tots, easy walks with lots of animals for kids, more-adventurous jaunts and surfing for tweens, and nightlife and adrenaline-charged activities (from rafting to zip-lining) for teenagers.

While almost anywhere in Costa Rica is good for family travel, the northwest part of the country and the central Pacific coast is easy to get to from the capital, San José, and offers tons of variety in a condensed space. In this exhilarating tropical playland you can explore Arenal's perfectly shaped volcanic cone and the surrounding Jurassic jungle before heading up to Monteverde for misty cloud forests filled with brightly colored birds, outrageously large insects, and weird animals, such as nocturnal, prehensile-tailed porcupines. Then head to the coast for tall, humid jungles that hide sloths, snakes and coatis. Look down from river bridges to see colossal crocodiles bathing in the sun or spend a day at the beach learning to surf in gentle waves. And expect plenty more expressions of awe.

ESSENTIAL EXPERIENCES

❋ **Hearing the dinosaur-like call of scarlet macaws before watching them land in a flash of brilliant red on a tree branch at sunset.**

❋ Gliding on a gentle wave while warm ocean water lightly sprays your face.

❋ **Feeling the mist of a 40ft (12m) waterfall before seeing it post-descent from the Arenal Observatory Lodge and its volcano views.**

❋ Gaining exhilarating speed as you zip-line through the myriad greens of the rainforest canopy.

❋ **Searching for critters in the mists of Monteverde's Middle Earth-like cloud forests.**

❋ Getting a touch of vertigo from your very solid bridge, while watching gargantuan sunbathing crocodiles in the river below.

LOCATION COSTA RICA, CENTRAL AMERICA | **BEST TIME OF YEAR** NOVEMBER TO APRIL | **IDEAL TIME COMMITMENT** TEN DAYS
ESSENTIAL TIP YOU CAN USE US DOLLARS ALMOST EVERYWHERE IN COSTA RICA | **PACK** SWEATERS FOR CHILLY NIGHTS; BINOCULARS FOR WILDLIFE WATCHING; INSECT REPELLENT.

COFFEE CULTURE

Cool highland mountains run down Costa Rica's interior and hold the country's often vast arabica coffee plantations. Become a coffee savant on a plantation tour in the Tarrazú province near Jacó or around Monteverde. Start by exploring the plants themselves, from sprout to mature, when the red fruit is picked by hand and gathered in baskets. Then enjoy the aromas while watching the roasting process and learning about the industry's history. At the end it's time to learn how to taste the coffee's nuances – which are only heightened by a view over the rows of plants surrounded by mist-covered jungles.

HIGH IN THE CANOPY

Click into the harness, hang on, and whooooooop! Zip-lining through the forest canopy in Arenal and Monteverde is a real adrenaline rush, offering another angle on the forests (and open to ages four-plus). If hanging from a wire 655ft (200m) up isn't your thing, don't despair: there are also open-air trams and suspension bridges that let you enjoy the serenity of the treetops. Will you see wildlife up here? Not much, but it's said that 90% of living organisms in the rainforest exist at this level. The beauty is in the details.

■ THE PERFECT GETAWAY

Get out of San José – quickly – and go straight to Parque Nacional Volcán Arenal. The volcano has stopped spouting lava and the views look like something out of a dinosaur-meets-unicorn fantasy. Walk or horseback-ride to waterfalls, explore the dark gray rubble of old lava flows, or windsurf, boat, or fish the 33-sq-mile (85-sq-km) volcanic lake. Meanwhile, trees with massive root buttresses hold troops of monkey comedians that will keep you laughing. See some of the world's most dangerous snakes and colorful frogs up close at the Arenal Eco Zoo.

Next, go to Monteverde for higher, mistier, lichen-draped forests with more critters. Take a walk along the family-friendly Bajo del Tigre trail to spot toucans and agoutis by day or tarantulas hiding in their ground lairs at twilight. There are specialist educational zoos here for butterflies, frogs, bats and snakes that allow you to see and learn about your favorite animals.

Then it's time to descend from the clouds to the sunny, humid coast. Jacó is touristy, yes, but it's a beachside town with enough sleeping and eating options to keep any family happy. Days can be spent exploring the nearby macaw-filled Parque Nacional Carara. If you haven't had enough animal and beach action, then Parque Nacional Manuel Antonio, about an hour down the coast from Jacó, is sure to deliver. Here, vine-covered trees harboring sloths give way to coconut palms and white sands where you can swim in warm blue water until an animal exciting enough (a spiny-tailed iguana, maybe?) draws you out. Again, this park is no secret but it merits its popularity through its beauty and density of animal life. Even at its most crowded it still feels as if the monkeys outnumber people.

■ PLAN IT

Fly into the Costa Rican capital of San José and rent a 4WD. Book your lodging well in advance if you'll be traveling during the peak months of December and January or June and July. The driest (and most popular) time to visit is November to April. Humpback whales migrate along the coast in September and October. Monteverde gets packed for the annual Monteverde Music Festival (includes jazz, Latin and classical artists), held on variable dates from January to early April.

■ DETOUR

Canoeing the canals of Parque Nacional Tortuguero is a boat-borne safari, where thick jungle meets the water and you can get up close with shy caimans, river turtles, crowned night herons, monkeys and sloths. In the right season, under the cover of darkness, watch the awesome, millennia-old ritual of turtles building nests and laying their eggs on the black-sand beaches. Sandwiched between wetlands and the Caribbean Sea, this is among the premier places in Costa Rica to watch wildlife.

189

OPENING SPREAD A footbridge cuts through the rainforest. **ABOVE (L)** The owner of Restaurante Elena Brown, where you can sample Costa Rican cuisine in Puerto Viejo de Talamanca. **ABOVE (R)** Surfing at sunset on the coast. **LEFT** A Central American squirrel monkey.

ARMCHAIR

✻ ***The Wildlife of Costa Rica: A Field Guide*** (Zona Tropical Publications) Packable illustrated fauna guide.

✻ ***The Old Patagonian Express: By Train Through the Americas*** (Paul Theroux) Late 1970s train voyage includes Limón and Puntarenas.

✻ ***The Umbrella*** (Jan Brett) Story and detailed art of the Costa Rican cloud forest. Ages four to eight.

✻ ***Nancy Drew: The Scarlet Macaw Scandal*** (Carolyn Keene) Nancy and friends volunteer in Costa Rica and find they have a mystery on their hands.

✻ ***The Divide*** (Elizabeth Kay) A 13-year-old boy falls into a world of legendary creatures while staying in Costa Rica with his family.

✻ ***There Never Was Once Upon a Time*** (Carmen Naranjo) Ten stories, narrated by children, by the widely translated novelist.

CELEBRATE LOST SOULS IN OAXACA

CEMETERIES COME ALIVE IN CENTRAL MEXICO AS LOCALS MAKE A MIDNIGHT PILGRIMAGE TO THE GRAVES OF THE DEPARTED DURING DÍA DE LOS MUERTOS (DAY OF THE DEAD) – A PARTY LIKE NO OTHER.

It's midnight. Among the crumbling headstones and the ruins of an old church there are shadows shuffling, swaying. Dark figures move in the moonlight, their voices rising into the air.

They're singing, these people. Some are even dancing, stepping through candles that throw flickering light across the busy cemetery. There's a mariachi band playing just outside the walls, where a crowd is dancing in the streets. Inside people are sitting on graves, some drinking and chatting, others are passing the night sedately with hands clasped in silent vigil.

Even stranger still, there's a small girl perched on one of the stones, dressed in a bridal gown and veil. She's sitting there stony-faced, flanked by two other young girls draped in the dark robes and black lace worn by widows in mourning. Peer a little closer and you can see their faces are caked in white, with scarlet gashes painted on their cheeks.

Death is all around. It's in the costumes and the painted faces of the revelers in the cemetery. It's in the fake skeletons and skull decorations that bedeck the town. Most of all, it's buried 6ft beneath the earth at everyone's feet.

Here, death isn't feared. It's not even the cause for sadness. At least, not today. It's a time for Mexicans to get back in touch with loved ones, friends and relatives, who have passed to the other side. For many people that means a couple of long, silent nights perched on the end of a grave, waiting to meet up with lost souls. For others it's a celebration of those who will never return, a time to indulge in their favorite activities – dancing, singing, drinking – in the presence of their spirits.

It's both a party and a pilgrimage, haunting and glorious.

ESSENTIAL EXPERIENCES

* **Spending a ghoulish night at Xoxo cemetery, with its gravestones, church ruins and mariachi band.**

* Painting your face like it's Halloween and joining a parade in Oaxaca City.

* **Checking out Day of the Dead–themed sand sculptures near Oaxaca's cathedral.**

* Settling back with a drink and taking in all of the action – from markets to parades – at the Zócalo (Oaxaca's main square).

* **Trying mole, Oaxaca's famously dark, complex sauce that's served with meats and vegetables year-round.**

* Enjoying the warmth of the people of Oaxaca, among the most hospitable in Mexico.

190

WHO'S THAT SKELETON?

One of the most striking and frequently seen images associated with the Day of the Dead is Catrina, the skeleton of an upper-class woman in a hat and a dress. It was originally sketched by Mexican printmaker José Guadalupe Posada in the early 1900s, and became part of Day of the Dead celebrations in the 1920s. Now 'La Catrina' images form a huge part of the festival, from the paintings and sculptures displayed throughout Oaxaca City to the costumes worn by festival-goers around town. The artist Diego Rivera even incorporated Catrina into one of his murals, *Dream of a Sunday Afternoon in Alameda Park,* in the 1940s.

WHY THE DAY OF THE DEAD?

As with many festivals in Latin America, the Day of the Dead is a blend of Catholicism and ancient Aztec and pagan rituals. While the Aztecs dedicated an entire month to remembering their dead ancestors, the modern form of the celebration takes place on All Saints and All Souls Days at the beginning of November: the first of the month is dedicated to deceased children and infants, while November 2 is dedicated to remembering adults. It's typical for Mexicans to celebrate those lives by practicing the things their loved ones held dear, including music and dancing, and visiting their graves to be closer to their souls. It's also become something of an artistic festival, where local artisans' Day of the Dead–themed works can be seen throughout cities.

■ THE PERFECT GETAWAY

Oaxaca City buzzes with life during the Day of the Dead, when the streets are constantly filled with people during the day, and the cemeteries are packed at night. The daylight hours are the perfect time to wander through town looking at the art displays: huge skulls are painted by local artists, while sand sculptures of skeletons dominate the space in front of Oaxaca's cathedral. As evening sets in there's no better place to be than the Zócalo, Oaxaca's main square and home to the markets and Day of the Dead parades. There's also room for an occasional political protest, in the form of more sculptures and posters – a reminder that all is not completely well in this sometimes turbulent country. Still, it's mostly a good-natured celebration, as cafes place 'Catrina' skeletons at their tables, and bags of bones laugh from balconies overlooking the square.

When night falls there are two cemeteries worth checking out, which visitors can split across the two days of the festival. Oaxaca's main cemetery, the Panteón General, is the easiest to get to (it's walking distance from the Zócalo) and the busiest. There's a full fairground outside it, and plenty of dark, costumed figures spending the night inside. It's an amazing experience to simply sit or stand by the walls of candlelit tombs and watch the festival's living celebrants pass by.

Out in Xoxo, a few miles south, it's even spookier. There's hardly any light here bar the flickering of tea-light candles on graves. Some groups of people sing songs in the ruins of an old church, while others sit on graves and chat, and others still choose to wait out the night in solo vigil. It will take a trip by bus or car to get here from Oaxaca, but it's worth the effort.

■ PLAN IT

The Day of the Dead is celebrated throughout Mexico and some parts of Central America on November 1 and 2. To get to Oaxaca City, fly to Mexico City and catch a six-hour bus transfer south. There are also flights between the two cities. Most Day of the Dead activities happen in Oaxaca itself; Xoxo cemetery is a short drive out of town. Plenty of tourist shops run bus trips out to Xoxo each night. Remember to behave respectfully in cemeteries and ask permission before taking photographs.

■ DETOUR

Those needing a change of scenery after all that ghoulishness should head west to the coast. The most popular destination is Puerto Escondido, a town with a relaxed vibe and plenty of empty sand. Off the beaten track (and about an hour south of Puerto Escondido), the former hippie haunt of Zipolite is as laid-back as it comes, with people doing yoga on the beach in-between munching on shrimp tacos from the local restaurants. (There's nothing else to do in Zipolite, and that's the point.)

MARK READ | LONELY PLANET ©

VW PICS | GETTY IMAGES ©

OPENING SPREAD The fabled Catrina, a common sight during the Day of the Dead. **ABOVE (L)** Traditional Oaxacan desserts are served. **ABOVE (R)** Locals gather at cemeteries to be close to departed loved ones. **LEFT** Participants don vivid costumes, like this man in Oaxaca.

ARMCHAIR

- ❋ **Ask a Mexican** (Gustavo Arellano) A tongue-in-cheek book for those with questions about Mexico's more interesting quirks.

- ❋ **The Power and the Glory** (Graham Greene) This classic, about a priest on the run at a time when Catholicism was outlawed in Mexico, provides excellent background to a fascinating country.

- ❋ **The Old Gringo** (Carlos Fuentes) The story of a US journalist living among the soldiers of famous revolutionary Pancho Villa.

- ❋ **Sliced Iguana: Travels in Mexico** (Isabella Tree) The travel writer's warm and perceptive account of Mexico and its indigenous cultures.

- ❋ **Frida** (2002) One of Mexico's most famous artists, Frida Kahlo, is immortalized in this biopic.

- ❋ **Spectre** (2015) The spectacular opening sequence of the Bond film was set during a Day of the Dead parade in Mexico City.

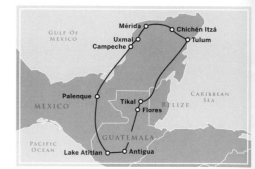

TRAVEL ALONG THE RUTA MAYA

FOR MILLENNIA THE MAYAN CIVILISATION SPREAD OVER JADE HILLS AND TANGLED JUNGLE, FLOURISHED ON SUGAR-WHITE BEACHES LAPPED BY TURQUOISE LAGOONS, AND LEFT BEHIND PYRAMID CITIES THAT WOULD FASCINATE EVERYONE FROM SPANISH CONQUISTADORES TO GEORGE LUCAS.

At its apex, Mayan civilization extended from the southern Mexican states of Tabasco, Yucatán, Quintana Roo, Campeche and Chiapas, through Belize and Guatemala, with a pinkie in both El Salvador and Honduras. Archaeologists believe the oldest of Maya's pyramids were built in present-day Belize in 2600 BC, but the lunar calendar, for which they have received most publicity, dates back to 3114 BC. The famed stepped pyramids and larger city-states, including Palenque (Chiapas), Tikal (Guatemala), and Copán (Honduras), were built during what scholars define as the Classic period (AD 250–900).

Jade and obsidian were Maya's earliest trade goods, soon supplemented by salt, sea shells, and cacao, which were traded with other early Mesoamerican cultures, including the Zapotecs to the north and Tainos to the southeast. The southern lowland cities went into decline and were eventually abandoned in the 8th and 9th centuries, while northern Yucatán cities survived until the Spanish arrived and conquered them. The last surviving city-states fell in 1697.

Initially the Spanish church torched all Mayan texts and art they found, but in the late 18th century Spanish officials began investigating former Maya sites. In 1839, John Lloyd Stephens, an American familiar with those investigations, visited Copán, Palenque and others, with English architect Frederick Catherwood. Their illustrations sparked popular interest worldwide.

Even today, many of the Maya ruins are hidden by dense jungle, so researchers have turned to satellite imagery that can detect limestone. As there are more than 70 restored Mayan sites in five countries, there are thousands of ways to tackle La Ruta Maya. We suggest starting at Chichén Itzá on the Mayan Riviera, moving on to Tulum before continuing south into Belize, and then Guatemala, where you'll enjoy mighty Tikal, the charming city of Antigua and Lake Atitlan, before turning back into Mexico to the jungle of Palenque and fabled Uxmal.

ESSENTIAL EXPERIENCES

❋ **Slaloming through the crowds in order to glean the secrets of the Mayan calendar at Chichén Itzá.**

❋ Checking out the enthralling ruins and spectacular beaches in sexy Tulum, the star of the Mayan Riviera.

❋ **Following La Ruta Maya into Belize where you'll glimpse the ancient trading hub of Altun Ha and massive Caracol, tucked away in the jungle.**

❋ Watching the sun drop into the misty jungle from the top of Temple IV in Tikal, arguably the most spectacular site on La Ruta Maya.

❋ **Looking back to the more recent past on a stroll through the sweet cobbled streets of old-town Antigua.**

194

DISTANCE 1190 MILES (1916KM) | **COUNTRIES COVERED** MEXICO, BELIZE, GUATEMALA | **IDEAL TIME COMMITMENT** TWO WEEKS
BEST TIME OF YEAR NOVEMBER TO APRIL | **ESSENTIAL TIP** GO DURING THE OFF-SEASON (MAY-OCT) TO AVOID CROWDS.

STAR GAZERS

More than a few researchers claim that the Maya are the only pre-telescopic civilization to demonstrate knowledge of the Orion Nebula as being fuzzy, rather than a pinpoint star. Such anthropologists point to a folk tale that deals with the Orion constellation, and their traditional hearths were oriented toward Orion. The Maya were also very interested in zenial passages – the time when the sun passes directly overhead – which at the latitude of the Mayan civilization happened twice annually, on a day equidistant between the two solstices. However, according to a recovered record, which anthropologists call the Dresden Codex, Venus was astronomically more important to the Mayans than the sun.

■ THE JOURNEY TODAY

This is a journey best made by mixing air and road travel. The most famous and best restored of the Yucatán Maya sites, Chichén Itzá (Mouth of the Well of the Itzáes), is overcrowded but still impressive, especially after the mysteries of the Maya astronomical calendar are explained in the 'time temples'. The ball court is flanked by temples at either end and bounded by towering parallel walls with stone rings cemented up high. A short drive away, the famed ruins at Tulum are found on a stunning stretch of white-sand beach, backed by the Si'an Kaan Biosphere Reserve where you can trek through pristine jungle and stumble on Mayan sites still in the grips of nature.

Belize's Altun Ha, close to Belize City and accessible from Cancun, was an important coastal trading hub and ceremonial center. The restored portion of Altun Ha has some 300 unexcavated mounds surrounding it. Belize's largest site, Caracol, set in a jungle and not far from Tikal, was found in the 1930s, and excavated in 1985. Its ceremonial center is dotted with massive pyramids and 20 major plazas. From here you can easily travel to Tikal, the largest of the restored Mayan ruins. At 236ft (72m), Temple IV is the highest of the numbered pyramids. Watch the sunset here amid temples rising above a jungle canopy screeching with howler monkeys, toucans and parrots. You may recognize the view, as Tikal was the setting for the rebel base in *Star Wars IV: A New Hope*.

A short flight from nearby Flores will land you in colonial Antigua, not far from stunning Lake Atitlan. Proceed north from the lake and into the mountains of Chiapas, where you'll find the city of Palenque, noted for its detailed architecture and tremendous stone carvings – particularly in the Temple of Inscriptions. In Campeche, the western flank of the Yucatán peninsula shapes up, and before you reach Merida, the portal to and from the Mayan Riviera, stop in Uxmal for a final fix.

■ SHORTCUT

Cut your Ruta Maya short by sticking to one country – one peninsula even. From Merida you can reach the sites of Chichén Itzá, Tulum and Uxmal in one long weekend. With one more day, you can diverge down to Chiapas – where Palenque and the finest Mayan carvings in the empire await.

■ DETOUR

Set in a highland valley surrounded by pine forest, five hours from Palenque, the colonial city of San Cristóbal de las Casas has cobbled streets and markets, and a unique ambience. Surrounded by dozens of traditional Tzotzil and Tzcltal villages, San Cristóbal is at the heart of one of the most deeply rooted indigenous communities in Mexico.

JUSTIN FOULKES | LONELY PLANET ©

MARK READ | LONELY PLANET ©

OPENING SPREAD The Mayan ruin of El Palacio in Palenque is one of many in the Yucatán. **ABOVE (L)** The colors of traditional Maya dress signify the village of origin. **ABOVE (R)** Ruins at Lubaantun in Belize. **LEFT** A guide leads the way deep into the Guatemalan jungle.

ARMCHAIR

✳ **2000 Years of Mayan Literature** (Dennis Tedlock) Mayan stories are some of the oldest in the world, and Tedlock was one of the first academics to treat ancient, Mayan-scripted myth as literature.

✳ **Breaking the Maya Code** (Michael D Coe) A true account about the eventual deciphering of the hard-to-crack Mayan language, written by a Yale professor who calls it 'one of the great intellectual adventures of our time.'

✳ **A Forest of Kings** (David Freidel and Linda Schele) Based on deciphered Mayan hieroglyphics and written by two archaeologists, this book tells tales of war, expansion and ritual that defined the Mayan civilization.

✳ **Apocalypto** (2006) Mel Gibson's film about the decline of the Mayan civilization and the harrowing escape of a young man trapped for human sacrifice.

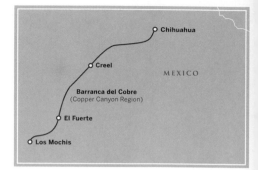

RIDE THE COPPER CANYON RAILWAY

THIS IS ONE OF THE MOST DRAMATIC TRAIN RIDES OF ALL: 407 MILES (655KM) OF RAILS RIGHT UP, OVER, AND THROUGH NORTHWEST MEXICO'S STUNNING COPPER CANYON (BARRANCA DEL COBRE). THIS SERIES OF 20 SPECTACULAR CANYONS IS FOUR TIMES LARGER THAN ARIZONA'S GRAND CANYON AND, IN PARTS, DEEPER.

The name 'Copper Canyon' was applied by the Spanish, who mistook the greenish-glow of lichen in the area for copper. As a physical location, it refers to the incredible Barranca de Urique, the canyon's deepest point at 6160ft (1879m) – although an altitude of only 1640ft (500m). That's not the only amazing detail. The Barranca de Urique has a subtropical climate with peaks 7500ft (2300m) above sea level and an ecosystem of conifers and evergreens. The region is also home to the Rarámuri, among Mexico's largest indigenous groups.

Imagine a big knife – a knife used by the gods. Now, imagine that gods have cars, and that one of them decides to scrape their big knife across a car the size of North Carolina. Finally, envisage the owner – some other god – coming home to find the damage: in scale, that scraped scar would be something along the lines of Copper Canyon's amazing chasms. OK, forget the metaphors, maybe you really do need to see it for yourself. Luckily, you can travel right through some of the steepest areas on the Ferrocarril Chihuahua al Pacífico – the fabled Copper Canyon Railway. It boasts 36 bridges and 87 tunnels and traverses 407 miles (655km) between Los Mochis at its western terminus and Chihuahua in the Midwest. It was opened in 1961, after taking many decades to build, and is the major link between Chihuahua and the coast, used heavily by passengers and for shipping freight. Two passenger trains ply the route: *clase económica* (economy class), and *primera express* (first class), which makes fewer stops and has a restaurant, bar and reclining seats. Alternatively, there is a privately operated rail car with an open-deck area.

Either way, the beauty of the landscape – sweeping mountain vistas, sheer canyon walls, sparkling lakes, fields of flowers, waterfalls and high desert plains (which are mostly free of human development) – will make any encounter truly priceless.

198

ESSENTIAL EXPERIENCES

✳ **Thrilling to each hairpin bend, deep tunnel and high bridge along the way.**

✳ Admiring the colonial ambience and Spanish architecture at the charming town of El Fuerte, which many use as either an end or start point for the journey.

✳ **Being unable to believe your eyes as you photograph endless dreamlike vistas, desert sunsets, and mystical cerulean skies.**

✳ Sucking in the brisk canyon air, as big an adrenaline hit as you're likely to find.

✳ **Getting to the end, only to ride all the way back and do it again.**

DISTANCE 407 MILES (655KM) | **COUNTRIES COVERED** MEXICO | **IDEAL TIME COMMITMENT** FIVE DAYS | **BEST TIME OF YEAR** LATE SEPTEMBER AND OCTOBER | **ESSENTIAL TIP** MAKE OVERNIGHT STOPS TO GET UP CLOSE TO THE CANYONS.

THE RARÁMURI

About 50,000 indigenous Rarámuri live in the Sierra Tarahumara's numerous canyons, including the Barranca del Cobre. You'll see mostly women dressed in colorful skirts and blouses, peddling beautiful handwoven baskets and carrying infants on their backs. 'Rarámuri' means 'those who run fast'. Their traditional hunting method is to chase and exhaust deer, driving them over cliffs to be impaled on wooden sticks placed at the bottom. Today, the Rarámuri run marathon footraces of at least 100 miles (160km) through the rough canyons, all the while kicking a small wooden ball ahead of them, and compete in ultra-distance races throughout the world.

■ THE JOURNEY TODAY

You arrive at the optimum time, when temperatures are not as hot at the bottom of the canyon or too cold at the top. You did your research – best to come just after the summer rains, late September and October, when vegetation is still green. You are on the train, heading inland to the east. You sit on the carriage's right side because that's where the best views are. Every so often you rise from your seat just to hang out in the vestibules between cars, where you enjoy the simple pleasure of the open windows and the cool, fresh mountain air whipping your face. Here, too, is your chance for unobstructed photos of the mighty landscape passing before your eyes. You thought the trip was all hype between Los Mochis and El Fuerte, when you passed through flat, gray farmland. 'That's it?' you thought, but you were impatient, and you knew it. Beyond El Fuerte, things got interesting quickly as the train clawed its way through fog-shrouded hills speckled with dark cacti pillars and you went snap-happy with your camera.

About three hours after leaving Los Mochis, you pass over the long Río Fuerte bridge and through the first of 87 tunnels. Along the way, you cut through small canyons and through three ascending loops at Témoris. 'That's La Pera,' you inform a fellow passenger, 'for its shape, like a pear.' The train hugs the sides of dramatic cliffs as it climbs higher and higher through the mountains of the Sierra Tarahumara. Finally, at Divisadero, you catch your first and only glimpse of the actual Barranca del Cobre. Everyone on board seems to exhale at the same time. Then that sound is replaced by the faintly surreal sound of a hundred camera shutters firing at once, like a flock of chirping mechanical birds.

ARMCHAIR

* ***Where the Air Is Clear*** (Carlos Fuentes) The first novel by Fuentes, one of the best-known Mexican writers, written in 1958 and one of his most highly regarded.

* ***Light Feet: A Rarámuri Tale*** (2008) Short film focusing on a Rarámuri boy who travels to the city after a parent dies.

* ***Pedro Páramo*** (Juan Rulfo) This 1955 short novel has been described as '*Wuthering Heights* set in Mexico and written by Kafka.'

* ***The Labyrinth of Solitude*** (Octavio Paz) Published in 1950, this collection of essays is an analysis of the Mexican character.

* ***Y Tu Mamá También*** (2001) Alfonso Cuarón's tale of two privileged teenagers from Mexico City embarking on a road trip is one of Mexico's highest-grossing films.

And then the train moves off again, circling back over itself in a complete loop inside the canyon at El Lazo before steaming onward into Creel and Chihuahua.

SHORTCUT

The best way to experience the Barranca del Cobre region is to make stops en route. Each stop will give you 24 hours before the train comes again: ample opportunity to get closer to those wonderful canyons. However, many people simply ride the train all the way through and then stop overnight before returning.

DETOUR

Cerocahui, a hub for local travelers, is a place where tourists are rarely found. Yet disembark here and you'll be rewarded by the sight of a tiny pueblo amid a verdant valley. Alongside Urique is where you'll first glimpse the Rarámuri, as well as Cerocahui's pretty yellow-domed church, San Francisco Javier de Cerocahui, dating from 1680. Today, the town is an *ejido* (communal landholding) devoted to forestry. There are a few good places to stay, a peaceful atmosphere and, best of all, proximity to the surrounding countryside, making it excellent for bird watching, hiking and horseback riding.

PETER VON FELBERT / LOOK-FOTO | GETTY IMAGES ©

OPENING SPREAD Heading east through the many crests and tunnels of the Copper Canyon by rail. **ABOVE** All aboard the Chihuahua Express. **BELOW** The vast Urique Canyon, one of 20 that make up the Copper Canyon trail.

THE SCHEDULE

The timetable is really very important on this trip. Well, not really. Both the *primera express* and *clase económica* trains run daily, but they tend to run late, although you will hear folk go on about 'normal' times as if they were the official word. You should listen to them: they're locals and they have the knowledge that can help you. Though the train can run on time, it has also been known to show up two hours earlier or later, so when all else fails, check with your hotel, at train stations, or with conductors.

SOUTH AMERICA

❋

1 HIKE THE INCA TRAIL TO MACHU PICCHU 2 CLIMB ARGENTINA'S MT ACONCAGUA

3 HAVE A GRAPE ESCAPE TO CHILE 4 CRUISE ARGENTINA'S PATAGONIAN HIGHWAY

5 ESCAPE TO ECUADOR'S CLOUD FOREST 6 EXPLORE COLOMBIA'S GHOST COAST

7 ICE TREK ARGENTINA'S MORENO GLACIER 8 HOT-AIR BALLOON OVER THE ATACAMA DESERT

9 DRIFT DOWN THE AMAZON RIVER 10 MOTORBIKE CHE GUEVARA'S DIARIES

11 GO CULTURE-CLUBBING IN PUNTA DEL ESTE 12 ENTER THE LOST WORLD OF MT RORAIMA

13 TREK CHILE'S TORRES DEL PAINE 14 KAYAK AND CRUISE ANTARCTICA

EXPLORE THE AMERICAS

HIKE THE INCA TRAIL TO MACHU PICCHU

THE INCA TRAIL IS A MYSTICAL AND UNFORGETTABLE EXPERIENCE. THINK VIEWS OF SNOWY MOUNTAIN PEAKS, DISTANT RIVERS AND RANGES, AND CLOUD FORESTS ACCENTED WITH ORCHIDS. THAT'S THE BACKDROP AS YOU WALK FROM ONE CLIFF-HUGGING PRE-COLUMBIAN RUIN TO THE NEXT.

It's the most famous trek in South America, and is hiked by thousands every year. Although the total distance is only about 26 miles (43km), it takes four days to navigate this ancient and narrow trail, laid by the Incas, from the Sacred Valley to Machu Picchu. It winds its way up and down and around the mountains, snaking over three high Andean passes en route. Although the journey alone is likely to inspire triumphant and poetic lifelong memories, the destination is equally magnificent.

Blessed with a spectacular location, the awe-inspiring ancient Inca city of Machu Picchu, which was hidden from Spanish conquistadores and remained virtually forgotten until the 20th century, is the best-known archaeological site on the continent. Apart from a couple of German adventurers in the 1860s, who apparently looted the site with the Peruvian government's permission, nobody except local Quechua people knew of Machu Picchu's existence until American historian Hiram Bingham was guided to it by locals in 1911. The Machu Picchu site was initially overgrown with thick vegetation, forcing Bingham's team to be content with roughly mapping the site.

He returned in 1912 and 1915 to carry out the difficult task of clearing the thick forest, when he also discovered some of the ruins on the so-called Inca Trail. Over the course of his various journeys, Bingham took thousands of artifacts back to the United States with him, which remains an international point of contention. Peruvian archaeologist Luis E Valcárcel undertook further studies in 1934, as did a Peruvian-American expedition under Paul Fejos in 1940–41. Although the Inca people laced hundreds of miles of similar trails throughout Andean Peru, the majesty of Machu Picchu, combined with the popularity of the trek to the old city, has resulted in this route being dubbed 'the Inca Trail'.

ESSENTIAL EXPERIENCES

* **Glancing over your shoulder at the icy Nevado Verónica at Wayllabamba.**

* Cresting Warmiwañusca pass at 13,780ft (4198m) above sea level, the highest point of the trek, with the Río Pacamayo (Sunrise River) snaking far below.

* **Descending from the ceremonial baths at Phuyupatamarka (Town above the Clouds), into dense and colorful cloud forests.**

* Winding through another stand of cliff-hanging cloud forest to reach Intipunku (Sun Gate), where you'll see the sunrise over Machu Picchu.

* **Walking in the footsteps of ancient Inca warriors and royalty through South America's greatest archaeological site.**

204

ORIGINS OF THE CITADEL

Despite scores of studies, knowledge of Machu Picchu remains sketchy. Some believe the citadel was founded in the waning years of the Incas as an attempt to preserve their culture or rekindle their predominance, while others think that it may have already become an uninhabited, forgotten city at the time of Spanish conquest. A more recent theory suggests that the site was a royal retreat or country palace abandoned at the time of the Spanish invasion. The site's director believes that it was an important city, a political, religious, and administrative center. Its location, and the fact that at least eight access routes have been discovered, suggests that it was a trade nexus between Amazonia and the highlands.

■ THE JOURNEY TODAY

After crossing the Río Urubamba at 7200ft (2195m), you'll climb gently alongside the river to the trail's first archaeological site, Llactapata (Town on Hillside), before heading south down a side valley to the hamlet of Wayllabamba (Grassy Plain), where you can look over your shoulder for views of the hulking, snowcapped, 18,860ft (5682m) Nevado Verónica. The trail crosses the Río Llullucha, and eventually emerges on the high, bare mountainside of Llulluchupampa where the flats are dotted with campsites. This is as far as you can reasonably expect to get on your first day.

From Llulluchupampa, it's a two- to three-hour ascent to the first pass of Warmiwañusca, which is also colorfully known as 'Dead Woman's Pass'. At 13,770ft (4197m) above sea level, it's the highest point of the trek. From here you can see the ruin of Runkurakay, a basket-shaped building, which you'll visit after a knee-jarring descent and a short climb. Above Runkurakay, the trail climbs past two small lakes to the top of the second pass at 12,960ft (3950m), which has views of the icy Cordillera Vilcabamba. The ecology falls under an Amazonian influence and your surroundings become lush as you descend to the ruin of Sayaqmarka (Dominant Town), perched on a small mountain spur.

After another river crossing you'll climb through magnificent cloud forest, and an Inca tunnel carved from the rock, to arrive at the third pass at almost 12,140ft (3700m), which has grand views of the Río Urubamba valley, and where some visitors take in a mind-blowing sunset and spend their final night.

Just below the pass is the stunning, well-named ruin of Phuyupatamarka (Town above the Clouds), with a series of ceremonial baths cascading with clear water. From Phuyupatamarka, the trail dives into the cloud forest below, following hundreds of Inca steps to Wiñay Wayna, and continuing through cliff-hanging cloud forest for another two hours to Intipunku (Sun Gate) – where it's traditional to enjoy your first glimpse of majestic Machu Picchu while waiting for the sun to rise over the surrounding mountains. The final triumphant descent takes less than an hour.

■ SHORTCUT

This 10-mile (16km) version of the Inca Trail gives an indication of what the longer trail is like. It's a real workout, and passes through some of the best scenery and most impressive terraced ruins. It begins with a steep three- or four-hour climb from km 104 to Wiñay Wayna, and continues another two hours on fairly flat terrain to Machu Picchu.

■ DETOUR

Consider a walk along any of the old Inca routes to Ollantaytambo through the dramatic Lares Valley. Starting at natural hot springs, wander through rural Andean villages, lesser known Inca archaeological sites, lush lagoons and river gorges. Finish off by taking the train from Ollantaytambo through to Aguas Calientes, the gateway to Machu Picchu. Although this trek is more cultural than technical, the scenery is breathtaking, and the highest mountain pass at 14,600ft (4450m) is certainly nothing to sneeze at.

207

ALLENG | SHUTTERSTOCK ©

OPENING SPREAD The awe-inspiring 15th-century Inca settlement, Machu Picchu. **ABOVE** A Quechua woman weaves alpaca wool. **LEFT** Stone terraces on the Inca Trail.

ARMCHAIR

✲ *Inca Land: Explorations in the Highlands of Peru* (Hiram Bingham) Bingham's 1922 account of his search for Vilcabamba, the Incas' last stronghold, which he thought he'd found at Machu Picchu.

✲ *The Royal Commentaries of the Incas* (Garcilaso de la Vega) The Inca empire's main expansion occurred in the 100 years prior to the arrival of the conquistadores in 1532. When the Spanish reached Cuzco, they chronicled Inca history as related by the Incas themselves. This, which is the most famous known account, was written by the son of an Inca princess and a Spanish military captain.

✲ *Porters of the Inca Trail* (2009) A documentary exploring the history and political struggle of the porters as well as cultural and traditional cornerstones of their Quechua heritage.

CLIMB ARGENTINA'S MT ACONCAGUA

QUITE SIMPLY, THIS IS THE HIGHEST HIKE IN THE WORLD. ARGENTINA'S 22,841FT (6962M) MOUNTAIN, LOFTIER THAN ANY SUMMIT OUTSIDE THE HIMALAYAS, IS IMMENSE BUT CONQUERABLE BY THOSE WITHOUT TECHNICAL CLIMBING SKILLS – IF YOU'RE UP FOR THE BREATHLESS BUT ULTIMATE CHALLENGE...

The Himalayas are greedy. Every 7000m-plus peak on the planet lies in this lofty range or in the neighboring Karakorams. Just. Aconcagua – at 6962m, the highest mountain outside Asia – comes tantalizingly close. (Indeed, the idea of erecting a 40m-high tower on the summit was once proposed.)

But Aconcagua (whose name is possibly derived from the Quechuan *ancho cahuac*, or 'white sentinel'), remains an intimidating prospect. Its air-depleting altitude, and the katabatic winds that lash and freeze the slopes, kept climbers from the top until 1897, when Swiss mountaineer Matthias Zurbriggen became the first to gaze down on all of the Americas. After a bit of trial and error, Zurbriggen ascended Aconcagua via the Horcones Valley. Today, most would-be summiteers follow his pioneering footsteps, along what has become known as the Normal Route. And several do indeed follow: approximately 3700 people a year attempt to ascend the mountain, which, despite its gargantuan proportions, is not considered a 'proper' climb but is essentially a really tough walk.

Unbelievably, Aconcagua requires no real technical skill. Both the Normal and slightly longer and less-used Vacas Valley routes can be attempted by trekkers – albeit physically and mentally super-fit ones. The final push may entail some crunching in crampons, but it's the extreme altitude, which makes every movement require momentous effort, that provides the biggest challenge.

There are prettier peaks. Much of the land here is bleak and dusty, the air is thin, those winds unremitting. But the prospect of such a trophy – the world's highest trekking peak! – is, for many, worth the cons. And if you do make it to the top (it's purported that only about 30% of hopefuls do), and when you're standing – or staggering – around the summit, looking across an ocean of other icy crests to the Pacific Ocean glittering in the distance, you'll feel on top of (most of) the world.

ESSENTIAL EXPERIENCES

✳ **Hiking from Confluencia camp and back, to acclimatize – and to glimpse Aconcagua's terrifying south face.**

✳ Staring out from Nido de Cóndores to the central valleys, endless mountains, and the twin peaks of Aconcagua.

✳ **Looking out for herds of wild guanacos on the Vacas Valley route.**

✳ Walking amid the mountain's *penitentes*, spikes of snow that are sculpted by the chill winds – like walking through oversized sharks' teeth.

✳ **Mastering La Canaleta, the punishing 984ft (300m) scree slope that must be faced at 21,325ft (6500m).**

✳ Standing atop the highest mountain outside the Himalayas, with views across glaciers and mountains to the Pacific Ocean beyond.

ELEVATION 22,481FT (6962M) | **LOCATION** MENDOZA PROVINCE, ARGENTINA | **IDEAL TIME COMMITMENT** THREE WEEKS
BEST TIME OF YEAR DECEMBER TO FEBRUARY | **ESSENTIAL TIP** ACCLIMATIZE, ACCLIMATIZE, ACCLIMATIZE.

MAN & MULE

Aconcagua's barren slopes are not conducive to wildlife – but one creature is found here in abundance. Hardy mules transport supplies up and down the mountain, capable of carrying 132lb (60kg) loads (and weary trekkers if necessary). Their *arrieros* (drivers) are an icon of rural Argentina, hardworking and loyal men who each handle three mules and guard them fiercely; learn a little Spanish and you'll have some interesting conversations. Every *arriero* carries a satchel containing his maté-making kit: a pouch of yerba maté tea leaves, a drinking vessel or gourd, and a *bombilla* (metal filter straw) through which to sip.

■ THE ADVENTURE UNFOLDS

Up. Down. Up again. Down again. Such is life on Aconcagua. Some record-seeking madman might have made the summit and back in a dumbfounding 20 hours but you'll be hiking on this Andean behemoth for almost 20 days. Acclimatization – trudging higher, sleeping lower – is essential if you're to reach the top. Even so, the escapade is perilously oxygen-parched from the start, with Confluencia, the very first camp, teetering at 11,122ft (3390m). At the medical center at Plaza de Mulas (13,943ft (4250m)), you've had your own oxygen levels tested – so far so good. You've researched the symptoms of acute mountain sickness: fatigue, headaches, disorientation. Fatigue seems inevitable, but you plan to climb slowly and eat like a mule to avoid the onset of the other symptoms. That way you have the best shot of making it to the top, wild weather willing.

You make friends fast on such a grueling shared mission. You've tried your pidgin Spanish on the muleteers and sipped their maté tea. You've embarked on day hikes with your trek-mates, to see pinnacles of ice and terrifying views of your distant goal. As the days pass, anticipation grows: now you just want to get there. Eventually you bed down in Camp Berlin, the Normal Route's final pause before the summit. It sits at 19,193ft (5850m), almost the height of Kilimanjaro. You try to sleep, praying it doesn't snow...

The next day's a blur. Setting off in the chill predawn, you huff and stumble up and up. On the callous scree of La Canaleta, two steps forward mean one step back. Your crampons scrape the ice; nausea scrapes your throat.

Finally, after 10 hours, you've reached the North Peak – Aconcagua's highest point. The understated cross that marks the spot is dressed up like Christmas, bedangled by the

ARMCHAIR

❋ ***Aconcagua: Summit of South America*** (Harry Kikstra) A practical guide to getting up the mountain, including planning tips and packing lists, historical background and route info.

❋ ***Altitude Illness: Prevention and Treatment*** (Stephen Bezruchka) Invaluable mountaineers' handbook, containing info on how to avoid AMS (acute mountain sickness) and how to spot the symptoms.

❋ ***Aconcagua: The Invention of Mountaineering on America's Highest Peak*** (Joy Logan) Easily readable examination of the social and cultural history of Aconcagua.

❋ ***Seven Years in Tibet*** (1997) Many of the mountain scenes in this Hollywood epic were filmed amid the peaks of Mendoza.

flags and bandanas of those who've been before. You add your own 'bauble' – proof, if only until the wind whisks it off into oblivion, that you mastered this mighty mountain.

■ MAKING IT HAPPEN

It's permissible to climb Aconcagua without a guide; you could just hire mules to carry your kit (or carry it yourself). However, you must be an experienced mountaineer to attempt a 22,481ft (6962m) peak alone. All climbers need a permit, available from the Aconcagua National Park Office in Mendoza. If you book an organized trek (either with a local company or back home), they will most likely arrange this, as well as the other logistics.

■ DETOUR

Raise a glass of rich red to your high-altitude achievements in Mendoza Province, Argentina's wine heartland, blessed with year-round sun thanks to the rain shadow provided by the mountain you've just climbed. Malbec is the grape of choice; pick up the Caminos del Vino maps (available from hotels and wine shops), which will help guide you down the area's winding, vine-flanked roads to bodegas offering tours, tastings, and boutique accommodations.

JASON MAEHL | SHUTTERSTOCK ©

OPENING SPREAD Two hikers begin to appreciate the full scale of Mt Aconcagua as it looms before them. **ABOVE** Further acclimatizing at camp 2, at a height of 18,209ft (5550m). **BELOW** Incredible views abound on the Aconcagua ascent.

MUMMIES ON THE MOUNTAIN

The first confirmed ascent of Aconcagua may have been in 1897, but the Inca at least part-scaled these mighty mountains much earlier, climbing them to make sacrifices to their gods back in the 15th and 16th centuries. In 1985, a well-preserved 500-year-old mummy was discovered at 17,060ft (5200m), on the southwest ridge of Cerro Pyramidal, one of Aconcagua's surrounding peaks. The mummy – a young boy, believed to be about seven years old – was wrapped in folds of cloth, the outer layer embroidered with yellow feathers. Buried with him were sandals, Inca statuettes, and some bags of cooked beans.

HAVE A GRAPE ESCAPE TO CHILE

YOU'VE HAD A NIP IN THE NAPA VALLEY AND YOU'VE IMBIBED IN BORDEAUX – BUT HAVE YOU EVER SIPPED SOME OF THE WORLD'S BEST RED WINES IN THE SHADOW OF THE ANDES?

'God was bringing the devil in his luggage.' So says Pablo, the tour guide at Viña Santa Cruz, as he strolls through the vines clinging to the rolling hills. He's referring to an old saying in Chile, used to describe how wine ended up in these parts. It was brought here by missionaries, Pablo says, to be used during mass as they sought to convert the locals. However, those locals showed just as much passion for the wine as they did the religion. And so here we are today, surrounded by acre after acre of grapes, with the Andes soaring high above on the horizon. Wine isn't the devil any more – instead it's a booming industry, and one Chileans are justifiably proud of.

This is the Colchagua Valley, one of Chile's premier wine-producing areas and a short drive south of Santiago. The area is famous for its cabernet sauvignon, which explains the fat bunches of ruby-red grapes hanging from the rows of vines that stretch as far as the eye can see. People come to Colchagua to try the wine – though it's mostly local Chilean tourists, as the area isn't widely visited by international travelers. But there are other reasons to come here. For example, how many vineyards have you been to that have both a DeLorean and a llama?

This is Viña Santa Cruz, home to 445 acres (180 hectares) of vines, and the aforementioned car and animal. The car – a replica of Marty McFly's time machine from the *Back to the Future* films – is in the display room and it's as popular with kids as the wine is with their parents. The llama is on top of a hill. When the tour of the winery concludes, Pablo points up to that summit. 'We've seen the heart of our wine,' he says. 'Now let's go and see its soul.' Up top are three pavilions, each dedicated to an ancient culture that left its mark on Chile: the Mapuche, the Aymara, and the Easter Islanders. It's a nice tribute to the land's former owners – the ones who were here before the devil arrived in God's luggage.

ESSENTIAL EXPERIENCES

❋ **Wandering through the Museo Colchagua and taking in thousands of years of ancient history.**

❋ Sampling wine, wine, and more wine in some of the region's 26 vineyards.

❋ **Trying the local Chilean cuisine at a restaurant in Santa Cruz, one of the area's more charming towns.**

❋ Riding the gondola at Viña Santa Cruz and walking through the pavilions dedicated to three of the area's ancient cultures.

❋ **Star-gazing at Viña Santa Cruz, or just marveling at the winery's meteorite collection.**

212

LOCATION COLCHAGUA VALLEY, CHILE | **BEST TIME OF YEAR** HARVEST (MID-MARCH UNTIL THE END OF APRIL); WINERIES ARE OPEN YEAR-ROUND | **IDEAL TIME COMMITMENT** THREE DAYS | **ESSENTIAL TIP** ORGANIZE A WAY BACK TO YOUR HOTEL BEFORE GOING TO THE WINERY: TAXIS ARE SCARCE IN SANTA CRUZ | **PACK** A JUMPER; TEMPERATURES DROP QUICKLY AT NIGHT.

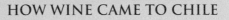

HOW WINE CAME TO CHILE

Blame the missionaries. When Spanish conquistadores decided to have their way with Chile, it opened the door for missionaries to begin preaching the good word. In order to conduct Mass, the missionaries needed wine, which prompted Diego García de Cáceres to plant the first vines in Santiago in 1554. By the 1800s the vineyards had grown from supplying merely the local Sunday Mass to exporting their product to Europe, and production peaked just before WWII. These days the industry has been scaled back slightly, but the country is still well known for its top-quality cabernet sauvignons.

PISCO INFERNO

While Chile is known around the world for its wine, local residents are even more passionate about another grape-based tipple: *pisco*. Produced in the vine-growing regions north of Santiago, pisco is a type of grape-based brandy whose native origins are fiercely fought over by Chile and neighboring Peru. Regardless of where it started, Chileans consume plenty of pisco, particularly in the famous cocktail, the pisco sour – a mix of pisco, egg whites, sugar syrup, lime juice, and bitters. If you want to try the very best, keep your eye out for Gran Pisco, the most sought after (and most alcoholic) version of the spirit.

■ THE PERFECT GETAWAY

Wine is undoubtedly the winner here. From the cabernet sauvignons to carménères, merlots and syrahs, there's something to suit almost every taste in reds. It's worth planning to visit at least four or five wineries during a trip to the Colchagua Valley, all of which can be reached from a base in the Spanish colonial town of Santa Cruz. The Viña Santa Cruz winery is an undoubted attraction, with its gondola, cultural exhibits, and observatory that houses the largest private meteorite collection in Latin America.

For pure liquid enjoyment, however, cast your net further afield. Most wineries in Colchagua are family-owned, including Viu Manent and Neyen de Apalta, and Viña Montes is a definite highlight of the area. Once the tasting is over, or maybe before it begins, there's plenty to keep visitors occupied in the town of Santa Cruz. The city's main square is the perfect spot to wander around for an hour or so, and the streets are filled with traveler-friendly shops.

Perhaps the town's centerpiece is Museo Colchagua, named the best private collection in South America. The museum houses a dazzling array of artifacts, from million-year-old fossils, Incan pottery, and Spanish colonial carriages, to steam locomotives and a curious collection of Nazi memorabilia. One section is dedicated to the 2010 Chilean mining disaster (when 33 miners were trapped underground for 69 days), with a recreation of events housed in a full-scale model of the chamber in which the men were trapped.

You could easily spend a whole day here taking it all in. Except, of course, you'd be missing out on all that wine tasting.

■ PLAN IT

It's possible to visit Colchagua Valley as a day trip from Santiago, and plenty of companies offer that service. A more enjoyable way to see the valley would be an overnight tour, giving you the chance to sample some of the region's cuisine over dinner. Those looking for a more independent experience can take a bus from Santiago down to Santa Cruz and hire a car to make their own way through the vineyards. An organized tour, however, will allow you to enjoy more of the product on offer.

■ DETOUR

There's no need to go all the way to the source to sample Chilean wines – Santiago boasts an appealing array of restaurants and wine bars that stock the local drop. The suburb of Bellavista, the city's creative hub, is home to its best dining. Try Restaurante La Pescadería, a seafood joint with a long wine list. In Santiago's old center, Bocanáriz has almost 400 Chilean wines on offer, including 36 by the glass. Over in upmarket Providencia, Baco's modern cuisine is a local favorite.

215

OPENING SPREAD An organic vineyard in Chile's Maipo Valley. **ABOVE (L)** Grapes ready for the picking to make another Chilean red. **ABOVE (R)** Gondolas over San Cristóbal hill give great views of Santiago. **LEFT** Barrels of Casillero del Diablo line the cellars of Concha y Toro.

ARMCHAIR

❋ **By Night in Chile** (Roberto Bolaño) A dying priest's rantings form a chilling indictment of Chile's brutal Pinochet regime in this novel by one of the country's foremost writers.

❋ **After-Dinner Declarations** (Nicanor Parra) Chileans are famously passionate about poetry, and Parra is one of the country's darlings.

❋ **Deep Down Dark** (Héctor Tobar) Compiled from interviews with the 33 men themselves, this tells the story of how the miners of Copiapó survived 69 days trapped underground.

❋ **La Buena Vida** (The Good Life; 2008) Chilean filmmaker Andrés Wood's story of four characters struggling through their lives in Santiago.

❋ **Se Arrienda** (For Rent; 2005) Alberto Fuguet's acclaimed movie follows the life of a fictional composer in Santiago.

CRUISE ARGENTINA'S PATAGONIAN HIGHWAY

IF YOU WANT TO SEE A SIDE TO ARGENTINA THAT MOST TRAVELERS NEVER DO, THE PATAGONIAN HIGHWAY IS A MUST. IT TRAVELS ALMOST THE LENGTH OF THE LAND AND THROUGH SOME OF ARGENTINA'S MOST REMOTE REGIONS.

Known officially as Ruta Nacional 40 (RN 40), the Patagonian Highway travels nearly the length of Argentina, a distance of more than 3000 miles (5000km). It begins in the north of the country, just south of the Bolivian border, and continues nearly to Tierra del Fuego in the south. To undertake the full trip requires a combination of vehicles, as much of the road is unpaved; on some stretches you will need a 4WD. Of course, walking is an option for part of the way, in which case good walking shoes, plenty of food and water, and an appetite for adventure are essential.

Save for the travel hubs of El Calafate and El Chaltén, rutted RN 40 is every bit a no-man's-land. It parallels the backbone of the Andes, where ñandú birds flit through sagebrush, trucks whip up huge storms of whirling dust, and gas stations dominate the horizon like oases. Nonetheless, the paving of RN 40 is underway, with long stretches of the road smooth enough for cycling. If you want to experience this lonely highway at its most evocative, get in quick before the renovations are complete. Its raw state is, after all, the mythical road to nowhere that has stirred the loins of many, including the writer Bruce Chatwin and outlaw Butch Cassidy.

The paving of RN 40 will clearly end this identity, which has defined a generation. When the reconstruction is finished, chances are most motorists will whiz from sight to sight, bypassing the quirky, unassuming settlements that provide so much joy for connoisseurs of the trip. For the moment, public transport stays limited to a few summer-only tourist shuttle services, and driving requires both preparation and patience.

ESSENTIAL EXPERIENCES

✳ **Becoming completely mesmerized by the magical, blue-hued Moreno Glacier, and entranced by icebergs crumbling with an almighty boom.**

✳ Stepping back in time to explore the wonderful, eternal millennial forest in the Parque Nacional Los Alerces.

✳ **Accepting the challenge and trekking the exciting Fitz Roy range near El Chaltén.**

✳ Communing with nature and enjoying the sight of southern right whales in the waters of Reserva Faunistica Península Valdés.

✳ **Pretending that you're a gaucho by riding the wide-open range and feasting on some firepit-roasted lamb at an *estancia* (ranch).**

DISTANCE 3000 MILES (5000KM) | **COUNTRIES COVERED** ARGENTINA | **IDEAL TIME COMMITMENT** ONE TO TWO MONTHS **BEST TIME OF YEAR** DECEMBER TO MARCH | **ESSENTIAL TIP** STOP TO HELP ANYONE STRANDED ON THE SIDE OF THE ROAD; THERE'S NO ROADSIDE ASSISTANCE AND CELL PHONES DON'T WORK IN THE AREA.

216

THE WELSH

Welsh settlers first came to Patagonia in 1865, though they quickly found themselves out of their depth. Few had farmed before and the arid steppe was a completely alien contrast to verdant Wales. After nearly starving, they survived with the help of the native Tehuelche, coming to occupy the entire lower Chubut valley and founding the towns of Rawson, Trelew, Puerto Madryn, and Gaiman. Today, around 20% of Chubut's inhabitants have Welsh blood and Welsh culture has made a revival, with yearly British Council appointments of Welsh teachers and exchanges for Patagonian students.

THE MORENO GLACIER

The Moreno Glacier (Glaciar Perito Moreno), the amazing centerpiece of the southern sector of Patagonia's Parque Nacional Los Glaciares, is a stunning natural wonder. It measures 18 miles (30km) long, 3 miles (5km) wide, and 195ft (60m) high, and is exceptional for its constant advance, creeping forward up to 6ft (2m) daily and causing icebergs the size of buildings to calve from its face. Watching it is thrilling, an auditory and visual adventure as the huge icebergs collapse into the Canal de los Tempanos (Iceberg Channel) and the glacier's appearance changes as shadows progress during the day.

■ THE JOURNEY TODAY

You've been on the road for a week and everything about the trip has been monumental, including the repairs. Gravel punctured your gas tank a while back, and you dodged flying rocks and sheep that think they own the road. You've negotiated blind curves on windy days when it seemed your car would fly right off the road, and all the while you've been struggling to process the sheer amount and variety of experiences that have come your way. You've seen massive frontier horizons dwarfing the gauchos that ride their horses on the steppe, and you've imbibed the monumental silence that accompanies such a space – a wild, barren emptiness as thrilling and as awesome as the craggy peaks and unspoiled rivers.

Now you've arrived in Patagonia itself, this unusual land. The map tells you it's a very large place and you've seen that for yourself. It's almost a country within a country with its oil boomtowns, ancient petrified forests, spectacular Península Valdés, and splendidly isolated Welsh settlements. You've heard about the trendy Patagonia, too: the tourist hubs with their designer shops, which seem worlds apart from the RN 40.

But it's been hours since the last town. You've been driving forever. The weather is cunning and the gravel dastardly. You're not in a hurry because the conditions won't allow you to be. The road seems to go on forever and your car is rattling, as are your teeth, as you trundle along this bumpy stretch. But then magic strikes: the view ahead suddenly cracks apart with brilliance and radiance as glacial peaks and gem-colored lakes make their presence felt with preternatural charm. And then it hits you, like a flying rock from the side of the road. This is why you came.

■ SHORTCUT

The Patagonian stretch of the RN 40 provides a potted summary of everything that makes the journey great. Through inland Patagonia, highlights include the Perito Moreno and Los Glaciares National Parks, the rock art of Cueva de las Manos, and remote ranches. From Esquel, the road continues paved until south of Gobernador Costa, where it turns to gravel. From there on it's mostly gravel, with some paved sections near population centers.

■ DETOUR

On the eastern seaboard, take the RN 3 south to Patagonia's famous Welsh settlements. Gaiman is a favorite, a quintessential Welsh river-valley village... in Argentina. A third of its residents claim Welsh ancestry and teahouses are popular for afternoon fare of cream pie, teacakes, fruit cake, and pots of black tea. Dolavon, 12 miles (19km) west of Gaiman, is a historic Welsh agricultural town, and less touristy than its neighbor. Its pastoral appeal derives from the waterwheels lining the irrigation canal and a historic center full of brick buildings.

219

G_OWIMAGES | GETTY IMAGES ©

PHILIP LEE HARVEY | LONELY PLANET ©

OPENING SPREAD The road stretches toward the tapered peaks of Mt Fitzroy and Cerro Torre. **ABOVE (L)** Prehistoric art at Cueva de las Manos. **ABOVE (R)** Patagonian gauchos ride out across the plains. **LEFT** The guanaco is native to – and plentiful in – the region.

ARMCHAIR

❋ **In Patagonia** (Bruce Chatwin) This classic is something of a tourist bible in this part of the world. It's a book of errant wanderings and musings on everything from hiking from Estancia Harberton to Viamonte, taking tea in Gaiman, and visiting the sacred mylodon cave.

❋ **The Old Patagonian Express** (Paul Theroux) This is the author's acclaimed account of his journey from Massachusetts,

across North America by train, through to Mexico, and into South America and the remote Andes.

❋ **La Historia Oficial** (The Official Story; 1985) Luis Puenzo's film is about a privileged couple who gradually realize that their adopted child was born to a victim of Argentina's 'Dirty War'.

❋ **Nueve Reinas** (Nine Queens; 2000) Fabián Bielinsky's film about a chance meeting between two criminals won numerous awards.

ESCAPE TO ECUADOR'S CLOUD FOREST

SOAR ABOVE QUITO TO CHECK OUT THE PLANET'S GREATEST CONCENTRATION OF ENDEMIC BIRDLIFE WHILE BOOKED INTO ECUADOR'S MOST LUXURIANT ECO-EXPERIENCE: THE GROUND-BREAKING, CLOUD-TOPPING MASHPI LODGE, SITTING SERENELY IN ITS OWN BIODIVERSITY RESERVE.

When you wake up that first steamy morning and look out the window – unavoidable given that your room's walls are floor-to-ceiling glass – what Mashpi Lodge is about sinks in, along, most likely, with the sun shafting through the cloud, creating an ethereal effect as if you're still floating through a dream. Sitting amid a 3200-acre (1295-hectare) tract of high-altitude forest, the lodge has been designed like a capsule, allowing you to feast your gaze on as much greenery as possible without being troubled by tiresome things such as creepy-crawlies (for better or worse, part of the package when you're sampling one of the world's most biodiverse locales).

And you have to rub your eyes more than once. How can such a remote refuge be three hours' drive from the capital? How can you be crashing in a wilderness lodge where 300-plus (and counting) bird species reside within a hummingbird's hoot yet have access to every conceivable creature comfort? How can this huge reserve, replete with birds found nowhere else, be just for the private viewing of you, your fellow guests, and a few dozen staff?

Good questions indeed. When Mashpi's creator, former Quito mayor Roque Sevilla, dreamed of establishing this paradise, he wanted to forge a reserve he could protect with his own principles yet share with nature lovers from around the globe, in a place that would stay at the summit of the ecolodge elect year upon year. Mashpi certainly has a rather remarkable location. Crowning the cusp of a cloud-forest ridge, it offers absolute arboreal immersion but oozes vistas, too – because of its design (all that glass) you can't look anywhere without imbibing them. Whether you're being spoiled in the spa, gorging in the restaurant, or – best of all – out exploring on a forest foray, a cacophony of nature is exploding before your eyes. Mashpi is luxury, sure, but it's also a classroom in the clouds.

220

ESSENTIAL EXPERIENCES

✱ **Relaxing in the hot tub while gazing out at panoramic jungle vistas.**

✱ Hearing the round-the-clock chatter of thousands of insects, birds, and large mammals – without even having to leave your room.

✱ **Whooshing across a forest gorge on the Mashpi sky bike, an original way to explore the canopy.**

✱ Admiring the spectacular flapping hues on display during a night-time butterfly walk and witnessing how the forest transforms after dark.

✱ **Chilling out in a waterfall plunge pool after a sticky day bird-spotting.**

✱ Gliding through and above the cloud-forest canopy on the 1.2-mile (2km) gondola system.

LOCATION PICHINCHA PROVINCE, ECUADOR | BEST TIME OF YEAR JULY TO SEPTEMBER | IDEAL TIME COMMITMENT THREE DAYS | ESSENTIAL TIP BRING A TOP-NOTCH CAMERA AND BINOCULARS TO TRACK WILDLIFE | PACK BINOCULARS, CAMERA, INSECT REPELLENT, FLASHLIGHT, SWIMWEAR, SUNGLASSES, LONG-SLEEVED SHIRT, AND A WATERPROOF JACKET.

GREEN TO THE GILLS

Mashpi Lodge helped to secure protected status for a far-larger slice of forest (a further 15,000-plus acres) around its own reserve: one of many pioneering projects that's been implemented to preserve this biome. Staying here, you're savoring and saving a place that would have been left to loggers and gold prospectors had Sevilla and co not intervened. Then there's the team of resident biologists, conducting critical ongoing research into wildlife hereabouts. The building itself got transported here mainly by hand to minimize pollution. And there's the little things: locally made furniture, subdued LED lighting to avoid enticing insects, and a work commitment with local communities to supply produce and have a staff that's 80% comprised of villagers from the vicinity.

■ THE PERFECT GETAWAY

Appetite for adventure whetted? Then Mashpi has achieved something: inspiring you to sally forth to see, to feel, and to think about the forest. However, staying here comes with responsibilities: you will need to blend into your environment to minimize disturbance to wildlife, much like the lodge building does.

Mashpi's most common package is the three-day/two-night stay (you can linger longer), so time-planning is of paramount importance. Some people favor a lodge-based break, and why not? The 22 rooms and suites are large and light, and the hot tub has panoramic views. The restaurant (all meals are included), bubbling with Ecuadorian coastal-mountain fusion cuisine, has two floors and views as alluring as the dining and Ecuadorian chocolate tastings. But would you waive the 1.2-mile (2km) canopy gondola ride? Glide up into the dense forest and down again, gawking at the birdlife and the preposterously varied plants. Or amble back on one of the hiking trails where, masterminded by naturalist guides, you'll likely garner your most memorable wildlife sightings. Hikes aren't just dense foliage and fleeting glimpses of fauna. They take in *leks* (locales where birds, such as the vibrant red Andean cocks-of-the-rock, gather to mate); they wind to viewpoints, where the reserve's 22 hummingbird species can be observed; and they lead to waterfalls, in which to cool off after the day's action.

The highlight? A stay here is a vault into the unknown. New species are constantly discovered, and just when you set your sights on the birds you could get sidetracked by night-time treks and butterfly flocks fanning out in luminous hues, or the nocturnal rustle of a puma or *tigrillo* (mini-tiger).

■ PLAN IT

Quito's Mariscal Sucre International Airport has direct flights to Central America, North America, Europe, and other South American transit hubs such as Lima and Bogota. Arrange with the lodge in advance which Quito hotel you want to be picked up from. Pick-up from other points in Ecuador needs to be arranged several weeks prior. Book well in advance, too: Mashpi is designed to get guests up close and personal to the forest, so it doesn't have that many rooms.

■ DETOUR

More jungle? Ecuador can slake your appetite. Its forested wildernesses are all the more interesting for being so accessible. Off the Quito–Mashpi road there's a bunch of them: such as the Pululahua Geobotanical Reserve, which features a cloud forest with a volcano (it last erupted 2500 years ago, but the soil's resultantly rich with endemic plants), and the Mindo-Nambillo Forest Reserve, another cloud-forest birding mecca fanning out from the tiny town of Mindo.

223

PHILIP LEE HARVEY | LONELY PLANET ©

MASHPI LODGE ©

OPENING SPREAD The rusty tipped page butterfly forms part of the forest's rich biodiversity. **ABOVE (L)** Clouds float about the canopy. **ABOVE (R)** Each of the bedrooms at Mashpi Lodge has floor-to-ceiling windows. **LEFT** The surrounding jungle offers a cacophony of nature.

ARMCHAIR

❋ ***The Birds of Ecuador*** (Robert S Ridgely and Paul J Greenfield) This bird-watcher's bible covers the feathered members of the entire country in two outstanding volumes.

❋ ***Cumandá*** (Juan León Mera) Considered to be the first novel (1879) by an Ecuadorian writer, this is a tragic tale of love set in Ecuador's steamy jungle.

❋ ***A la Costa*** (To the Coast; Luis A Martinez) Another seminal Ecuadorian work: the first to deal literarily with Ecuador's two regions of *selva* (forest) and *costa* (coast) and the protagonist's journey between the two to find meaning in life.

❋ ***El Ultimo Rio*** (Pastrana's Last River; Nelson Estupiñan Bass) About the only work translated into English by one of the most important exponents of Afro-Latino writing.

EXPLORE COLOMBIA'S GHOST COAST

ONCE THE SOLE DOMAIN OF ESCAPED SLAVES AND DRUG RUNNERS, COLOMBIA'S LUSH PACIFIC COAST IS BECOMING A HAVEN FOR INTREPID BEACH LOVERS, SURFERS, WHALE-WATCHERS, AND ANYONE WITH A DESIRE TO GET FAR, FAR AWAY FROM IT ALL.

224

Nestor Tello is bucking waves like an aquatic rodeo cowboy. The local guide is standing on the bow of the *panga*, casually holding on to the bow line, trusting his compadre, Pozo Briceño, not to flip him out of the boat as Briceño guns the double outboards in the back. The two men, employees of El Cantil, a dreamy seven-casita ecolodge sitting on a half-moon bay on Colombia's Pacific coast, have spotted a giant humpback whale. But out here, a mile off the coast, where sunlight shimmers on steely water, every giant wave looks like a whale. This particular crest, however, gracefully arcs its massive body 15ft (4.5m) out of the sea, then thwaps its tail on the water, showering its surrounds in a frothy spray before it disappears.

There are many elusive creatures along this 62-mile (100km) coastline, which runs south from Ensenada de Utría National Park to Cabo Corrientes. The steamy wetness from rivers, volcanic springs, mountain rain, and sea infuses the humid air, creating a jungle so thick with coconut palms, starfruit, and trees such as La Palma Que Camina ('the palm that walks'), that you can almost see it breathe.

Hiding in the foliage are thousands of species, including an indigenous bird colloquially known as the Baja Tomo. It's so evasive that even the locals have never set eyes on one. The same goes for the drug runners who ply this empty stretch of coastline, transporting their wares north – they exist, but are practically invisible. And they prefer to keep it that way. The legend of their presence has been enough to keep this tangled coast of coconut palms (up to 69ft or 21m tall) and 3-mile (5km) volcanic black-sand beaches almost completely unexplored. But that's changing quickly. Urban Colombians and expat gringos alike – from surfing aid-workers to visiting university professors and mining executives – pilgrimage to El Cantil to play in their own private Eden. It's high time to join them.

ESSENTIAL EXPERIENCES

❋ **Renting a stand-up paddleboard and syncing up with the rolling Pacific at the half-moon bay in front of El Cantil.**

❋ Hiking 3 miles (5km) south on the sand to the village of Termales to meet the locals and soak in their jungle hot springs.

❋ **Surfing famous Pacific breaks such as Pico de Loro, Pela-Pela, and El Chorro with Guillermo Gomez, the owner-surfer of El Cantil.**

❋ Photographing arcing humpback whales from a *panga* in the Pacific.

❋ **Flopping in your hand-woven hammock to read *One Hundred Years of Solitude* and let the day fly by.**

❋ Eating pastries topped with *miel de panela*, a sweet syrup derived from sugarcane juice.

LOCATION EL CANTIL ECOLODGE, COLOMBIA | **BEST TIME OF YEAR** SUMMER MONTHS (JANUARY, FEBRUARY, MARCH) AND AUGUST **IDEAL TIME COMMITMENT** THREE NIGHTS, FOUR DAYS | **ESSENTIAL TIP** EL CANTIL IS OFF THE GRID; THERE'S LIMITED CELL PHONE SERVICE BUT DON'T EXPECT WI-FI | **PACK** SWIMSUIT, LIGHTWEIGHT RAIN JACKET AND MOSQUITO REPELLENT.

WET & WILD

The Chocó-Darien Rainforest, where El Cantil
Ecolodge sits, stretches from Panama, in the
north, down the Pacific coast of Colombia and
into Ecuador. It covers 72,394 sq miles (187,500
sq km) and has the highest volume of rainfall on
Earth. Some areas of this region, thankfully not
where El Cantil is located, receive as much as
43ft (13m) of rainfall per year. The Chocó-Darien
has 8000 plant species, 97 reptile species, 127
amphibian species, roughly 600 bird species,
and some of the highest numbers of endemic
plants in South America. Roaming the jungle
are jaguars, ocelots, giant anteaters, tapirs, and
cotton-top tamarins, one of the most endangered
primates in Colombia. You'll know one when you
see it: they have a crown of white fur pouffing
from the top of their heads.

LARGER THAN LIFE

Officially the 'The City of Eternal Spring', Medellín is unofficially 'The City of Sensual People' – allegedly home to the most beautiful women on Earth and also the birthplace of Fernando Botero, the iconic Colombian sculptor and painter of wide-girthed, well-endowed humans. 'I fatten my people to give them sensuality,' Botero has said. See his curvy bronze creations at the Plaza Botero, a busy, downtown square that fronts the Museo de Antioquia, a light-filled art-deco building that holds Botero's most famous paintings, such as *La Casa de Amanda Ramirez*, in which a large man holds a fleshy naked woman on his shoulders as a couple make love on a bed behind them.

■ THE PERFECT GETAWAY

Backed by roadless jungle and facing a bay ringed by a black-sand beach, El Cantil Ecolodge is a far-out oasis, built by Guillermo 'Memo' Gomez and his family in the 1990s. At El Cantil, life beats at a barely perceptible pulse. The lodge's seven small *palafitos* – wood-framed, one-bedroom casitas with oil lamps, open-air windows, a bathroom, and a deck strung with two hammocks – lead to El Cantil's open-air restaurant. Sound idyllic? It is.

The restaurant, which sits high in the canopy and has views of the Pacific, is where local women (who walk about 3 miles every morning from the village of Termales) work their magic, producing family-style Chocoan meals like the *plato tipico*: fish, coconut rice, fried plantains, and fruit. They also serve frosty Aguila beers. It's easy to let lunch roll through to dinner and sit in the high breeze listening to the cacophony of crashing waves and squawking toucans, but save the second beer and the reverie for later. There's way too much to explore.

Surfers should enlist Memo for a dawn expedition, which requires a jungle hike or a boat ride, to one of the local breaks such as La Cascada del Amor. Or take a whale-watching ride in the lodge's *panga*: from July to September humpback whales, sometimes six at a time, rise out of the water. To meet the locals, walk to the village of Termales. The fishing community of a few hundred people, with its sand lanes and gardens sprouting oregano, chili, and onion, have capitalised on its hottest asset – a sulfuric hot spring in its backyard jungle – by building a spa, complete with pebbled tubs and mud baths. Back at El Cantil, there's only time for a nap in the hammock before dinner and that second Aguila.

■ PLAN IT

There are direct flights to Medellín from some US cities, including New York (five hours). El Cantil is 120 miles (193km) from Medellín as the crow flies, but it requires an hour-long flight from Medellín's Enrique Olaya Herrera Airport on Satena Airlines to Nuquí. Someone from the lodge will be waiting to transfer you 40 minutes south by boat. All activities can be arranged at the lodge for an additional fee.

■ DETOUR

For a Caribbean equivalent, try Ecohabs, 22 miles (35km) north of the city of Santa Marta in Tayrona National Park. Its breezy, thatch-roofed cabanas sit on a cliff overlooking Canaveral Beach. The 58-sq-mile (150-sq-km) park rises from the sea to 2953ft (900m) peaks in the Sierra Nevada de Santa Marta. It's home to 300 species of bird; ruins from the Tayrona tribe, here long before the Spaniards came; and beaches lined with coconut palms. Hike stone-paved trails to indigenous settlements or take a 15-minute walk to Playa Grande, a white-sand beach. (Surfers: beware the fierce riptides.)

227

KRIS DAVIDSON | LONELY PLANET ©

KRIS DAVIDSON | LONELY PLANET ©

OPENING SPREAD Secluded Puspanita Beach in Tayrona National Park. **ABOVE (L)** Wax palm trees line the hills inland. **ABOVE (R)** Take your pick from hammock or bed in a thatched-roof cabana at Ecohabs. **LEFT** Fernando Botero's curvaceous statues dot Medellín's Plaza Botero.

ARMCHAIR

✳ **One Hundred Years of Solitude** (Gabriel García Márquez) Get lost in the creative genius of Colombia's Nobel Prize–winning novelist.

✳ **Love in the Time of Cholera** (Gabriel García Márquez) Follow the lifelong love affair between Florentino Ariza and Fermina Daza to its fitting conclusion.

✳ **Killing Pablo** (Mark Bowden) Gripping read about capturing and killing the world's most notorious drug lord.

✳ **Tropical Nature** (Adrian Forsyth and Ken Miyata) Fascinating primer on the ecosystems of Central and South America.

✳ **Even Silence Has An End** (Ingrid Betancourt) Frightening memoir by former Colombian presidential candidate about her six-year captivity by the FARC in the Amazon jungle.

✳ **Romancing the Stone** (1984) An entertaining romp through the Colombian jungle in search of buried treasure.

ICE TREK ARGENTINA'S MORENO GLACIER

DON'T JUST OGLE THE WORLD'S MOST FAMOUS GLACIER – STRAP ON SOME CRAMPONS AND WALK ATOP IT. SO-CALLED 'MINI TREKS' WILL HAVE YOU CRUNCHING ACROSS THE ICE, DISCOVERING A WORLD OF SERACS, CREVASSES AND SINKHOLES.

Spilling down from the Chilean border on Cerro Pietrobelli, in the chilly heights of the Patagonian Andes, Perito Moreno Glacier is a pin-up of world ice. In tourism terms, it is a phenomenon, every summer's day drawing thousands of people who arrive from the nearby gateway town of El Calafate. Most of them simply wander around the maze of walkways and viewing platforms on Peninsula Magallanes, watching and hoping for calving ice, but a few of the more adventurous types among them boat across to Lago Argentino's opposite shore to explore the glacier at much closer quarters.

Among the rock rubble at the edge of the glacier you'll be equipped with crampons – a set of spikes that are fitted to your shoes to give you grip and traction while hiking on the ice. If you have never used crampons before, this is the perfect adventure to trial them, as treks here follow smooth and safe lines across the ice. At this level, it's as simple as remembering to walk with your legs slightly further apart than normal to avoid catching a spike in your trousers or leg.

Once crampons are fitted, trekkers spend about 90 minutes on the ice, exploring just a tiny sliver of this remarkable glacier. Around 19 miles (30km) in length and up to 2300ft (700m) deep, Moreno advances at an average of about 6.5ft (2m) per day at its center, pushing inexorably forward, issuing thunderous booms as ice topples from its snout into Lago Argentino seemingly every few minutes.

The trek across the ice provides a showcase of glacial features as you wander past crevasses, seracs, and sinkholes, with views back over the glacier to the grey surface of Lago Argentino. At trek's end you'll even get to taste the glacier, with a final stop at a makeshift bar for a gut-warming whiskey on ice… ice that's been chipped straight from Moreno Glacier.

ESSENTIAL EXPERIENCES

* **Watching seracs crash and splash down from the glacier into Lago Argentino.**
* Peering into the depths of a sinkhole as you wonder just how deep this glacier really is.
* **Standing in a shower of ice as the guide ahead of you cuts steps into the glacier with his ice axe.**
* Toasting your glacial prowess with a whiskey and alfajores biscuit at trek's end.

LOCATION PERITO MORENO GLACIER, LOS GLACIARES NATIONAL PARK, ARGENTINA | **IDEAL TIME COMMITMENT** ONE DAY
BEST TIME OF YEAR NOVEMBER TO MARCH | **ESSENTIAL TIP** WEAR BOOTS WITH RIGID SOLES, AS THESE FIT BEST INTO CRAMPONS.

GLACIARIUM

The Argentinian town of El Calafate thrives on glacier tourism, with buses radiating out each morning to the various glaciers that surround it. In 2011, El Calafate took the icy relationship another step, with the opening of the Glaciarium museum on the outskirts of town. Featuring displays about glaciation and glaciers around the world, the well-designed museum places particular focus on the many glaciers of Patagonia and nearby Los Glaciares National Park. When you're done browsing the displays, head downstairs to the Glacio Bar, with its chairs, tables, and bar carved from a Moreno Glacier iceberg, for a drink in subzero temperatures.

■ THE ADVENTURE UNFOLDS

At Bajo de las Sombras on Lago Argentino you board the *Perito Moreno*, the boat threading between icebergs as it sails across the lake. As you climb out onto the rocky shores, there's an explosion that you seem almost to feel rather than hear. A serac has calved from the front of the glacier, creating a mighty splash like fireworks.

A short walk through the forest and along the pebbly beaches brings you to the front edge of the glacier. Here, you're fitted with your crampons, and you waddle out like a duck toward the ice. At first you wonder how you're going to walk on something as slippery as ice, but immediately you feel the bite of the crampons into the glacier. It's as though you've been velcroed to the thing.

In a line of trekkers you snake across the glacier, climbing slowly higher. What strikes you most is the color. It doesn't have the transparency of water or other ice. Instead, it's blue, having been so tightly compressed that only the blue photons of light penetrate to its depths. You look up at the mountains around you. A condor circles a summit, and the nearest rock face is scarred by the movement of the glacier millennia ago. You are standing atop a natural powerhouse – a bit of ice so strong and relentless it has all but shaped this mountainous land – yet it seems so peaceful.

As you become more confident on your crampons, you also grow bolder. You lean into a sinkhole, a guide anchoring you by the arm as you watch meltwater pour deep into the hole, disappearing into a blue abyss. You have no wish to follow it. This hole looks as if it goes on forever, and yet you know you can only see a part of it. You step back and feel your nerves resettle, though you could still do with that whiskey you've been promised.

■ MAKING IT HAPPEN

Mini treks on Moreno Glacier are operated exclusively by Hielo y Aventura. The company – which also runs the boat transfers – operates a bus services to the glacier from El Calafate, about 50 miles (80km) away. El Calafate has flights to and from Buenos Aires.

■ AN ALTERNATIVE CHALLENGE

If spending 90 minutes out on the ice in the smooth, ironed-out stuff has simply whetted your appetite for a more challenging glacier experience, Hielo y Aventura also has a Big Ice adventure, which involves spending four hours on the glacier. This trip accesses more remote and wilder sections of the enormous Moreno Glacier. After hiking along the lateral moraine for about 90 minutes, the group are led out onto the expanse of undulating ice. It's a surreal feeling being out there, surrounded by white statues and ice caves, with electric blue light shining through their ephemeral flanks. It's like being a figurine on a gigantic Christmas cake, tucked away in the most beautiful freezer on Earth.

MATT MUNRO | LONELY PLANET ©

OPENING SPREAD A trekking tour is guided across the Moreno Glacier. **ABOVE** The glacier is about 19 miles (30km) long, and moves some 6.5ft (2m) each day. **LEFT** Visitors take the less adventurous option of simply gazing at the glacier, an awesome spectacle nonetheless.

ARMCHAIR

※ *Handbook of Lago Argentino & Glaciar Perito Moreno* (Miguel Angel Alonso) Guidebook specific to the Los Glaciares National Park region and Moreno Glacier in particular.

※ *The Physics of Glaciers* (Kurt Cuffey & WSB Paterson) Definitive book on the what, why, and how of glaciers.

※ *Los Glaciares National Park Travel & Trekking Guide* (Colin Henderson) A regional guide that includes Moreno Glacier.

※ *Perito Francisco Pascasio Moreno, Un Heroe Civil* (Hector Fasano) If you read Spanish, and can track it down, this biography tells the life of the eponymous Argentinian explorer and surveyor.

※ *Alpine Climbing: Techniques to Take You Higher* (Mark C Houston & Kathy Cosley) If the feel of crampons has you thinking about bigger mountaineering challenges, start here.

HOT-AIR BALLOON OVER THE ATACAMA DESERT

SEEN AT GROUND LEVEL, CHILE'S ATACAMA DESERT COUNTS AS ONE OF MOST SUBLIME LANDSCAPES IN THE AMERICAS. SEEN FROM THE HEAVENS ABOVE, IT'S EVEN MORE EXTRAORDINARY.

Imagine you're the first human to land on Mars. Above is a cloudless sky. Down below hostile terrain looms into view: parched canyons and arid plains. It is a lifeless expanse without water – only barren red rock as far as the eye can see. Subtract your spaceship and any little green men, add in a big sheet of canvas and a little wicker basket and, hey presto, this what it's like taking a hot-air balloon ride over Chile's Atacama Desert (well, more or less).

The Atacama is a regular stand-in for the Red Planet for TV and movie productions: scientists have even road-tested Mars Rovers here before they are dispatched across the solar system. Though the environment may look Martian, this is a proudly Chilean wilderness – the driest, most lifeless, and probably most ancient desert on Earth, forming the northern frontier of the South American nation. The Atacama is set on a high-altitude plateau, flanked by two mountain ranges that keep out incoming rainclouds. There are some parts of the desert where rain has never been recorded.

Hiking, horseback riding, and mountain biking have been the traditional ways to explore the Atacama Desert's dusty trails – but in recent years hot air ballooning has taken off, with companies operating dawn flights out of San Pedro de Atacama. From up in the sky, the drama of the desert becomes heightened. In the basket, you can be eye-to-eye with the summits of volcanoes that straddle the Chile–Bolivian border. They are mountains which, according to indigenous Atacameno legends, have distinctive personalities – capable of love, rage, and jealousy. You can scan the pancake-flat salt-pans for bursts of pink: the flocks of endangered flamingoes that come to feed on algae in brackish pools. And you can gaze out at the canyons and dunes and imagine yourself bound for extraterrestrial worlds – were it not for the creaking of the wicker basket and the gentle desert breeze on your face.

ESSENTIAL EXPERIENCES

* **Watching leaping flames inflating the balloon envelope in the pre-dawn darkness.**

* Experiencing the giddy thrill as your hot-air balloon becomes airborne for the first time.

* **Peeking through the tiny holes in the wicker basket to see the ground hundreds of meters beneath your feet.**

* Squinting into the distance to try to spot Bolivia.

* **Coming back down to earth with a gentle thud and a small cloud of dust.**

* Spending the rest of the morning swinging in a hammock, gazing up at the skies from whence you descended.

232

ELEVATION 7900FT (2408M) | LOCATION SAN PEDRO DE ATACAMA | IDEAL TIME COMMITMENT ONE WEEK, WITH ONE MORNING FOR BALLOONING | BEST TIME OF YEAR JULY, WHEN THE DESERT IS AT ITS COOLEST | ESSENTIAL TIP TAKE PLENTY OF WATER AND SUNSCREEN WHEREVER YOU GO – SHADE CAN BE SCARCE.

GHOST TOWNS OF THE DESERT

The Atacama suffers no shortage of surreal sights, but Humberstone has a legitimate claim to be the strangest. Established in 1879 as a nitrate-mining settlement, it lay abandoned after the industry collapsed in the mid 20th century. Today it's a bona fide ghost town where a trickle of visitors pace the deserted streets: exploring houses with no inhabitants, schools with no pupils, hotels with no guests, and a theater in which no performances are held (although it does claim a resident cast of ghosts). The neighboring ghost town of Santa Laura – just over a mile away – is equally peculiar.

◼ THE ADVENTURE UNFOLDS

The Atacama Desert covers some 40,000 sq miles (103,600 sq km) – the overwhelming majority of which goes untrammelled by tourists. At its heart is the town of San Pedro de Atacama: a pre-Colombian settlement where drovers once rested on journeys from the Andes to the Pacific. The town is still a staging post for modern travelers, many of whom use it as a base from which to embark on day trips into the desert.

As luck would have it, most of the headline attractions of the Atacama are accessible on short (and sometimes bumpy) roadtrips from San Pedro. Two hours to the north is the El Tatio geyser field, where 64 geysers send scalding jets of water into the air. Most local operators organize visits at dawn, when the slanting sunlight catches the clouds of steam. An hour in the opposite direction is the Laguna Chaxa – a sulfurous pool in the salt flats, where three species of flamingo stalk the shallow pools. And on the outskirts of San Pedro itself is the Atacama's best-loved attraction: the Valle de la Luna – the Valley of the Moon. Encompassing rolling sand dunes and rocky monoliths, it is best visited at sunset when its fierce-looking forms take on terracotta hues and look (slightly) more serene.

San Pedro de Atacama itself merits a day or two of idle exploration – with lively restaurants and shops lining its narrow streets. In a quiet plaza off the busy main drag stands the Iglesia San Pedro – a 17th-century church with a cactus wood ceiling and stout adobe walls. San Pedro offers a broad range of accommodations in which to hang up your dusty boots – from backpacker digs to bank balance-sinking luxury lodges. A favorite among the latter is Tierra Atacama – a high-concept hotel set in shady gardens, with cabins that face the exquisitely conical Licancabur volcano. And

ARMCHAIR

✳ *Poema de Chile* (Gabriela Mistral) One of South America's best-loved writers, Gabriela Mistral grew up in Elqui, south of the Atacama, and mentioned the desert in her poetry.

✳ *The House of the Spirits* (Isabel Allende) The Chilean-American author, a distant relative of the country's president brutally overthrown by Pinochet in 1973, weaves a magic-realist tale drawing on those events, while celebrating Chile's people.

✳ *Quantum of Solace* (2008) Admittedly not the best James Bond film of recent times, but the closing scenes feature Daniel Craig crash-landing a plane in the Atacama Desert, before dynamiting the Cerro Paranal Observatory (which stars as a villain's lair).

THE ATACAMA GIANT

The greatest celebrity in the Atacama is El Gigante – the giant. Not a mythical creature, nor a wrestler, El Gigante is an 282ft (86m) geoglyph – a giant depiction of a human figure etched into the hillside, and the largest prehistoric representation of a person in the world. Little is certain about his past; carved roughly a millennia ago, he is thought to represent a deity or a shaman, and was used to measure the passage of the sun and determine when to plant certain crops. He's in good company – thousands of other, smaller geoglyphs are spread across the Atacama.

for those seeking an instant overview of all
the attractions in and around San Pedro de
Atacama, fear not: the launch pad for hot-air
balloon flights is 30 minutes out of town.

■ MAKING IT HAPPEN

Getting to the Atacama requires some patience.
The Chilean capital Santiago is served by
connections from around the world, and has
regular departures for the northern town of
Calama, taking two hours. From here, it's just
over an hour's drive to San Pedro de Atacama.
A number of operators offer balloon flights.

■ A DETOUR

The Atacama's lack of moisture not only
defines its landscapes, it also means the
region has some of the clearest skies in the
world – scientific institutes consider it a global
epicenter of stargazing. Three hours' drive
south from Calama is the European Southern
Observatory's Paranal base, open for free tours
on Saturdays and home to one of the world's
most powerful telescopes. It's also easy to
arrange astronomical tours in San Pedro, with
groups training (rather smaller) telescopes
on the constellations and understanding how
indigenous Andean peoples viewed the cosmos.

PHILIP LEE HARVEY | LONELY PLANET ©

OPENING SPREAD A hot-air balloon floats across the vast expanse of the Atacama
Desert. **ABOVE** A pilot inflates his vessel in preparation for another ride. **BELOW**
Chile's incredible desert landscape as seen from the Tierra Atacama Hotel.

DRIFT DOWN THE AMAZON RIVER

THE AMAZON. PHYSICALLY, IT'S IMMENSE AND MYTHICALLY IT'S THE VERY SAME. A RIVERINE AMAZON JOURNEY NEVER FAILS TO EVOKE OVERLAPPING IMAGERY: EXOTIC, DENSE RAIN FOREST; INDIGENOUS TRIBES; ABUNDANT WILDLIFE; ENVELOPING MYSTERY; SOMETIMES EVEN MENACE.

In 1541, a Spanish expedition ran short of supplies while exploring east of the Andes. To look for more, a detachment floated down the Río Napo to its confluence with the Amazon and then to the mouth of the Amazon. Placed under attack by native tribes, the Spanish were shocked that some of the warriors were female. To them, it seemed the warriors were like the Amazons of Greek mythology, an observation that gave the world's greatest river its name (Río Amazonas in Spanish).

Fittingly, for a river named from mythology, its physical characteristics are truly awe-inspiring. The Amazon is over 3800 miles (6200km) long, containing about a fifth of the world's fresh water. At its greatest, it is 25 miles (40km) across, dumping 60 million gallons of fresh water into the ocean per second, more than the next eight largest rivers in the world combined. If you count its numerous tributaries, the Amazon crosses seven countries, from its inconspicuous source in the Peruvian highlands to its mouth near Belém in Brazil.

Yet often travelers' expectations outweigh the reality. Many arrive for an Amazon cruise expecting to hop onto the riverbanks for casual, Discovery Channel–like encounters with jaguars, anaconda, and spear-toting locals. They then need to adjust their attitude fast, for the Amazon's quintessential experiences are more sublime. The river is massive and unrelenting, as much a life form as the plants and animals that depend on it for their survival. Wildlife is hard to spot amid this intricate, organic superstructure, but is all the more special when it makes itself known. The rain forest is awesome in scope and atmosphere. Indigenous tribes are withdrawn, but the Caboclo (mixed Amazonian and European) populating the riverbanks buck the trend to an extent. Within its infinite folds, the Amazon contains wonders galore.

236

ESSENTIAL EXPERIENCES

❋ **Canoeing through a flooded forest.**

❋ Dozing in a hammock on a slow boat to nowhere.

❋ **Listening to the song of a thousand birds and the eerie cry of howler monkeys.**

❋ Imagining you're Aguirre battling the river, and then being thankful you're not.

❋ **Learning to tolerate the insistent rhythm of forró music, played incessantly on the riverboats.**

❋ Stopping at a riverside town and hiking through the lush rainforest.

❋ **Bringing a rod and fishing from the boat when you grow weary of the bland food on board.**

DISTANCE 800 MILES (1300KM) | **COUNTRIES COVERED** BRAZIL, PERU | **IDEAL TIME COMMITMENT** ONE WEEK
BEST TIME OF YEAR MAY TO SEPTEMBER | **ESSENTIAL TIP** DON'T SHELL OUT FOR A STUFFY RIVERBOAT CABIN. SLEEP IN YOUR HAMMOCK INSTEAD.

THE FLOW

The Amazon has not always flowed west to east. About 150 million years ago, when South America and Africa went their separate ways, it flowed east to west. Then, 15 to 20 million years ago, the Andes shot up and blocked the water's exlt. At the same time, a smaller ridge of land, now called the Purus Arch, rose like a spine in the middle of the continent. East of the Purus Arch, the river started draining into the Atlantic Ocean, but west of there the water was trapped and a huge inland sea formed. Eventually the water poured over the Arch, gouging a deep channel near present-day Parintins, and the Amazon returned to being a river, but now flowing west to east. Confirming the theory, biologists showed that Amazonian stingrays are more closely related to Pacific species than Atlantic ones.

SURFING THE RIVER

Every month or so, a certain alignment of the sun and moon ensures tides are at their strongest. In the Amazon, this means powerful waves can form at the mouth of certain rivers and barrel upstream with tremendous force. This phenomenon, which occurs when the tide briefly overpowers the river's force, is called a 'tidal bore', but in Brazil they know it as the *pororoca*, meaning 'mighty noise'. Indeed, waves can reach heights of 13ft (4m) and speeds of 18 miles (30km) per hour, and can rip fully grown trees right off the bank. All of which pleases extreme surfers (and kayakers) in search of the archetypal 'endless wave'. For more, catch the National Pororoca Surfing Championship held at São Domingos do Capim, 75 miles (120km) east of Belém, usually in March.

■ THE JOURNEY TODAY

As you string up your hammock on the *gaiola* (riverboat) you boarded back in Belém, at the mouth of the great river, you watch the rainforest and local life glide effortlessly by. You marvel at the activity on the Amazon's edges, crowded with jungle and settlements. Most major towns along the Amazon have a port and an airstrip – but no roads in or out – so travel is limited to plane or boat. In effect, the Amazon is a road – popular, crowded and functional – but what a road!

The boat stops in Monte Alegre and everyone gets off to see the ancient rock paintings there, the Amazon's oldest-known human creations. Across river, there's beautiful, unspoilt countryside near Alenquer, but you'll save that for another time. Another traveler tells you she is going to hike to the virgin rainforest at Floresta Nacional do Tapajós, while another thinks of heading to the fabulous lagoon with white-sand beaches at Alter do Chão, but you're already thinking of life back on the boat. Because you're hooked.

So you're back on board, and the *gaiola* is suddenly insanely crowded with new passengers, plus there's a fierce Amazonian rainstorm on the way. It hits and, due to the boat's open sides, you and everyone else get thoroughly soaked. Someone tells you that *gaiola* means 'bird cage' and suddenly it all makes sense. You chalk it up to experience, like everything else on board, until finally the storm dies down and you're back on deck.

You climb into your hammock, just near the railing, enjoying the sounds of boat life, and once again lose yourself in the sight of the world's greatest rainforest seductively passing by.

■ SHORTCUT

The beauty of an Amazon trip is that it can be as long or as short as you make it. Most people do the journey between Brazilian cities Belém and Manaus in four to six days, although the cruise can be extended easily to six weeks, including stopovers, detours, and excursions to multiple countries.

■ DETOUR

Every June, the river island town of Parintins hosts Boi Bumba, Brazil's premier folklore festival. This vibrant event tells the tale of the death and resurrection of an ox, and is performed by two samba schools, Caprichoso and Garantido. Expect a typically Brazilian clash of color, music, and lavish carnivalesque hijinks. Actually, the whole festival is really a cover for a competition between the opposing schools, but don't expect to understand the complex rules, which are indecipherable to casual outsiders. Just become a slave to the rhythm and enjoy the party. Parintins can be reached by riverboat from Manaus.

OPENING SPREAD The Amazon wends its way through the Peruvian rainforest. **ABOVE (L)** Surfers ride the *pororoca* tidal bore, an Amazonian phenomenon. **ABOVE (R)** The sun breaks the canopy in early morning. **LEFT** The jaguar is the dominant predator in the Amazon rainforest.

ARMCHAIR

❋ ***Indiana Jones and the Kingdom of the Crystal Skull*** (2008) Good ol' Indy uses the Amazon as part of his quest to find the storied crystal skull.

❋ ***Aguirre, the Wrath of God*** (1972) and ***Fitzcarraldo*** (1982) The brilliant madcap-director Werner Herzog is the ultimate Amazon film-maker. The first tells the story of the unhinged conquistador Aguirre and his attempt to find the legendary city of El Dorado.

The second tells of loopy Irishman, Fitzcarraldo, and his attempt to build an opera house in the middle of the Amazon. Both utilize the uncanny river to astounding effect, as metaphor for the dashed, elusive hopes of these flawed protagonists.

❋ ***The Lost City of Z*** (2016) Jungle adventure loosely based on English explorer Percy Harrison Fawcett's obsessive early 20th-century search for an ancient Amazonian civilization.

MOTORBIKE CHE GUEVARA'S DIARIES

ERNESTO 'CHE' GUEVARA WAS, IN HIS YOUNGER DAYS, A HARDY AND INSATIABLE TRAVELER. HIS MEMOIR, THE MOTORCYCLE DIARIES, DOCUMENTS A 5000-MILE (8000KM) RIDE ACROSS SOUTH AMERICA ON A BATTERED NORTON MOTORCYCLE, A JOURNEY FILLED WITH REVOLUTIONARY DERRING-DO.

Ernesto Guevara de la Serna – 'Che' to his friends – divided public opinion more deeply than just about any figure in the 20th century. There are many 'Ches': hero of the third world and the Sierra Maestra; the CIA's most-wanted man; a handsome and often misunderstood pop figure. His image can still be seen all over Cuba (and beyond), on everything from key rings to billboards.

Che graduated from the University of Buenos Aires in 1953 with a medical degree, but the year before, he embarked on a transcontinental motorcycling odyssey with his friend Alberto Granada. The pair's nomadic wanderings were documented in *The Motorcycle Diaries*, which, when published in 1996 by Verso, carried the flip, though appropriate, tag: '*Das Kapital* meets *Easy Rider*'. It was a momentous journey because it planted the seed that would change irrevocably the course of Latin American history. When it was over, Che was convinced that Latin America needed to be united as one super state, a belief that drove him to play a critical role in the Cuban revolution.

Che and Alberto traveled through Argentina, Chile, Peru, Ecuador, Colombia, Venezuela, Panama, and Miami, before returning to Buenos Aires, the trip opening his eyes to the grinding poverty and stark political injustices prevalent in Latin America. When he later traveled to Guatemala in 1954 on the eve of a US-backed coup against Jacobo Arbenz' leftist government, he was enthusiastically devouring the works of Marx and nurturing a deep-rooted hatred of the US. In 1955, he was deported to Mexico for his pro-Arbenz activities, falling in with a group of Cubans that included Moncada veteran Raúl Castro, a longstanding Communist Party member impressed by Che's sharp intellect and unwavering political convictions. Raul introduced him to his charismatic brother, Fidel, and the rest, as they say, is history.

240

ESSENTIAL EXPERIENCES

❋ **Paying homage at the apartment building at Entre Ríos 480 in Rosario, Argentina, where Che was born in 1928.**

❋ Visiting Cuba – enough said.

❋ **Traveling to the Museo Casa Ernesto 'Che' Guevara in Alta Gracia, Argentina, which focuses heavily on Che's early life.**

❋ Crossing the Cruce de Lagos, as Che did, in Parque Nacional Vicente Perez Rosales.

❋ **Taking up the trail of Che in Chile's Lakes District.**

❋ Locating the exact spot where Che was killed in the village of La Higuera, Bolivia.

DISTANCE 5000 MILES (8000KM) | **COUNTRIES COVERED** ARGENTINA, CHILE, PERU, ECUADOR, COLOMBIA, VENEZUELA, USA, PANAMA
IDEAL TIME COMMITMENT SIX MONTHS | **BEST TIME OF YEAR** WHENEVER THE DESIRE GRIPS YOU
ESSENTIAL TIP LEAVE YOUR REVOLUTIONARY IDEALS AT HOME.

CHE'S LAST STAND

Serious Che pilgrims will want to further explore the three countries most associated with the revolutionary. Cuba's Che sites are legion, of course, while in Argentina stops include Rosario, where he was born, and the Guevara family maté plantation in Misiones. In Bolivia, the Ruta del Che takes in the hotel in which an incognito Guevara stayed when he arrived in the country, the jungle location where he was captured, the village schoolhouse where he was executed, and his burial place at Valle Grande. Journey Latin America can provide tailor-made tours.

THE IMAGE

Che was immortalised in a 1960 Alberto Korda photograph that skilfully captured his iconic qualities: that now-famous defiant expression and wistful eyes gazing far into the future. It's perhaps the world's best-known photograph, but it wasn't until seven years after Che's death that it took off, when an Italian publisher cropped it and reworked it into a poster to publicise Che's Bolivian diaries. Ever since, everyone from Andy Warhol to Smirnoff and rock band Rage Against the Machine has been riffing off it, and ripping it off. Korda, a lifelong socialist and Che supporter, steadfastly refused to ever take a cent in payment for his photograph and even sued Smirnoff for commercial exploitation.

■ THE JOURNEY TODAY

You've made it to Chile, arriving from Argentina through the Parque Nacional Vicente Perez Rosales, a zone of celestial lakes and soaring volcanoes. You're following the route Che and Alberto took, except they had to lake hop when and where they could, helping out with bilge-pumping.

On your hired motorbike, you arrive in Petrohué, with its majestic lakeside setting and all-enveloping serenity, then you take the road skirting the enormous Lago Llanquihue and past the huge Volcán Osorno, a prime destination for mountain climbers and skiers, with its perfect conical peak towering above azure glacial lakes. You pause for a while, struck by its idyllic shape, a serendipitous result of the 40 craters around its base, ensuring that the volcano's eruptions have never taken place at the top. You imagine Che similarly lost in thought, perhaps thinking of the volcano's unique structure as a metaphor for the united nations of Latin America, a superstructure working to preserve the whole...

From Osorno, Che and Alberto rode to the lively port of Valdivia, the most attractive city in Chile's Lakes District, with its touches of German influence, mist, and rain. You pause there, relaxed and refreshed, and then push on for Temuco, where the pair paid homage to poet Pablo Neruda, although it was at this point their ancient motorbike reached the end of its life. Che and Alberto then rode a truck to the beautiful colonial city of Valparaíso, and again you follow their lead, minus the truck, before traveling north to Chuquicamata's breathtaking copper mine and the nitrate ghost towns around the Iquique. These towns were still functioning when Che visited, and their psychic trace is heavy in the air, as is his, everywhere you go.

Finally, you wash up at beachside Arica, the end of your Chilean adventure. There, as you watch the sea and sand, you take it easy for a while, contemplating the next country in your Guevarian adventure.

■ SHORTCUT

If don't have time for the whole *Motorcycle Diaries* journey, try the Chile loop as outlined in the previous section. Allow one to two weeks.

■ DETOUR

It wasn't part of the original journey, but a visit to Cuba should be compulsory, as you're already in that part of the world. Cuba is full of bombastic Che iconology as well as Santa Clara's Monumento Ernesto Che Guevara, a monument, mausoleum, and museum complex in a square guarded by a bronze statue of 'El Che'. The mausoleum below contains 38 stone-carved niches dedicated to guerrillas killed in the failed revolutionary attempt in Bolivia that cost Che his life, along with the remains of 30 of them, including the man himself. The adjacent museum holds Che ephemera.

243

OPENING SPREAD Following in the tire marks of Che Guevara in view of Mt Sajama, near the Bolivia–Chile border. **ABOVE (L)** Chile's Volcán Osorno, a landmark on Che's route. **ABOVE (R)** Che rode on through Chile's Lake District. **LEFT** That iconic image adorns a wall in Havana.

ARMCHAIR

* ❋ *The Motorcycle Diaries* (Che Guevara) Became the basis for the 2004 film of the same name, directed by Walter Salles.

* ❋ *Traveling with Che Guevara: The Making of a Revolutionary* (Alberto Granado) Che's companion wrote his version of the journey, which would also serve as a reference for Salles' film.

* ❋ *Chasing Che: A Motorcycle Journey in Search of the Guevara Legend* (Patrick Symmes) Details the journalist and Latin American specialist's efforts to retrace Che's famed journey.

* ❋ *Che* (2008) Steven Soderbergh's two-part epic is an exhaustive account of Che's life, from his first meeting with Fidel to his death in Bolivia. This timeline was also covered in the 1969 film *Che!*, with Omar Sharif in the lead role, widely considered an ill-conceived production.

GO CULTURE-CLUBBING IN PUNTA DEL ESTE

URUGUAY'S PUNTA DEL ESTE IS NOTORIOUS FOR ITS JET-SET REVELRY, BUT BEYOND THE NONSTOP PARTY MORE SUBTLE PLEASURES AWAIT, FROM CONTEMPORARY ART TO ROLLING WINE COUNTRY.

Bronzed, bikini-clad sylphs sip cocktails while their well-fed sugar-daddies convene over cigars, and a shirtless DJ in mirrored aviators spins thumping house music under a makeshift canopied booth in the sand. It's just another afternoon on the beach in 'Punta', as regulars call it. By turns referred to as the St-Tropez or Hamptons of South America, Punta del Este is exactly what you'd expect from those comparisons: a high-end festival of flesh and flash. Attracting Brazilian millionaires and high Buenos Aires society, the area explodes into one continuous beach bash from December through to the end of February. Outside of this frenzied high season, when hotel prices skyrocket and traffic jams are commonplace, many local businesses are shuttered and vacation homes sit empty.

As in Spain and Argentina, the dinner rush starts at 10pm and the clubs likely won't be bumping until well after 2am. Punta del Este proper, a built-up small peninsula of hotels, low-lying residential and commercial buildings, and a small marina, isn't entirely where it's at any more. The party has shifted east to the surf town of La Barra, with its scene-y Bikini Beach, and the formerly sleepy fishing village of José Ignacio, where a small number of modernist inns, smart hotels, and the odd seafood restaurant now exist. Beyond the sand and socialising, Punta del Este has cultural cachet that the average merrymaker is blissfully unaware of. One need only head inland a few minutes to hit up a sculpture park, working cattle ranch, or winery.

Punta's quieter side is just as compelling, from the natural splendor of the windswept coves, dunes, and cliffs along the coast to the green pastureland and sun-dappled, canopied country roads that snake through it – a refreshing respite from that thumping house beat.

244

ESSENTIAL EXPERIENCES

❋ **Lingering over a sunset dinner at a beachside *parador* (restaurant) and sampling freshly caught *brótola* (a local white fish) or grilled octopus.**

❋ Visiting the kitschy, colorful Museo del Mar for the weird and wonderful sea creatures preserved in bottles, the shells, and the vintage beach paraphernalia.

❋ **Splashing about, then sprawling and gaping at the eye-candy on the beaches in La Barra, Punta, and José Ignacio.**

❋ Shaking a tail feather till the sun comes up in a downtown Punta club or at a La Barra beach party.

❋ **Exploring Casapueblo, a rambling, gleaming-white Gaudí-esque villa housing a hotel and art gallery built on the water in Punta Ballena.**

LOCATION PUNTA DEL ESTE, URUGUAY | **BEST TIME OF YEAR** IF YOU WANT TO PARTY: HIGH SEASON (DECEMBER TO FEBRUARY) **IDEAL TIME COMMITMENT** FOUR TO SEVEN DAYS | **ESSENTIAL TIP** BOOK WELL IN ADVANCE DURING HIGH SEASON, INCLUDING ANY FLIGHTS OR THE FERRY FROM BUENOS AIRES | **PACK** SUNSCREEN, TEENY BIKINI, CAMERA, CASH.

CLASSIC COCHES

A popular pastime in Uruguay is lovingly restoring and maintaining classic cars from the 1920s through to the 1960s. Keeping cars running as long as possible has also been a necessity in the country: import taxes and sky-high insurance rates keep new cars prohibitively expensive. Founded in 1996, the Punta del Este Sport and Classic Car Club holds rallies and races in the summer so people can parade their treasures and admire each other's workmanship. It's also not uncommon to find an abandoned, rusted-out shell of a 1940s' Ford pick-up adding visual interest to a roadside field.

■ THE PERFECT GETAWAY

Punta del Este's South Beach–esque condos and nightclubs are just a part of this resort town, but it's a good idea to start your explorations here. Climb the giant concrete fingers emerging from the sand on Playa Brava, sample the *asado* (charcoal-grilled beef) at a traditional *parrilla* (grill) restaurant, and then check out the yachts in the marina. Listen out for the name and location of the summer's happening club, then make a game of getting past the ever-humorless bouncer.

Over to the east, the striking Museo-Taller Casapueblo, perched on Punta Ballena, is artist Carlos Páez Vilaró's workshop, gallery, and hotel. Now head west to visit youthful La Barra, where a lively combination of art galleries, surf emporiums, and ice-cream shops attract glitterati, backpackers, and families alike. Go inland to discover the delightful Museo del Mar, which is a treasure trove of whalebones and sea-creature taxidermy, in addition to thousands of collectibles.

In José Ignacio, lunch at beachfront hot spot La Huella may entail a long wait, but the people-watching and impossibly fresh seafood, like the white-fish *brótola*, make up for it. The serene Pablo Atchugarry sculpture park is 3 miles (5km) inland and includes local sculptor Atchugarry's studio. Venture further west and you'll hit sleepy Garzon, a tiny town in *gaucho* (cowboy) country now best known as the home of Argentine celebrity-chef Francis Mallmann's eponymous restaurant.

There are also places with a feral beauty to them, like the hippie-magnet village of Cabo Polonio, which has no roads into it, just 4 miles (7km) of dunes from Hwy 10 (walk or hitch a ride on the open-air dune-rider bus to get there). Other things Cabo Polonio does not have: electricity; running water; beefy bouncers...

ARMCHAIR

* ***Open Veins of Latin America: Five Centuries of the Pillage of a Continent*** (Eduardo Galeano) A famously scathing indictment of American and European exploitation of Latin America.

* ***Seven Fires: Grilling the Argentine Way*** (Francis Mallmann) Experience Mallmann's fiery magic first-hand at his restaurant-hotel in the village of Garzon.

* ***The Rest is Jungle and Other Stories*** (Mario Benedetti) This cross-section of tales spans five decades of work by the late respected Uruguayan journalist, poet, and author.

* ***Miracle in the Andes: 72 Days on the Mountain and My Long Trek Home*** (Nando Parrado) Parrado tells of surviving the crash that killed most of his Uruguayan college rugby team in 1972.

* ***Montevideo, Taste of a Dream*** (2010) Story of the Yugoslav soccer team's tour to Montevideo for the first World Cup in 1930.

SANDWICH OF CHAMPIONS

The *chivito*'s story of origin involves an Argentine woman vacationing in Punta del Este in the 1960s who ordered a 'chivito' (baby goat) sandwich. The chef didn't have any baby goat on hand so he improvised this dazzlingly extreme sandwich instead, which quickly rose to unofficial national sandwich status. Make sure that you don't have anything to do after eating one – you will need to lie down for a while once you've ingested the lethal combination of fried meats (steak, ham, bacon), mayo, egg, and sundry fried and grilled toppings such as olives and peppers, squashed into an oil-sodden bun.

PLAN IT

Fly into Montevideo (the capital of Uruguay) or Buenos Aires (the capital of Argentina). From Montevideo, take a bus or rental car to Punta. From Buenos Aires, take a quick direct flight (less than an hour) or ferry across to Uruguay. The ferry will either take you to Colonia or Montevideo, then take a rental car or bus to Punta. Book accommodation well in advance in high season (December to February); avoid the crowds by going in the shoulder season (November and March).

DETOUR

Though overshadowed by grape-growing giants such as Argentina and Chile, Uruguay shares these countries' temperate climes and great vine-growing conditions, and is South America's fourth-largest producer of wine. The closest winery to Punta del Este is the award-winning Alto de la Ballena, which has around 20 acres (8 hectares) of vineyards at the foothills of the Sierra de la Ballena. Here, owners Paula Pivel and Alvaro Lorenzo grow merlot, tannat, cabernet franc, syrah, and viognier. You can visit their incredibly scenic estate and taste wines by appointment only. Be sure to contact the winery in advance of turning up.

MARTIN ARNOLD | 500PX ©

OPENING SPREAD Casapueblo, designed by the artist Carlos Páez Vilaró in Punta Ballena. **ABOVE** Le Mano (the hand), a sculpture by Mario Irarrázabal, reaches through the sand at Punta del Este. **BELOW** Punta del Este's beach and skyline.

ENTER THE LOST WORLD OF MT RORAIMA

HERE BE DRAGONS – AT LEAST, THAT'S HOW IT FEELS. TO ASCEND VENEZUELA'S MIGHTIEST TABLETOP MOUNTAIN, VIA A TANGLE OF FOREST, AN ARMY OF SANDFLIES, AND PUNISHINGLY SLIPPERY SLOPES, IS TO DISCOVER A PREHISTORIC AND UTTERLY UNIQUE LOST WORLD.

'Inaccessible, except by means of balloon.' That was the verdict on Mt Roraima in 1872. By the latter half of the 19th century, several Western explorers had set their eyes on the highest of Venezuela's strange table-shaped mountains, and all had determined it quite insurmountable – its foliage too dense, its situation too remote, its upper flanks too extraordinarily sheer.

In this era of pioneering and adventure, however, 'impossible' was just a challenge. In 1884, multitasking botanist, curator, author, and photographer Everard Im Thurn and his assistant Harry Perkins finally made it to the top. Actually, it wasn't that hard. Roraima was, and still is, the simplest to climb of the 115 tepuis (flat-topped mountains) in Venezuela's sweeping Gran Sabana. A sloping ledge naturally hewn into Roraima's southern flank means that those of reasonable fitness willing to brave its humidity, downpours, slippery rocks, and biting flies can negotiate the vertical cliffs of the upper reaches and attain the summit without recourse to climbing ropes or hot-air balloons. Hikers attempting to top this 9219ft (2810m) massif today still follow Im Thurn's historic route.

In 1912, Sir Arthur Conan Doyle, inspired by this alien realm, penned his non-Sherlock classic, *The Lost World*. In Doyle's imagination, this was a place where pterodactyls swooped and stegosaurus clomped. They don't, but you can believe they might. There's an eerie atmosphere on Roraima's singular summit – nightmarish rocks, strange sands and streamlets, a crystal valley, and bug-eating plants that have evolved in lofty isolation from the land around.

Then there are the views – clouds permitting. Often the mesa is draped in a dramatic tablecloth of wispy white (it rains virtually every day). But when the linen is whipped off, the vastness is revealed; from here, you can look out over three countries – Roraima marks the meeting point of Venezuela, Guyana, and Brazil – and across to other tepuis, which all have their own secret summits.

ESSENTIAL EXPERIENCES

✳ **Watching waterfalls tumble off the top of neighboring tepui Kukenán – which, in Pemón, means 'Place of Death'.**

✳ Spending the night in a Roraima 'hotel', sandy areas sheltered by rock overhangs.

✳ **Scouring the tepui top for curious indigenous species – tiny black toads and unusual blooms.**

✳ Taking a dip in the jacuzzis – ice-clear, icicle-cold pools on Roraima's summit.

✳ **Waiting for the mist to clear, to give sweeping, international views of where Venezuela, Guyana, and Brazil meet.**

✳ Nursing wobbly legs, a sunburned nose and myriad *jejene* (sandfly) bites with a cold beer back in Paraitepui, after a climb well done.

248

ELEVATION 9219FT (2810M) | **LOCATION** CANAIMA NATIONAL PARK, SOUTHEAST VENEZUELA | **IDEAL TIME COMMITMENT** FIVE TO SIX DAYS | **BEST TIME OF YEAR** NOVEMBER TO APRIL | **ESSENTIAL TIP** PACK OUT ALL WASTE.

WEIRD WORLD

There may not be dinosaurs lurking on the tepuis, but they still feel prehistoric. These flat-topped mesas are two billion years old, formed when South America, Australia, and Africa were still joined as the super-continent Gondwana. Over time the surrounding sandstone has eroded, leaving these tables to tower over the plateau. High and sheer-sided, each tepui has evolved in isolation, resulting in many unique species. Roraima has many endemic bromeliads, bellflowers and carnivorous heliamphoras, plus the *Oreophrynella quelchii* – a little black toad with an unusual defense mechanism: when faced with danger it doesn't hop away, but rolls into a ball.

TRIBE OF THE TEPUI

The Pemón people have long lived in the shadow of Roraima. Inhabiting a remote region of the Gran Sabana, bounded by mountains on all sides, they were not known to the Western world until the mid-18th century; today the Pemón number around 16,000. The tribe has its own ideas about the tepuis, believing them to be home to the *mawari* (spirits). According to Pemón legend, an enormous Wazacá tree once grew here, on which all the world's fruit and vegetables grew. One day, one of their creator-ancestors chopped it down, causing a great flood. The remaining stump is Mt Roraima.

■ THE ADVENTURE UNFOLDS

You've finished counting and you're pretty sure you've numbered 43 *jejene* (sandfly) bites on your left leg; you can't bear to tally those on the right. These little blighters are impervious to DEET, and the termite chili sauce – which is the locally recommended prophylaxis – doesn't seem to be deterring them either. You're hot and sweaty, and very nervous about the black rock wall lurking outside your tent: tomorrow's steep and precipitous path to the top...

The two-day trek here from Paraitepui afforded intermittent views of Roraima. When the skies were clear, its anvil-like hulk was revealed in all its seemingly impenetrable glory; when the mists gathered about its upper flanks it was like spirits amassing for a malevolent coven. Now, you're just one night's sleep and four hours' clamber away from joining them.

The upward haul is exceptionally tough going. You squelch through red clay, get tangled in tree-roots, splish under waterfalls, and battle unforgiving scree. Cheerful orchids line the path, but you barely see them. Finally, one last push, and you've made it.

Life is weird up here. The 12 sq mile (31 sq km) summit isn't a smooth plateau, but a netherworld made up of scant vegetation, creepy and uneven rocks, tiny black toads, and chill air. You'd soon get lost wandering alone,

so you're grateful for your guide's direction as he leads you to a glittering canyon of crystals, a series of freezing quartz-lined pools (where you dare not take a dip), and to La Ventana – the window. You lie down, belly first, on the dark stone and crawl to the edge of the ledge for the most vertiginous, though spectacular, views.

That night you stay in a 'hotel' – though, unfortunately, the word means something quite different up here to en-suite bathrooms and room service. These rocky overhangs will protect your tent from the elements, so you can sleep soundly amid the strange stillness and be ready to embark on the leg-juddering descent the next day. Your time on top of Roraima has been brief. But, truly, you have had a glimpse into another world.

■ MAKING IT HAPPEN

Roraima is located within Canaima National Park, in southern Venezuela. You cannot climb it independently – you must book a tour or hire a local guide. Tours depart from Santa Elena de Uairen. Most trips take six days: three days up (though this could be squeezed into two); a day on the summit; two days back down. Santa Elena is 15 minutes from the border with Brazil. You can fly into Boa Vista, Brazil, and catch a bus or shared taxi to the border.

■ DETOUR

Angel Falls was discovered by the outside world when an American pilot named Jimmie Angel crash-landed on Auyantepui in 1937. Tumbling 3212ft (979m) off the side of this tepui, it's the highest waterfall on the planet. It's not easy to reach, buried deep in the jungle of Canaima National Park. To get there, fly from Ciudad Bolívar to the indigenous village of Canaima, then take a scenic flight over the falls. More fun is an overnight boat trip from Canaima, sleeping in hammocks at a rustic *campamento* and hiking to Mirador Laime for fine falls views.

251

MARCELO ANDRE | GETTY IMAGES ©

OPENING SPREAD The Kukenan River flows past Venezuela's flat-topped tepuis.
ABOVE Trekkers atop Mt Roraima. **LEFT** Angel Falls cascades down Auyentepui.

ARMCHAIR

* ***Quest for the Lost World*** (Brian Blessed) The larger-than-life actor fulfils his childhood dream of mastering Mt Roraima.

* ***The Lost World*** (Sir Arthur Conan Doyle) This classic novel, first published in 1912, is a romp with dinosaurs across South American plateaus, inspired by Venezuela's tepuis.

* ***Birding in Venezuela*** (Mary Lou Goodwin) Comprehensive field guide, including details of the country's best bird-watching sites.

* ***Comandante: Hugo Chávez's Venezuela*** (Rory Carroll) A warts and all analysis of the populist president's 14 years in power, published shortly after his death.

* ***Up*** (2009) Oscar-winning cartoon movie about a man who ties balloons to his house and floats off to see South America; beautifully animated, with luscious Roraima-esque scenery.

URUGUAY
○ Buenos Aires

PACIFIC
OCEAN

ARGENTINA

SOUTH
ATLANTIC
OCEAN

○ Torres del Paine National Park
○ Punta Arenas

TREK CHILE'S TORRES DEL PAINE

TREK AROUND OR INTO THE HEART OF ONE OF THE WORLD'S MOST FANTASTICALLY SHAPED MOUNTAIN RANGES, PUSHING THROUGH PATAGONIA'S NOTORIOUS WINDS TO VIEWS THAT WILL WOW EVEN THE MOST SEASONED MOUNTAIN TRAVELERS.

Near the southern tip of South America, the Torres del Paine rises like a fistful of broken fingers, its multitude of peaks and spires tortured into otherworldly shapes by time and wild weather. Trekkers who journey south to the national park invariably come to hike one of two routes: the Paine Circuit or the W Trek. The latter is named for its shape as it angles into a trio of valleys cut deep into the range. The most striking of these are the Ascencio and Frances valleys, which provide the finest trekking views on offer in the Torres del Paine. The Ascencio valley rises to meet an enormous terminal moraine, atop which is found a lake set beneath the trio of towers that give the mountains and the national park their name. The trail through the Frances valley skirts the crevassed base of the Frances Glacier, climbing onto a lookout set inside a ring of impressive peaks.

The Paine Circuit does exactly as its name suggests, looping around the Torres del Paine. It's more committing than the W Trek, but is also less busy – in summer there can be more than 2000 people in Torres del Paine National Park every day. For the extra effort, trekkers add a string of lakes and glaciers, as well as a wild pass crossing above Grey Glacier. Stepping onto Paso John Garner on a fine day can be a sublime experience, staring directly down onto Grey Glacier. On a foul day, with gale-force winds spearing ice into your face, it can feel as perilous as the poles.

In early 2012, a huge fire tore through the national park, burning most of the land between the Frances valley and Refugio Grey, about a 10-mile (16km) stretch of both treks. The devastated area will take decades to recover, though fortunately the bulk of the Torres del Paine's natural attractions lie outside the fire zone.

252

ESSENTIAL EXPERIENCES

✳ **Viewing the eponymous towers from the lakeside lookout above the Ascencio valley.**

✳ Battling winds at the aptly named Paso de los Ventos (Pass of the Winds) or atop the Frances Glacier lookout.

✳ **Bracing for the brawn and beauty of nature on the exposed crossing of Paso John Garner.**

✳ Celebrating day's end with a pisco sour in one of the refuges.

✳ **Listening for ice falls as you walk high above Grey Glacier.**

DISTANCE PAINE CIRCUIT, 62 MILES (100KM); W TREK, 42 MILES (69KM) | **LOCATION** TORRES DEL PAINE NATIONAL PARK, CHILE
IDEAL TIME COMMITMENT PAINE CIRCUIT, EIGHT DAYS; W TREK, FOUR DAYS | **BEST TIME OF YEAR** DECEMBER TO MARCH
ESSENTIAL TIP THE NATIONAL PARK AUTHORITY, CONAF, DOESN'T ALLOW SOLO HIKERS TO CROSS PASO JOHN GARNER, SO JOIN UP
WITH OTHER TREKKERS AT CAMPAMENTO LOS PERROS IF WALKING ALONE.

SENDERO DE CHILE

Conceived as a multidistance adventure on the scale of the USA's Appalachian or Pacific Crest trails, Chile's Sendero de Chile will, when all sections are connected, become one of the longest pathways in the world. Stretching for over 5300 miles (8500km) from Arica, in the country's north, to its southern tip at Cape Horn, it is designated for hiking, mountain biking, and horseback riding. Note that some stretches follow gravel roads instead of beautiful trails, so it's worth researching the parts you wish to undertake before setting out – there are updates and maps on the trail's official website: www.fundacionsenderodechile.org.

■ THE ADVENTURE UNFOLDS

You have climbed steeply up from your sublime lodge accommodation at Hostería Las Torres and instead of feeling as though you're on the fringe of these mighty mountains, you feel as though you're about to step into them. The wind rages through the Ascencio valley, which you can now glimpse below you for the first time. Rock slopes reach down to beech forests and grassy slopes in a scene that looks as if it could have been transplanted from the Swiss Alps. From the small pass, you descend to Refugio Chileno, sited on the banks of the Río Ascencio, then continue onward up the valley through beech forest. Sunlight peeps through the leaves, and the trail criss-crosses the river and the tributaries that pour down from the hanging glaciers that rise above you.

About an hour's walk past the refuge, the trail turns uphill, winding skyward beside the massive rubble heap of the ancient glacial moraine. Near its head, you step out onto the moraine – there are boulders here larger than some houses – and finally up onto its summit. You knew it was close to the towers – the Torres of legend – but still the view is more astounding than you could ever have imagined. A brilliant turquoise lake lies pooled at the base of the three towers, which point at the sky as if a trio of missiles ready to be fired. You immediately understand why the nomadic Tehuelche people, who roamed Patagonia, viewed these peaks with reverence and fear.

You lie about on the boulders that fringe the lake, watching clouds and shadows float and swirl around the peaks. Bursts of sunlight extract new and changing colors from the rock – rust-red, gray, yellow. Only the shapes stay the same. Other trekkers come and go from this mesmerizing place, but you linger,

ARMCHAIR

❋ **The Voyage of the Beagle** (Charles Darwin) A vivid chronicle of the graduate geologist's five-year expedition aboard the HMS *Beagle*, observing native flora, fauna, and volcanoes.

❋ **Birds of Chile** (Alvaro Jaramillo) Most wildlife you'll see in the Torres del Paine is feathered; this detailed guide covers them all.

❋ **In Patagonia** (Bruce Chatwin) Classic travel account about Patagonia and its characters – the mylodon skin that inspired Chatwin's journey was found near Torres del Paine.

❋ **Against the Wall** (Simon Yates) Account of a punishing climb of the 4000ft (1220m) high rock face on the Central Torre by Yates (of **Touching the Void** fame).

❋ **Patagonia: Wild Land at the End of the Earth** (Tim Hauf and Conger Beasley Jr) Photographic essays about Patagonia, including Torres del Paine.

boulder-hopping your way down to the shore of the lake, where water pours furiously through the moraine and down into the Ascencio valley. You follow its lead, finally turning your back on these mighty towers for the walk back to your base at Las Torres.

■ MAKING IT HAPPEN

Camping grounds and refuges surround the Torres del Paine. It's easily possible to walk the W Trek staying only in refuges – sleeping bags or quilts are supplied, meaning you only require a sleeping sheet – though you'll need to bring camping equipment for the Circuit. Torres del Paine treks are a staple item in the brochures of many adventure-travel companies.

■ AN ALTERNATIVE CHALLENGE

Mountains might be the dominant feature of Torres del Paine, but look closely and there's actually as much water here as there is land, which makes kayaking out from the park an appealing option. Commercial trips follow the Río Serrano as it squirms its way towards the sea from the mountains, with paddling deviations to the likes of the Tyndall and Serrano Glaciers. It's a fulfilling way to obtain a new view of an old favorite.

PATRICK_GIJSBERS | GETTY IMAGES ©

OPENING SPREAD The singularly stunning landscape of the Paine Massif. **ABOVE** The Andean condor, a frequent sight here, has the second-longest wingspan of any bird. **BELOW** Lake Pehoé is one of many jewels to be found in the Torres del Paine.

ANDEAN CONDORS

Even if you've come to Torres del Paine National Park to see only the mountains, you'll undoubtedly leave impressed by the vision of Andean condors cruising through its skies. Seen regularly around the Torres' peaks, this vulture is all black except for white feathers around its neck and the tips of its wings. Nesting on inaccessible rock ledges that afford protection and easy takeoffs, its most striking feature (apart from its rather hideous looks) is its wingspan – at 8ft (2.5m), it's second only to the wandering albatross.

KAYAK AND CRUISE ANTARCTICA

A WORLD OF GLISTENING WHITE, WHERE ICEBERGS CALVE, WHALES BREACH, AND PENGUINS MINGLE IN THEIR MILLIONS… TO VISIT ANTARCTICA, BY EXPEDITIONARY VESSEL AND SEA KAYAK, IS TO LEAVE THE WORLD OF MAN AND SUBMIT ENTIRELY TO THE WONDER OF NATURE.

A continent that no one owns, with no permanent human population and no capital – Antarctica (cliché alert) is the planet's last true wilderness. In this frozen zone at the bottom of our world, Mother Nature is still totally in charge. She seems to be venting her fury here, though: Antarctica is the coldest, windiest, and driest continent. Arable land? 0%. Ice cover: 98%; the other 2% is barren rock. In short, over 5 million sq miles (14 million sq km) of freezing, hostile nothing. So why is it so beautiful? The existence of this gargantuan land was not known until the 19th century. Maoris, whalers, and Captain Cook had previously nibbled at the region's edges, spying sub-Antarctic isles. But it wasn't until 1820 that the main landmass was first glimpsed, then confirmed as a continent in 1840. There followed a flurry of expeditions, keen as Boy Scouts to tick off firsts in this unwelcoming but irresistible new world.

Getting to Antarctica is less perilous these days. Tourist cruises began in the 1960s, and boomed from the '80s. Today, during the November to February austral summer, fleets of vessels carrying around 34,000 passengers set sail for the Antarctic Peninsula, surrounding southern isles and, most intrepid of all, the Ross Sea. Antarctica is busier than it was. You'll spot other visitors: the birds, seals, penguins, and whales that breed and feed amid the floes.

Cruising is a physical doddle. There are no Shackleton-type exertions; you just need to be able to get in and out of a Zodiac, the rigid-hulled inflatables that whisk explorers from big ship to shore. But there are ways to up the adrenalin levels: many vessels carry kayaks, so you can sidle into coves for extreme ice close-ups. There may also be opportunities for tougher hikes or even (shudder) ice diving. But even if your most strenuous task is lifting your binoculars to focus on a blue whale flicking its tail, this is still the adventure of a lifetime.

ESSENTIAL EXPERIENCES

* **Mingling among the noisy, stinky, enormous king penguin colonies on South Georgia.**

* Zipping past the face of a skyscraper-high iceberg in Paradise Harbour, aboard a tiny Zodiac.

* **Squeezing through the mile-wide Lemaire Channel, flanked by mountains.**

* Viewing the bergs, seals, and penguins from sea-level, on a kayak expedition.

* **Sharing a beach on the South Shetland Isles with Adélie, chinstrap, and gentoo penguins, and elephant and crabeater seals.**

* Raising a dram to Shackleton – the explorer is buried in the whalers' cemetery at Grytviken, South Georgia.

DISTANCE FROM 2000 NAUTICAL MILES (3700KM) | **LOCATION** ANTARCTIC PENINSULA | **IDEAL TIME COMMITMENT** TWO TO THREE WEEKS | **BEST TIME OF YEAR** NOVEMBER TO FEBRUARY | **ESSENTIAL TIP** TAKE GINGER TO COMBAT SEASICKNESS.

A PLACE OF PEACE

On 23 June 1961, a dozen countries signed the Antarctic Treaty, a landmark agreement to demilitarize and preserve the White Continent. Today, 53 countries (comprising 80% of the world's population) are members. The treaty's aims are clear: to ensure Antarctica is used only for peaceful purposes, and that it's not exploited for nuclear testing or waste disposal; to guarantee the freedom of scientific research; and to remove the potential for sovereignty disputes over its territories. Each year, members meet to discuss pressing issues, such as environmental pressures and the impact of tourism, in the hope of safeguarding this wilderness for the future.

A PLACE OF PENGUINS

Seven species of penguin are found on Antarctica and the sub-Antarctic islands. Adélies, named after the wife of French explorer Dumont d'Urville, are small black-and-white birds with white eye rings. Chinstraps have a black line across their throats; they're the second most numerous species. Macaronis are the first – there are 12 million breeding pairs of these orange-tufted creatures. Rockhoppers, the smallest species, also have head tassels. Emperors are the largest, growing up to 3.2ft (1m); kings are nearly eight inches (20cm) shorter and breed in vast numbers on South Georgia. Small gentoos flock here too, identifiable by their orange bills and white eye flashes.

◼ THE ADVENTURE UNFOLDS

You've found your sea legs. Crossing the dreaded Drake Passage to get from Ushuaia to the South Shetland Islands was a rocky ride. Dramatic, though, watching waves crash on deck, feeling the full force of Poseidon in a strop. But then – calm. The tidal torrents became mirror-smooth. The last ripple you saw turned out to be a humpback flexing its fluke.

You haven't decided what you like best yet. The elegant Arctic terns are a contender, as are the elephant seals, guarding the beaches with cantankerous grunts, and the orcas, the albatrosses, the minkes, and the penguins, who don't care for rules and peck at your boots when you're trying to keep your distance.

Then there's the land itself. How can there be so many shades of white? Icebergs glitter and glow blue or emerald green; some are carved into elegant shapes, while others loom like mountains. It's gorgeously terrifying. Yesterday, as you passed an ice wall, a chunk the size of a caravan plunged into the water with a mighty boom.

Your favorite moment, though, has been your small piece of peace. There are only 100 passengers on your ship – more intimate than the vast vessels carrying thousands, and you can get ashore more frequently. But still, that's 100 people, plus naturalists, guides, and other crew. So you join a kayak excursion. The land felt vast before, now it feels infinite; from kayak-level you feel like a microscopic krill. You paddle to a quiet cove. A crabeater seal bobs up, watching your progress. You paddle on, under an ice arch, past a berg of dazzling blue. And, for a moment, you lose sight of the others – it's just you, that crabeater, and the world's wildest place.

◼ MAKING IT HAPPEN

Most Antarctic cruises disembark from Ushuaia, south Argentina, where they can be booked, often at discounted rates. But advance booking is advised. Itineraries range from one to three weeks. Shorter trips go to the Antarctic Peninsula; longer routes also visit South Georgia and the Falkland Islands (Islas Malvinas). Choose your ship based on its itinerary, facilities, and size (bigger boats are more stable, smaller vessels enable more shore landings).

◼ AN ALTERNATIVE CHALLENGE

Today, reaching the South Pole is more about hard cash than hard graft. With US$50,000, it's possible to fly there aboard a ski-plane – covering in hours the wilderness that took early explorers many months to cross. Fly from Punta Arenas in Chile to Union Glacier Camp, to acclimatize to life on Antarctica; from there it's a four- to five-hour flight to the Geographic South Pole, to walk round the globe in a few footsteps, visit the Amundsen–Scott Station and, of course, buy souvenirs. For details, visit antarctic-logistics.com.

ANDREW PEACOCK | GETTYIMAGES ©

OPENING SPREAD A Zodiac takes a group of adventurers for a close up look at the Antarctic ice shelf. **ABOVE** Penguin spotting via kayak. **LEFT** King penguins are one of seven species of penguin found on the Antarctic peninsula.

ARMCHAIR

❋ **Antarctica** (Lonely Planet) Handy guidebook to the continent, including planning advice and maps.

❋ **The Worst Journey in the World** (Apsley Cherry-Garrard) The Antarctic classic; tells the tale of Scott's ill-fated polar expedition.

❋ **Terra Incognita: Travels in Antarctica** (Sara Wheeler) The travel writer joined the USA's Antarctic Artists' and Writers Program, and then the British Antarctic Survey; the results are a thoughtful meditation on the White Continent.

❋ **Frozen Planet** (2011) The BBC's breathtaking TV series shows the poles in all seasons, bursting with life and battered by katabatic winds – essential viewing.

❋ **Scott of the Antarctic** (1948) Black-and-white movie retelling of Scott's journey, filmed largely in Norway. Ralph Vaughan Williams' rousing score was later reworked into his *Sinfonia Antarctica*.

INDEX

INDEX

INDEX

INDEX

INDEX

INDEX

wildlife
alligator 86-9
Amazon parrot 152
Andean condor 255
anteater 181-2, 225
bald eagle 31, 138
bear 27, 28-31, 35, 52, 70-73, 146
beluga whale 39
bighorn sheep 27
black bear 28-31, 52
blue lizard 164
blue whale 256
capuchin monkey 181
Carib hummingbird 153
coatimundi 184
cotton-top tamarin 225
crocodile 86-9, 186
deer 52, 89, 96, 141
Ecuador's Cloud Forest 220-23
egret 89
elk 27, 70-73, 141
flamingo 164-7
Florida panther 86, 88
grizzly bear 31, 70-73, 146
ground squirrel 52
guanaco 208
heron 89
howler monkey 184
hummingbird 223
humpback whale 28-31, 189, 224-7
iguana 164
jaguar 182, 184, 225, 239

jaguarundi 181, 184
margay 184
marmot 52
moose 24
ocelot 184, 225
Olive Ridley turtle 189
orca 36-39, 90-93
owl 52
penguin 256-9
peregrine falcon 138
polar bear 35
porcupine 186
prairie dog 133
puma 184
raccoon 52, 89
red-tailed hawk 52
river otter 78
scarlet macaw 186
sea lion 78
spirit bear 28-31
squirrel monkey 189
Steller's jay 52
tapir 182-4, 225
turkey vulture 52
whale 28-31, 36-39, 78, 90-93, 189, 216, 224-7
wolf 70-73